The Wine Spectator
GUIDE TO SELECTED WINES

Edited by
Marvin R. Shanken

A FIRESIDE BOOK
Published by Simon & Schuster, Inc.
New York

A Fireside Book

Published by Simon & Schuster, Inc.
Simon & Schuster Building
Rockefeller Center
1230 Avenue of the Americas
New York, New York 10020

FIRESIDE and colophon are registered trademarks
of Simon & Schuster, Inc.

Designed by Stanley S. Drate/Folio Graphics Co. Inc.

Material in this book is based on reviews that appeared in *The Wine
Spectator* newspaper. Editorial offices are located at Opera Plaza,
Suite 2040, 601 Van Ness Avenue, San Francisco, California 94102

Manufactured in the United States of America

10 9 8 7 6 5 4 3 2 1

Library of Congress Cataloging in Publication Data

The Wine spectator guide to selected wines / prepared and compiled
by the Wine spectator staff.—
San Francisco, Calif.: Wine Spectator,
    v: ill.; 28 cm.
    Annual.
    Cover title: Guide to selected wines

    ISSN 0749-033X = The Wine spectator guide to selected wines.

    1. Wine and wine making—Directories. I. Wine spectator. II. Title:
Guide to selected wines.
TP546.5.W56   641.2′22—dc19   84-643378
                              AACR 2   MARC-S

ISBN: 0-671-54247-8

Acknowledgments

The editor wishes to acknowledge the editorial staff of *The Wine Spectator* for their participation in the preparation of this wine guide. Staff members include managing editor Harvey Steiman and senior editors James Laube, James Suckling, and Gregory S. Walter. Special appreciation is extended to assistant editor Sabrina Harryman Hellman who diligently logged the thousands of wines tasted each year and performed all of the other record-keeping tasks for this project.

CONTENTS

Preface

For many of us wine is becoming a part of daily life.

From the least expensive jug wine to the most ravishing Trockenbeerenauslese, wine can brighten existence and ease the way through life's scenarios, whether as a catalyst to conversation between friends, as a means of "breaking the ice" for less-than-amiable acquaintances, or as a source of aesthetic enjoyment. Wine can help you impress an important client eyeing you coolly over an expensive business luncheon. And wine can add just a little more spice to those romantic interludes with a friend, whether at home or on the town. Wine heightens the enjoyment of special events; often special bottles are saved through the years for those occasions.

Buying good wine at reasonable prices is hard work. It takes knowledge, experience, and good advice. Consumers are faced with literally thousands of wine labels competing for attention on retail shelves across America. It can all be very confusing—and very intimidating.

The Wine Spectator, a national consumer newspaper for people serious about wine, recognizes this problem—and has helped to solve it with this *Guide to Selected Wines.* The 1985 edition contains more than one thousand recommendations from the pages of the twice-monthly newspaper's "New Releases" section, recommendations which can eliminate much of the guesswork involved in buying wine.

Included is information necessary to making an informed purchase—vineyard name, price, availability, and an evaluation based on the appearance, nose (aroma), and taste of the wine. The description will assist in determining whether a wine is worth a try.

In preparation for each issue of *The Wine Spectator,* the editors taste more than one hundred wines in a series of "blind" tastings (that is, without knowledge of producer). They only know the wine type, vintage, and retail price. After each taster evaluates the wines and records his or her impressions, the group discusses them and votes on the rating that each should receive. Only wines that have some degree of national distribution are reviewed.

The four ratings or classifications used by the panel and this book are as follows:

Spectator Selection: These wines are considered by the staff panel to be outstanding achievements in winemaking—of the highest quality. They are worth making a special search for.

Best Buy: These wines have outstanding quality but also are a tremendous value. Price, high quality, and availability are the important considerations for this rating.

Highly Recommended: These wines display excellence in any or all of the criteria, and are recommended without reservation.

Recommended: Displaying solid structure and character without major defects, these wines are always a safe purchase. Wines that carry our "Bacchus" symbol represent the best in that category.

The guide is organized by the wine's country of origin. Its California wine selections are arranged by type of grape (varietal—e.g., Cabernet Sauvignon, Gewürztraminer). Other wine-producing areas are organized by region. Within a section entries are ordered alphabetically by producer (e.g., Château Carbonnieux, Drouhin, Robert Mondavi). Vintages are stated for each wine, and where the wine is of no single vintage the letters "NV" are used to designate "non-vintage."

Prices listed are suggested retail prices from the wine producer or importer. Prices and availability may vary throughout the country, as some of the wines recommended are produced in small quantities. Your local retailer can tell you whether a particular wine is available in your area.

The "Cellar Selections" section features wines that the editors strongly recommend for home wine cellars. These wines will benefit from further bottle age and can be purchased now for substantially less than when ready to drink.

An interest in wine can accompany us through life and become an enjoyable and rewarding avocation. With this book the consumer can develop his or her own palate based on tasting notes and recommendations that are trustworthy. No longer need the wine consumer buy wine "blind."

U.S.: California

CABERNET SAUVIGNON

Spectator Selections

Beaulieu Vineyard

From Beaulieu Vineyard, Rutherford:

Cabernet Sauvignon, Napa Valley, Georges de Latour Private Reserve, 1979, $18.

Best Beaulieu private reserve in years.

Sight: clear, deep ruby.

Nose: complex, deep cherry aromas, tobacco, cassis.

Taste: dry, full body, soft but firm fruit, rich, viscous, chocolaty, balanced, good acid, elegant, great structure, long finish.

Burgess

From Burgess Cellars, St. Helena:

Cabernet Sauvignon, Napa Valley, Vintage Selection, 1980, $15.95.

Mixture of power and elegance, long life ahead.

Sight: clear, deep purple.

Nose: deep, complex, vanilla, spicy, anise.

Taste: dry, big, woody, complex and powerful, floral, cassis fruit, good structure, long finish, beautiful balance, young feel.

Chateau Montelena

From Chateau Montelena Winery, Calistoga:

Cabernet Sauvignon, Napa Valley, 1979, $16.

Classic Cabernet.

Sight: clear, deep-dark ruby.

Nose: closed, some oak, tobacco aromas.

Taste: dry, full body, great fruit flavor, very intense oak, balanced, tannic, long full finish.

CHATEAU MONTELENA
ESTABLISHED 1882
Cabernet Sauvignon

NAPA VALLEY
Cabernet Sauvignon
ESTATE 1979 BOTTLED
GROWN, PRODUCED & BOTTLED BY CHATEAU MONTELENA
WINERY · CALISTOGA, NAPA VALLEY, CALIFORNIA
ALCOHOL 13.5% BY VOLUME

Heitz Cellar

From Heitz Wine Cellars, St. Helena:

Cabernet Sauvignon, Napa Valley, Martha's Vineyard, 1979, $30.

Truly great Cabernet—outclasses the field around it.

Sight: clear, deep red garnet.

Nose: minty, eucalyptus, complex aromas, cassis.

Taste: dry, full body, clean fruit, very well balanced, eucalyptus, minty, has great complexity and depth, long finish.

Kenwood

From Kenwood Vineyards, Kenwood:

Cabernet Sauvignon, Sonoma Valley, Artist Series, 1980, $25.

Classic Sonoma Cabernet; has tremendous potential.

Sight: clear, deep purple-ruby.

Nose: herbal, currants, cassis, earthy, complex.

Taste: dry, big, fat, full body, lots of fruit, tannic, clean, good structure, lots of character, long full finish.

St. Clement

From St. Clement Vineyards, St. Helena:

Cabernet Sauvignon, Napa Valley, 1981, $12.50.

Rough edges, but gorgeous flavors.

Sight: clear, deep purple.

Nose: closed, vanilla, wood and fruit.

Taste: dry, full body, intense chocolaty fruit, balanced, good wood and acid, rich flavors.

1981
ST. CLEMENT
NAPA VALLEY
CABERNET SAUVIGNON
Alcohol 13.0% by Volume
Produced and Bottled by St. Clement Vineyards
St. Helena, California, U.S.A.

Simi

From Simi Winery, Healdsburg:

Cabernet Sauvignon, Alexander Valley, 1979, $9.

Great Cabernet at any price. A tightly knit wine.

Sight: clear, medium ruby.

Nose: clean, tobacco, herbal, complex.

Taste: dry, full body, lots of finesse, depth and complexity, good balance, intensity without being raw, subtle, clean.

Cabernet Sauvignon, Alexander Valley, Reserve, 1978, $17.

Excellent value in high-quality Cabernet.

Sight: clear, medium garnet.

Nose: rich, weedy, some dill.

Taste: dry, clean, deep fruit, full body, moderate tannin, good acid, well balanced, long full finish.

Stag's Leap Wine Cellars

From Stag's Leap Wine Cellars, Napa:

Cabernet Sauvignon, Napa Valley, Stag's Leap Vineyards, Cask 23, 1977, $30.

Still has a long way to go.

Sight: clear, deep garnet.

Nose: rich, complex, herbal, woody aromas.

Taste: dry, rich, deep, lots of fruit, well balanced, closed, complex, long finish.

Best Buys

Estrella

From Estrella River Winery, Paso Robles:

Cabernet Sauvignon, San Luis Obispo County, Estate Bottled, 1979, $6.

Tremendous value in a clean Cabernet for current drinking.

Sight: clear, deep garnet.

Nose: rich, woody, leathery, spicy fruit.

Taste: dry, full body, clean, balanced, great soft fruit, long finish, lots of varietal character.

Glen Ellen

From Glen Ellen Winery, Glen Ellen:

Cabernet Sauvignon, Sonoma County, Proprietor's Reserve, 1981, $3.49.

Great price and good structure.

Sight: clear, deep red ruby.

Nose: simple, fruity, varietal.

Taste: dry, good fruit, very assertive, clean, fresh, grapy, good acid, some complexity, long finish.

Liberty School

From Caymus Vineyards, Rutherford:

Cabernet Sauvignon, Napa Valley, Lot 10, NV, $5.99.

Hard, young Cabernet that's tough to beat for the price.

Sight: clear, deep red ruby.

Nose: herbal, peppery, clean aromas.

Taste: dry, full body, tannic, lots of fruit underneath, hard, young flavors, herbal character, long finish.

Seghesio Winery

From Seghesio Winery, Healdsburg:

Cabernet Sauvignon, Northern Sonoma, 1976, $4.50.

Excellent value in a mature Sonoma County Cabernet.

Sight: clear, medium brick red.

Nose: clean, spicy, peppery, some oak.

Taste: dry, medium body, rich, delicate flavors, fully mature, herbal, varietal, good fruit flavors, balanced, short finish.

Stephen Zellerbach Vineyard

From Stephen Zellerbach Cellars, Healdsburg:

Cabernet Sauvignon, Alexander Valley, 1979, $7.50.

Good potential for aging—excellent value.

Sight: clear, medium-to-deep ruby.

Nose: fruity, fragrant, bit of mint.

Taste: dry, soft, fruity, good acid, full body, clean, moderate tannin, well balanced.

Highly Recommended

Buena Vista

From Buena Vista Winery, Sonoma:
Cabernet Sauvignon, Sonoma County, 1980, $16.
A classic Cabernet.
Sight: clear, deep ruby.
Nose: herbal, fruity, tobacco aromas.
Taste: dry, full body, soft, great fruit, balanced, good acid and tannins, long finish.

Caymus Vineyards

From Caymus Vineyards, Rutherford:
Cabernet Sauvignon, Napa Valley, 1980, $12.50.
A classic Cabernet that needs some cellaring—also a relative bargain at the price.
Sight: clear, deep purple-ruby.
Nose: clean, ripe, rich Cabernet aromas, tobacco and bell-pepper aromas, complex.

Taste: full body, rich fruit, tart, cassis flavors, a bit closed and hard, tannic, complex flavors. rich structure.

Diamond Creek

From Diamond Creek Vineyards, Calistoga:
Cabernet Sauvignon, Napa Valley, Gravelly Meadow, 1981, $20.
Has the potential to be even greater, needs time.
Sight: clear, deep ruby.
Nose: closed, spicy, oaky.
Taste: dry, full body, very well balanced, intense cassis and chocolate, great structure, complex fruit flavors, long finish.

Estrella

From Estrella River Winery, Paso Robles:
Cabernet Sauvignon, San Luis Obispo County, NV, $4.50.
A super wine at a super price.
Sight: clear, medium ruby.
Nose: varietal, slightly raisiny, very low herbal character.
Taste: dry, medium body, soft fruit, moderate wood, varietal, good acid, balanced.

Franciscan Vineyards

From Franciscan Vineyards, Rutherford:
Cabernet Sauvignon, Napa Valley, 1979, $8.50.

Great value in a Cabernet.
Sight: clear, medium deep ruby.
Nose: herbal, nice olives.
Taste: dry, full body, good character and fruit, soft, low tannin, balanced, long finish.

Gran Val

From Clos du Val Wine Co., Napa:
Cabernet Sauvignon, Napa Valley, 1982, $7.50.
Young, rich Cabernet at a great price.
Sight: clear, deep purple-ruby.
Nose: herbal, berries and fruit, vanilla, oak.
Taste: dry, full body, lots of fresh fruit and acid, firm backbone, balanced, clean finish.

Guenoc

From Guenoc Winery, Middletown:
Cabernet Sauvignon, 70 percent Lake County, 30 percent Napa County, 1980, $8.
Good value in a complex, drink-now Cabernet.
Sight: clear, deep inky purple.
Nose: herbal, berries, clean aroma.
Taste: dry, full body, assertive, good fruit and acid, herbal, good wood complexity, balanced, long finish.

Gundlach-Bundschu

From Gundlach-Bundschu Winery, Vineburg:
Cabernet Sauvignon, Sonoma Valley, Batto Ranch, 1981, $12.
Drinks very well now, will age well.
Sight: clear, deep purple.
Nose: young, minty, perfumy, cherry.
Taste: dry, good fruit, clean, tannic, full body, forward, well balanced, very young.

M. Marion

From M. Marion, Los Gatos:
Cabernet Sauvignon, California, 1980, $3.99.

Great Cabernet value for current drinking.

Sight: clear, medium-to-deep ruby.

Nose: herbal, spicy, anise, olives.

Taste: dry, nice fruit, medium body, balanced, some wood, soft, clean flavor.

Joseph Phelps Vineyards

From Joseph Phelps Vineyards, St. Helena:

Cabernet Sauvignon, Napa Valley, 1980, $10.75.

Great structure in mouth-filling Cabernet, good price.

Sight: medium deep garnet.

Nose: clean, spicy, herbaceous, anise, cumin seed, varietal.

Taste: dry, full body, ripe mouth-filling black-cherry fruit, good acid and balance, nice tannin, good structure.

Round Hill

From Round Hill Vineyards, St. Helena:

"House" Cabernet, California, NV, $4.50

Perfect for current drinking.

Sight: clear, deep ruby.

Nose: weedy, herbal, full.

Taste: dry, good Cabernet character, full body, herbal, weedy character, soft flavors, clean, balanced.

Sequoia Grove

From Sequoia Grove Vineyards, Rutherford:

Cabernet Sauvignon, Napa Valley, 1980, $12.

This is an ager.

Sight: clear, deep dark ruby.

Nose: herbal, weedy, dill, some berries.

Taste: dry, full body, fruity, good acid, lots of wood, tannin, great balance, long finish.

Stonegate

From Stonegate Winery, Calistoga:

Cabernet Sauvignon, Alexander Valley, Vail Vista Vineyard, 1980, $8.50.

Lots of potential for greatness.

Sight: clear, deep ruby.

Nose: perfumy, closed, good Cabernet aroma.

Taste: dry, full body, assertive, stylish, good fruit and balanced, good structure.

Recommended

Adelaída

From Adelaída Cellars, Paso Robles:

Cabernet Sauvignon, Paso Robles, 1981, $7.25.

Intense without being heavy.

Sight: clear, deep ruby.

Nose: ripe Cabernet, some wood, closed aromas.

Taste: dry, rich, hardy, a bit tannic, good structure, needs time, long on palate, clean, long finish.

Ahlgren Vineyard

From Ahlgren Vineyard, Boulder Creek:

Cabernet Sauvignon, Napa Valley, 1980, $10.50.

This wine really needs more time to smooth out.

Sight: clear, dark ruby.

Nose: floral, waxy, mostly closed.

Taste: dry, full body, tannic, huge wine, lots of fruit and character, hard, smoky, long finish.

Almadén

From Almadén Vineyards, San Jose:

Cabernet Sauvignon, Monterey County, 1980, $5.35.

Bargain-priced Cabernet with higher aspirations.

Sight: clear, medium ruby.

Nose: clean, dill herbal, varietal.

Taste: dry, full body, good fruit, clean flavors, moderate tannin, balanced, lingering finish.

Cabernet Sauvignon, Monterey County, 1981, $5.85.

Another in a line of reasonably priced, easy-drinking Cabernets.

Sight: clear, medium ruby.

Nose: resinous, turpentine, piney aromas, floral.

Taste: dry, berries, herbal, stemmy, resinous character comes through, otherwise clean flavors, lingering finish.

Ballard Canyon

From Ballard Canyon Winery, Solvang:

Cabernet Sauvignon, Santa Ynez Valley, 1981, $9.

Stylish for current drinking.

Sight: clear, deep ruby.

Nose: asparagus.

Taste: dry, medium body, intense asparagus, almost sweet impression because of intense fruit, lingering finish.

Beaulieu Vineyard

From Beaulieu Vineyard, Rutherford:

Cabernet Sauvignon, Napa Valley, Georges de Latour Private Reserve, 1978, $16.

Pricey.

Sight: clear, medium ruby.

Nose: oaky, clean, good varietal character, herbal.

Taste: dry, full body, clean, moderate fruit, good acid, very woody, a bit closed now and awkward, though seems thin.

Beringer Vineyards

From Beringer Vineyards, St. Helena:

Cabernet Sauvignon, Napa Valley, State Lane Vineyard, 1979, $9.50.

Needs time.

Sight: clear, deep ruby.

Nose: clean, closed, anise and spice aromas.

Taste: dry, full body, great fruit, young, very tannic, varietal anise and spice, balanced, long finish.

Cabernet Sauvignon, Sonoma County, Knights Valley Estate, 1980, $8.

Lots of potential at a good price.

Sight: clear, deep ruby-purple.

Nose: grapy, berry, slight tobacco aroma.

Taste: dry, full body, lots of berry fruit, woody, some harshness, high in extract, rich, awkward, long finish.

Boeger

From Boeger Winery, Placerville:

Cabernet Sauvignon, El Dorado, 1980, $8.50.

Lacks finesse at this stage, grapy and simple.

Sight: brilliant, deep ruby-purple.

Nose: clean, grapy, pruney, stemmy.

Taste: dry, full body, pruney, dried apricots/fruit, balanced, good tannin, tannic finish.

Davis Bynum

From Davis Bynum Winery, Healdsburg:

Cabernet Sauvignon, Sonoma County, 1980, $8.

Good value in Cabernet—needs time.

Sight: clear, deep ruby.

Nose: clean, earthy, herbal, eucalyptus.

Taste: dry, a bit hot, tannic, full body, good fruit and acid, lacks balance, long finish.

Cakebread Cellars

From Cakebread Cellars, Rutherford:

Cabernet Sauvignon, Napa Valley, 1980, $14.

Great wine for the cellar.

Sight: clear, deep inky purple.

Nose: herbal, closed, berries.

Taste: dry, full body, big and tannic, great structure, high in fruit and acid, lots of oak extract, long full finish.

Caparone Winery

From Caparone Winery, Paso Robles:

Cabernet Sauvignon, Santa Maria Valley, Tepusquet Vineyard, Unfined and Unfiltered, 1981, $10.

Big and brawny but stylish.

Sight: clear, deep garnet.

Nose: intense, green pepper, herbal, some fruit.

Taste: dry, full body, lots of fruit, dense flavors, rich and tannic, mostly balanced, long and tannic finish.

J. Carey

From J. Carey Vineyards and Winery, Solvang:

Cabernet Sauvignon, Santa Ynez Valley, Alamo Pintado Vineyard, 1981, $9.50.

Herbaceous style, balanced yet needs time.

Sight: clear, deep ruby.

Nose: herbaceous, bell pepper.

Taste: dry, full body, tannic, woody, herbal, rich, balanced.

Carneros Creek Winery

From Caneros Creek Winery, Napa:

Cabernet Sauvignon, Amador County, 1980, $10.

High in alcohol.

Sight: clear, deep inky purple.

Nose: closed, spicy, deep.

Taste: dry, full body, tannic, clean, a bit hot, lots of berries and herbal flavors, good acid, balanced.

Cabernet Sauvignon, Napa Valley, 1980, $12.50.

Needs time, well structured.

Sight: clear, inky purple.

Nose: closed though clean.

Taste: dry, full body, lots of tannin, herbal, clean, oaky, complex, long finish.

Cabernet Sauvignon, Napa Valley, Fay/Turnbull Vineyards, 1980, $15.

Rough young wine with good potential.

Sight: clear, deep ruby.

Nose: deep, herbal, mint, green pepper, cassis.

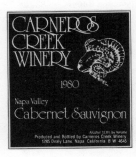

Taste: dry, full body, intense, ripe fruit, tannic, young and coarse, good complex flavors.

Cabernet Sauvignon, Napa Valley, Truchard Vineyards, 1980, $13.50.

A lot of wine for the money.

Sight: opaque purple.

Nose: closed, some oak and fruit.

Taste: dry, full body, deep intense concentrated fruit, oily with lots of fruit, good acid and structure, lots of wood, tannic finish.

Cassayre-Forni Cellars

From Cassayre-Forni Cellars, Rutherford:

Cabernet Sauvignon, Napa Valley, 1980, $12.

Lay this down for a while.

Sight: brilliant, clear, deep opaque purple.

Nose: intense, dill, ripe fruit aromas.

Taste: dry, full body, intense ripe fruit, lots of extract, huge, very tannic, good acid, long, tannic finish.

Cabernet Sauvignon, Napa Valley, 1981, $10.25.

Huge, may need eons.

Sight: clear, deep purple, ruby edge.

Nose: closed, herbal-earthy nuances.

Taste: dry, soft, tannic, full body, awkward, good acid, closed fruit, very tannic finish.

Chalk Hill Winery

From Chalk Hill Winery, Healdsburg:

Cabernet Sauvignon, Sonoma County, 1981, $8.

Full and rich Cabernet with lots of grapy flavor.

Sight: clear, deep dark ruby.

Nose: deep, anise, floral aromas.

Taste: dry, rich fruit, clean, minty flavor, a bit alcoholic, good acid, vanilla, long finish.

Chappellet

From Chappellet Vineyard, St. Helena:

Cabernet Sauvignon, Napa Valley, 1980, $18.

Lots of wood, needs lots of time.

Sight: clear, deep ruby-purple.

Nose: closed, coffee, minty.

Taste: dry, huge, full body, tannic, very woody, long tannic finish, fruit buried.

Chateau Chevalier

From Chateau Chevalier Winery, St. Helena:

Cabernet Sauvignon, Napa Valley, 1980, $11.25.

Needs time; stylish wine.

Sight: clear, deep ruby.

Nose: rich, pruney, dense, closed.

Taste: dry, full body, ground pepper, full fruit, a bit hot, tannic, long finish.

Chateau St. Jean

From Chateau St. Jean, Kenwood:

Cabernet Sauvignon, Sonoma Valley, Wildwood Vineyards, 1979, $17.

Old-style Cabernet Sauvignon: big, grapy and full.

Sight: clear, deep dark, ruby.

Nose: deep, woody, concentrated fruit.

Taste: dry, very tannic and grapy, woody, lots of fruit, reduced, long and full on palate, long finish, very closed.

Cilurzo

From Cilurzo Vineyard & Winery, Temecula:

Cabernet Sauvignon, Temecula, 1980, $5.

Stylish vegetal flavors.

Sight: clear, medium garnet, orange edge.

Nose: asparagus, vegetal, slightly cooked aromas.

Taste: dry, medium body, vegetal, woody, slightly sour on finish, balanced, different style.

Clos du Bois

From Clos du Bois Winery, Healdsburg:

Cabernet Sauvignon (55 percent) & Merlot (45 percent), Alexander Valley, Marlstone Vineyards, 1980, $15.

Has potential; needs time.

Sight: clear, deep purple.

Nose: herbal, fruity, spicy, complex aromas.

Taste: dry, full body, soft, closed but intense fruit, high extract, tannic, full finish.

Cabernet Sauvignon, Sonoma County, 1980, $9.

Good complexity in reasonably priced Cabernet Sauvignon.

Sight: medium-deep ruby.

Nose: deep, woody, herbaceous and varietal.

Taste: dry, full body, tannic, lots of complex fruit and flavor, but good acid and balance, rough, raw flavors now, coffee finish.

Clos Du Val

From Clos Du Val Wine Co., Napa:

Cabernet Sauvignon, Napa Valley, 1981, $12.50.

Hard and tight structure; not showing much now except potential.

Sight: medium ruby-red.

Nose: cherry, herbaceous, varietal.

Taste: dry, hard, young tannic, good fruit flavors, floral flavor, nice structure, long finish.

Coast Range

Coast Range Négociants, Rutherford:

Cabernet Sauvignon, Napa Valley, 1981, $6.50.
Nice flavors; reasonable price.
Sight: clear, deep purple.
Nose: fruity, woody, accessible.
Taste: dry, soft, full fruit, full body, herbal, varietal, balanced lingering finish.

Conn Creek

From Conn Creek Winery, St. Helena:

Cabernet Sauvignon, Napa Valley, 1980, $13.75.
Needs time but has great structure—will reward further aging.
Sight: clear, deep purple.
Nose: floral, intense, berries.
Taste: dry, tannic, full body, very big and fruity, good structure, long finish.

Crystal Valley Cellars

From Crystal Valley Cellars, Modesto:

Cabernet Sauvignon, Lake County, 1980, $5.50.
Lacks depth, otherwise pleasant.
Sight: clear, medium-to-deep ruby.
Nose: clean, a bit closed, some berries.

Taste: dry, fruity, tannic, short in middle, medium body, balanced, lingering finish.

Dehlinger Winery

From Dehlinger Winery, Sebastopol:

Cabernet Sauvignon, Sonoma County, 1980, $9.
Simple style.
Sight: clear, medium-to-deep ruby.
Nose: closed, some herbal, fruity aromas.
Taste: dry, medium body, soft, good fruit, balanced tannin and acid, medium finish.

Devlin

From Devlin Wine Cellars, Soquel:

Cabernet Sauvignon, Sonoma California, 1980, $9.
Very different, vegetal style.
Sight: clear, deep, dark purple.
Nose: green peppers, asparagus.
Taste: dry, full body, high extract, full flavor, lots of wood.

Diamond Creek

From Diamond Creek Vineyards, Calistoga:

Cabernet Sauvignon, Napa Valley, Red Rock Terrace, 1981, $20.
Will improve with age.
Sight: clear, deep, ruby.
Nose: closed, young, berryish, complex.
Taste: dry, full body, complex fruit, great structure, lots of oak, long lingering finish.

Cabernet Sauvignon, Napa Valley, Volcanic Hill, 1981, $20.
Pricey but solid Cabernet.
Sight: clear, deep ruby.
Nose: closed, berryish, spicy.
Taste: dry, full body, good austere fruit, tannin, balanced, complex flavors, needs time.

Domaine Laurier

From Domaine Laurier, Forestville:

Cabernet Sauvignon, Sonoma County, Green Valley, 1980, $12.
Nose detracts slightly, full-flavored.
Sight: clear, deep ruby.
Nose: intense dill, weedy, slightly stinky.
Taste: dry, full body, soft ripe fruit, herbal, balanced acid and fruit, lingering finish.

J. Patrick Doré Selections

From Coastal Wines, Ltd., Sausalito:

Cabernet Sauvignon, Mendocino County, 1981, $6.
Needs more aging.
Sight: clear, medium ruby-red.
Nose: closed, woody aromas.
Taste: dry, full body, tannic, lots of oak, varietal, woody on finish, full, hard flavor.

Cabernet Sauvignon, Napa Valley, 1978, $4.
Well-balanced, drink now.
Sight: clear, deep garnet, light browning on edge.
Nose: herbal, woody, varietal.
Taste: dry, woody, medium to full body, soft fruit, clean, good balance, lingering finish.

Dry Creek Vineyard

From Dry Creek Vineyards, Healdsburg:

Cabernet Sauvignon, Sonoma County, 1980, $9.50.
Young and raw, may come together in time.
Sight: medium deep garnet.
Nose: weedy, light herbal fruit.
Taste: dry, full body, some soft fruit, but very harsh and woody, flabby.

Dunn Vineyards

From Dunn Vineyards, Napa:
Cabernet Sauvignon, Napa Valley, Howell Mountain, 1980, $12.50.
Has tannin and wood to burn—may balance out, may not.
Sight: clear, very deep ruby-purple.
Nose: deep, herbal, bell-pepper aromas, cassis.
Taste: dry, very woody, full body, fruit is buried beneath high wood and tannin, fine structure, long finish.

Fetzer

From Fetzer Vineyards, Redwood Valley:
Cabernet Sauvignon, Lake County, 1981, $5.50.
Well made, drink now.
Sight: clear, medium ruby.
Nose: young, oak, berries, tobacco.
Taste: dry, full, fruity, low wood, soft flavors, moderate tannin, balanced, tart finish.
Cabernet Sauvignon, Lake County, 1982, $5.50.
A young wine that needs some bottle age.
Sight: clear, deep ruby.
Nose: floral, tarry, violets.
Taste: dry, medium, body, young and green, stemmy, good fruit underneath, balanced, short tannic finish.
Cabernet Sauvignon, Mendocino, 1981, $7.
Simple wine with too much wood and tannin.
Sight: clear, medium-deep ruby.
Nose: clean, ripe berries, spicy.
Taste: dry, full body, lots of tannin overshadows fruit, tannic finish, too much wood.

Fisher Vineyards

From Fisher Vineyards, Santa Rosa:
Cabernet Sauvignon, Sonoma County, 1980, $12.
Needs lots of age.
Sight: clear, deep purple, ruby rim.
Nose: closed, some Cabernet fruit.

Taste: dry, full body, tannic, good extract and fruit, balanced, tannic, puckering finish.

Flora Springs

From Flora Springs Wine Co., St. Helena:
Cabernet Sauvignon, Napa Valley, 1980, $11.
Needs lots of time—everything's here.
Sight: clear, deep purple.
Nose: woody, eucalyptus.
Taste: dry, fruity, full body, clean, lots of varietal character, strong acid and tannin, balanced.

Louis J. Foppiano

From Louis J. Foppiano Winery, Healdsburg:
Cabernet Sauvignon, Sonoma County, 1980, $6.
Still young, great value.
Sight: clear, medium to deep ruby.
Nose: full, rich cassis and herbal aromas.
Taste: dry, clean, full body, lots of tannin, round varietal flavors, concentrated fruit, wood in background, long finish.

Franciscan

From Franciscan Vineyards, Rutherford:
Cabernet Sauvignon, Napa Valley, Private Reserve, 1978, $13.50.
Needs time—a complex Cabernet.
Sight: clear, medium garnet.
Nose: complex, dill aromas.
Taste: dry, full body, good Cabernet character, good acid, woody, lots of extract, anise, balanced, long finish.

Freemark Abbey

From Freemark Abbey Winery, St. Helena:
Cabernet Sauvignon, Napa Valley, 1979, $10.50.
Young classic Napa Cabernet.
Sight: clear, deep garnet.
Nose: herbal, weedy.
Taste: dry, full body, woody, herbal style, clean, good structure and balance.

Gallo

From Ernest and Julio Gallo, Modesto:
Cabernet Sauvignon, California, Limited Release, 1978, $9.
Needs more time in bottle.
Sight: clear, deep ruby, garnet edge.
Nose: closed, some wood and fruit.
Taste: dry, full body, tannic, ripe but closed fruit, awkward, good acid, tannic finish.

Geyser Peak Winery

From Geyser Peak Winery, Healdsburg:
Cabernet Sauvignon, California, 1978, $6.35.
Good for current drinking.
Sight: clear, medium ruby.
Nose: some ripe fruit, low intensity.
Taste: dry, fruity, medium body, comes alive on the palate, good acid, moderate wood, balanced.

Glen Ellen

From Glen Ellen Winery, Glen Ellen:
Cabernet Sauvignon, Sonoma Valley, Glen Ellen Estate, 1981, $9.75.
Needs time, still very young.
Sight: clear, deep purple ruby.
Nose: young herbal, weedy aromas.
Taste: dry, closed, very tannic, young, bit hot, woody, still too young.

Grand Cru Vineyards

From Grand Cru Vineyards, Glen Ellen:
Cabernet Sauvignon, Alexander Valley, 1979, $14.50.
Needs lots of aging.
Sight: clear, deep purple ruby.
Nose: intense, currants, earthy.
Taste: dry, full body, tannic, complex fruit, lots of extract, closed, full, long finish.
Cabernet Sauvignon, California, 1981, $8.50.
Will come together in a few years.

Sight: clear, medium-to-deep ruby.

Nose: good fruit, some wood, mostly closed.

Taste: dry, good varietal character, full body, slightly hot, closed, long finish, very young.

Guenoc

From Guenoc Winery, Middletown:
Cabernet Sauvignon, Lake County, 1981, $8.50.
Has a sweet flavor.
Sight: clear, deep garnet.
Nose: woody, minty.
Taste: dry, tannic, lots of fruit, has a sweet impression, vanilla flavors.

Hacienda Wine Cellars

From Hacienda Wine Cellars, Sonoma:
Cabernet Sauvignon, Sonoma Valley, 1981, $11.
Moderate bitterness detracts.
Sight: clear, deep purple.
Nose: fruit, peppery, herbal.
Taste: dry, bitter, lots of wood, full body, herbal, long finish, balanced.

Haywood

From Haywood Winery, Sonoma:
Cabernet Sauvignon, Sonoma Valley, 1980, $9.75.
This wine needs lots of bottle time.
Sight: clear, deep dark ruby.
Nose: grapy, fermentation bouquet.
Taste: dry, full body, inky, intense raw fruit and wood, lots of character, long finish.

Heitz Cellar

From Heitz Wine Cellars, St. Helena:
Cabernet Sauvignon, Napa Valley, 1979, $11.25.
Woody style—simple fruit.
Sight: clear, deep red-garnet.
Nose: woody, resinous.
Taste: dry, ripe fruit, full body, woody, chocolaty, simple, long finish.

William Hill

From William Hill Winery, Napa:
Cabernet Sauvignon, Napa Valley, Mt. Veeder, 1980, $17.
Needs time; woody style.
Sight: clear, rich ruby color.
Nose: complex, woody, herbal.
Taste: dry, tannic, full body, woody, balanced, full fruit flavors, long finish.

HMR

From HMR Ltd., Paso Robles:
Cabernet Sauvignon, Paso Robles, 1979, $12.50.
Balanced now but with potential.
Sight: clear, medium-deep ruby.
Nose: clean, varietal, herbal.
Taste: dry, tart, full body, herbal character, bit closed on palate, all components in balance, long finish.

Inglenook Vineyards

From Inglenook Vineyards, Rutherford:
Cabernet Sauvignon, Napa Valley, 1980, $8.
Another in a long string of fine, Inglenook Cabernets.
Sight: clear, medium red-ruby.
Nose: clean, complex, currants, cigar-box aromas.
Taste: dry, full body, tannic, full fruit, a bit soft on middle, good structure, nice full flavors.

Jekel Vineyard

From Jekel Vineyard, Greenfield:
Cabernet Sauvignon, Monterey County, Private Reserve, 1979, $16.

Needs considerable time; great potential.
Sight: clear, deep ruby red.
Nose: intense, herbal, green olives.
Taste: dry, full body, big and tannic, closed, very ripe fruit, good acid, balanced, long finish.

Jordan

From Jordan Vineyard and Winery, Healdsburg:
Cabernet Sauvignon, Alexander Valley, 1980, $16.75.
Rambunctious young wine, early signs of complexity, pricey for what you get now.
Sight: clear, deep ruby-purple.
Nose: waxy, tarry, peppery, berries.
Taste: dry, young and tarry, grapy and woody, awkward, rough and raw, some heat on finish.

Robert Keenan Winery

From Robert Keenan Winery, St. Helena:
Cabernet Sauvignon, Napa Valley, 1980, $13.25.
Very hard and closed now.
Sight: opaque, deep purple.
Nose: closed, pepper, deep.
Taste: dry, huge, tannic, full body, lots of fruit and acid, long woody finish.

Kenwood

From Kenwood Vineyards, Kenwood:

Cabernet Sauvignon, Sonoma Valley, Jack London, 1980, $12.50.
Big, rough Cabernet that needs to age.
Sight: cloudy, opaque.
Nose: green pepper, minty, toasty.
Taste: dry, full body, dried fruit, tannic, bitter, chocolate, awkward, tannic finish, needs time.

Konocti

From Konocti Winery, Kelseyville:
Cabernet Sauvignon, Lake County, 1980, $5.50.
A tannic wine with a lot of young flavor.
Sight: clear, deep garnet.
Nose: green stemmy.
Taste: dry, tannic, clean, good fruit, woody, pungent, lingering finish, chocolaty.

Lakespring

From Lakespring Winery, Napa:
Cabernet Sauvignon, Napa Valley, 1980, $11.
Awkward now, needs time to develop.
Sight: clear, deep ruby.
Nose: closed, varietal.
Taste: dry, soft Cabernet fruit, full body, hot, tannic, needs time.

Lambert Bridge

From Lambert Bridge, Healdsburg:
Cabernet Sauvignon, Sonoma County, 1980, $12.50.

Drinks well now and will age.
Sight: clear, medium-to-deep garnet.
Nose: green pepper, some berries, slightly closed.
Taste: dry, full body, some vegetal green-pepper aromas, varietal, good acid, round, full, balanced flavors.

Landmark

From Landmark Vineyards, Windsor:
Cabernet Sauvignon, Alexander Valley, Estate Bottled, 1980, $8.50.
A bit awkward now.
Sight: clear, deep purple-ruby.
Nose: earthy, dill, closed, ripe fruit.
Taste: dry, full body, tannic, ripe fruit but closed, balanced, medium finish.
Cabernet Sauvignon, Sonoma County (75 percent) & Napa County (25 percent), 1978, $7.50.
Wait for this one, you can afford to.
Sight: clear, deep purple.
Nose: closed, very herbal.
Taste: dry, full body, intense jammy flavor, lots of character though closed, ripe, tannic, long finish.

Leeward Winery

From Leeward Winery, Oxnard:
Cabernet Sauvignon, San Luis Obispo County, Nepenthe Vineyard, 1981, $9.
Has a distinctive South Coast varietal character.
Sight: clear, deep garnet.
Nose: dill aromas.
Taste: dry, full body, dill flavor carries through, good acid, lots of tannin, long finish, almost overpowering dill character.

J. Lohr

From Turgeon & Lohr Winery, San Jose:
Cabernet Sauvignon, California, NV, $4.50.
Stylish character that may not be for everyone.
Sight: clear, deep ruby-purple.
Nose: weedy, herbal, Central Coast character.
Taste: dry, tart, very soft,

good fruit, lots of green pepper, weedy, balanced.
Cabernet Sauvignon, Napa County, Keig Vineyard, 1980, $10.
Lighter style—worth trying.
Sight: clear, deep purple-ruby.
Nose: minty, perfumy, sweet aroma.
Taste: dry, fruity, full body, tart, very tannic in middle, falls off slightly on finish.

Lower Lake Winery

From Lower Lake Winery, Lower Lake:
Cabernet Sauvignon, Lake County, 1980, $8.50.
Heavy-handed raisiny character.
Sight: clear, deep garnet.
Nose: cough syrup, ripe fruit.
Taste: dry, full body, heavy, ripe fruit, slight medicinal character, good structure.

Maddalena Vineyard

From San Antonio Winery, Los Angeles:
Cabernet Sauvignon, Sonoma County, 1981, $5.95.
Lots of Zinfandel character in a Cabernet.
Sight: clear, deep inlay amber.
Nose: dull, jammy, minty.
Taste: dry, full body, more Zinfandel character than Cabernet Sauvignon, good flavors, balanced, lingering finish, decent structure.

Marietta Cellars

From Marietta Cellars, Healdsburg:
Cabernet Sauvignon, Sonoma County, 1981, $9.
Very tannic, has good structure, needs time.
Sight: clear, deep purple.
Nose: minty, deep, eucalyptus.
Taste: dry, tannic, full body, chocolaty, grapy fruit flavor, long finish.

Markham

From Markham Vineyards, St. Helena:
Cabernet Sauvignon, Napa

Valley, Yountville Vineyard, 1979, $12.85.

Very hard wine; needs a long time.

Sight: clear, deep purple.

Nose: intense, overripe, jammy.

Taste: dry, full body, very tannic, fruity, jammy flavors, ripe, good acid, tannin overpowering, long finish.

Louis M. Martini

From Louis M. Martini, St. Helena:

Cabernet Sauvignon, North Coast, 1979, $6.

Good price, simple.

Sight: clear, medium ruby, garnet edge.

Nose: spicy, herbal, woody.

Taste: dry, light body, some fruit, lots of wood, soft, decent balance.

Cabernet Sauvignon, Sonoma Vineyard Selection, Monte Rosso Vineyard, Lot 1, 1979, $10.

Needs time.

Sight: clear, medium-to-deep ruby.

Nose: simple, good fruit, spicy.

Taste: dry, full body, full wood flavor, deep fruit, balanced, long finish.

Matanzas Creek Winery

From Matanzas Creek Winery, Santa Rosa:

Cabernet Sauvignon, Sonoma Valley, 1980, $16.

Needs time; has the backbone for aging.

Sight: clear, deep inky purple.

Nose: spice, cassis, complex, fruity.

Taste: dry, full body, tannic, lots of fruit, good acid, still young, long finish.

Mill Creek Vineyards

From Mill Creek Vineyards, Healdsburg:

Cabernet Sauvignon, Sonoma County, 1979, $8.50.

Seems to fall off toward the finish.

Sight: clear, medium-to-deep ruby.

Nose: woody, herbal, varietal.

Taste: dry, full body, tannic, high acid, solid fruit, seems a bit out of balance, lingering finish.

Cabernet Sauvignon, Sonoma County, 1980, $9.

Intense dill flavor.

Sight: clear, medium ruby.

Nose: clean, dill, weedy.

Taste: dry, full body, tannic, good balance, some fruit, full finish.

Cabernet Sauvignon Sonoma County Estate Bottled 1979, $8.50.

Big style Sonoma Cabernet.

Sight: clear, deep purple-ruby.

Nose: clean, peppery mint, herbal.

Taste: dry, full body, herbal, peppery, lots of fruit, tannic, complex, long finish.

Mirassou

From Mirassou Vineyards, San Jose:

Cabernet Sauvignon, Central Coast Cuvée, NV, $7.

Old-style vegetal Monterey Cabernet.

Sight: clear, deep ruby.

Nose: herbal, vegetal.

Taste: dry, full body, round, full, vegetal flavors, soft, lingering finish.

Robert Mondavi Winery

From Robert Mondavi Winery, Oakville:

Cabernet Sauvignon, Napa Valley, 1980, $12.

Will age well.

Sight: clear, medium ruby.

Nose: herbal, earthy, some eucalyptus.

Taste: dry, good fruit, very clean, full body, tannic, lots of currants and cassis flavors, balanced, long finish.

Cabernet Sauvignon, Napa Valley, Reserve, 1979, $25.

An elegant wine which is balanced enough to drink now.

Sight: clear, deep ruby, garnet edge.

Nose: clean, assertive, perfumy, eucalyptus.

Taste: dry, elegant, soft, round, full flavors, varietal, good acid, well balanced, long finish.

The Monterey Vineyard

From The Monterey Vineyard, Gonzales:

Cabernet Sauvignon, San Luis Obispo, 1979, $7.99.

Pleasant Cabernet for price.

Sight: clear, deep ruby purple.

Nose: herbal, olive, wood, anise.

Taste: dry, medium body, nice herbal character, lots of wood, wood bitterness on finish.

Monticello Cellars

From Monticello Cellars, Napa:

Cabernet Sauvignon, Napa Valley, 1980, $9.75.

Drink now or hold.

Sight: clear, deep black-purple.

Nose: floral, perfumy, woody.

Taste: dry, full body, intense

fruit and acid, not tóo tannic, balanced, short finish.

Cabernet Sauvignon, Napa Valley, 1981, $13.50.
Everything is here but the fruit.
Sight: medium garnet.
Nose: coffee, green pepper.
Taste: dry, young, full-bodied wine that offers good structure, acid but seems a bit shy.

Mont St. John

From Mont St. John Cellars, Napa:
Cabernet Sauvignon, Napa Valley, Private Reserve, 1980, $11.50.
Big stylish wine, hot and heavy.
Sight: deep, dark ruby.
Nose: minty wood, alcohol.
Taste: dry, full body, lots of tannin, fruit clouded by tannin and alcohol, hot, tannic finish.

Mountain House

From Mountain House Winery, Cloverdale:
Cabernet Sauvignon, Sonoma, 1980, $10.
Intensely varietal, price is reasonable.
Sight: clear, deep garnet, red edge.
Nose: herbal, good fruit, floral.
Taste: dry, full body, intense herbal, lots of wood, bit raw, rich, round, blackberry, long finish.

Mountain View Vintners

From Mountain View Vintners, Windsor:
Cabernet Sauvignon, Napa Valley, Special Selection, 1981, $7.50.
Big wine, raw flavors, young but balanced.
Sight: deep purple.
Nose: floral, grape fermentation bouquet.
Taste: dry, full body, lots of fruit, balanced tannic finish.

Mount Veeder Winery

From Mount Veeder Winery, Napa:
Cabernet Sauvignon, Mt.

Veeder–Napa Valley, Bernstein Vineyards, 1980, $13.50.
Needs time, but lots of complexity.
Sight: clear, medium-deep ruby.
Nose: perfumed, cassis, vanilla, spicy.
Taste: dry, full body, soft, rich, complex fruit, good tannic backbone, good structure, some heat on finish.

Napa Cellars

From Napa Cellars, Oakville:
Cabernet Sauvignon, Alexander Valley, 1980, $16.
Very stylish wine, expensive though.
Sight: opaque, deep purple-black.
Nose: closed, ripe fruit in background.
Taste: dry, full body, tannic, too intense, closed, herbal, good structure, very long finish.
Cabernet Sauvignon, Napa Valley, 1979, $16.
Price is high; not yet ready to drink.
Sight: clear, deep black-purple.
Nose: nice, woody-peppery, herbal.
Taste: dry, intense fruit, full body, tannic, herbal, jammy full fruit, strong acid, good structure, long finish.
Cabernet Sauvignon, Napa Valley, 1980, $12.
Huge wine, may need too much time.
Sight: clear, deep purple.
Nose: intense, ripe, full berries.
Taste: dry, tannic, full body, ripe, raisiny, jammy flavors, good acid, some bitter woody flavors on finish.

Napa Sun Winery

From Napa Sun Winery, Napa:
Cabernet Sauvignon, Napa Valley, 1980, $5.99.
Simple Cabernet—a safe buy.
Sight: clear, medium ruby.
Nose: light varietal, oak and dill aromas.
Taste: dry, full body, tannic, good fruit, balanced, simple flavors, good acid, finish falls off.

Parducci

From Parducci Wine Cellars, Ukiah:
Cabernet Sauvignon, Mendocino County, 50th Anniversary Bottling, 1980, $8.
Much more complex than usual Parducci Cabs.
Sight: clear, deep purple.
Nose: ripe, fruity, dill, assertive.
Taste: dry, full body, varietal, tannic, good acid, beginnings of complexity, balanced, young, long finish.

Pat Paulsen Vineyards

From Pat Paulsen Vineyards, Cloverdale:
Cabernet Sauvignon, Sonoma County, 1981, $8.
Herbal, young and raw.
Sight: clear, deep ruby-purple.
Nose: jammy, bell pepper, herbal.
Taste: dry, full body, raw, harsh, dumb, lots of fruit and tannin, long finish.

Joseph Phelps Vineyards

From Joseph Phelps Vineyards, St. Helena:
Cabernet Sauvignon, Napa Valley, Eisele Vineyard, 1979, $30.
Needs time; a bit high priced.
Sight: clear, deep dark ruby.
Nose: intense, jammy aromas, closed, cedar.
Taste: dry, full body, very tannic, good fruit/acid balance, closed flavors, long finish.
Insignia, Napa Valley, 1979, $25.
Needs time, but has lots of potential—when price is no object.
Sight: clear, medium-to-deep ruby.
Nose: spices, herbal, fresh woody aroma.
Taste: dry, big, full body, clean, softness of flavor aided by 30 percent Merlot, woody, complex, well balanced but young.

Pine Ridge

From Pine Ridge Winery, Yountville:

Cabernet Sauvignon, Napa Valley, Rutherford District, 1980, $12.

Big style—another ager.

Sight: clear, deep, purple-ruby.

Nose: dill, herbal, closed though fragrant.

Taste: dry, tart, tannic, full body, lots of varietal character, chocolaty flavors, balanced, long finish.

Cabernet Sauvignon, Napa Valley, Rutherford Cuvée, 1981, $13.

Price is a bit high for a wine that is rough now but should settle down.

Sight: clear, deep ruby-purple.

Nose: clean, alcoholic, fruit and oak.

Taste: dry, full body, tannin overshadows fruit now, good structure, lots of extract, some alcoholic and tannic flavors on finish.

Raymond

From Raymond Vineyard and Cellar, St. Helena:

Cabernet Sauvignon, Napa Valley, Estate Bottled, 1980, $11.

Hard to evaluate now, has potential.

Sight: clear, deep ruby-purple.

Nose: pruney, raisiny.

Taste: dry, full body, pruney, raisiny, ripe, rich fruit, balanced, tannic, closed, long finish.

Richardson

From Richardson, Sonoma:

Cabernet Sauvignon, Sonoma Valley, 1981, $10.

Drink soon, seems short on palate.

Sight: clear, dark purple.

Nose: closed, intense, peppery.

Taste: dry, intense, seems low in tannin, lots of fruit and acid, long finish.

Ridge

From Ridge Vineyards, Cupertino:

Cabernet Sauvignon, California, Tepusquet Vineyards, 1981, $9.

Intense color and flavor gives this lots of potential.

Sight: deep purple.

Nose: clean, jammy, herbaceous, minty.

Taste: dry, intense jam fruit, lots of extract, good structure and balance, good flavors, tannic finish.

Cabernet Sauvignon, Mendocino, 1981, $7.50.

Simple, very enjoyable Cabernet.

Sight: clear, medium ruby.

Nose: berries, minty, pepper.

Taste: dry, full body, tannic, lots of varietal fruit, good acid, balanced, somewhat short finish.

Cabernet Sauvignon, Monte Bello, 1978, $30.

Will live for a decade, at least.

Sight: clear, deep garnet-red edge.

Nose: ripe, cassis, wood, varietal.

Taste: dry, good fruit, full body, cassis and pepper flavors, tannic, complex, oak in background, balanced, long finish.

Cabernet Sauvignon, Napa County, York Creek Vineyards, 1981, $12.

Big intense Cabernet that needs time to round off rough edges.

Sight: deep purple-ruby.

Nose: smoky, cedary, varietal aromas.

Taste: dry, very intense, tight smoky Cabernet Sauvignon fruit, tannic, but balanced by fruit and acid.

Cabernet Sauvignon, Napa County, York Creek, 1980, $12.

Needs patient cellaring.

Sight: clear, nice ruby-purple.

Nose: rich, jammy, anise on nose.

Taste: dry, full body, lots of wood, nice fruit, jammy flavors, long finish.

River Oaks

From River Oaks Vineyards, Healdsburg:

Cabernet Sauvignon, Sonoma County, 1979, $5.95.

Woody style, good value.

Sight: clear, medium-to-deep garnet.

Nose: olives, menthol, woody aromas.

Taste: dry, soft, medium body, full, clean, woody flavors, balanced.

Cabernet Sauvignon, Sonoma County, 1981, $6.

Grapy style of Cabernet without a lot of structure. Pleasant flavors.

Sight: purple-garnet.

Nose: plummy, grapy, spicy, Beaujolais-like aroma.

Taste: dry, full body, ripe, raw fruit, fat and grapy, tannic but balanced, finish falls off.

Ross-Kellerei

From Ross-Kellerei, Buellton:

Cabernet Sauvignon, Santa Barbara County, 1980, $8.

Good for current drinking.

Sight: clear, deep purple.

Nose: rich, ripe, very herbal, spicy, peppery.

Taste: dry, full body, very herbal, peppery flavors, good acid, nice fruit, well balanced.

Roudon Smith Vineyards

From Roudon-Smith Vineyards, Santa Cruz:

Cabernet Sauvignon, Sonoma Mountain, 1981, $12.

For long-term cellaring.

Sight: clear, deep purple-ruby.

Nose: jammy, herbal, bell peppers.

Taste: dry, big full body, hot, hard to drink, very young, long finish.

Round Hill

From Round Hill Vineyards, St. Helena:

Cabernet Sauvignon, Napa Valley, 1980, $7.50.

Nice Cabernet fruit, drink in a few years.

Sight: deep purple.

Nose: deep, jammy Cabernet, herbal, oak.

Taste: dry, full body, good herbal, tobacco fruit, lots of extract, tannic astringent finish.

Rutherford Hill

From Rutherford Hill Winery, Rutherford:

Cabernet Sauvignon, Napa Valley, 1979, $10.50.
Needs time.
Sight: deep purple-ruby.
Nose: closed, bit of spice.
Taste: dry, full body, very closed, some complexity, good fruit, varietal.

San Martín

From San Martin Winery, San Martin:

Cabernet Sauvignon, San Luis Obispo County, 1981, $7.75.
Nice Cabernet, soft, simple, pleasant to drink already.
Sight: medium ruby.
Nose: weedy, spicy, herbal.
Taste: dry, hard, full body, good Cabernet, good fruit, some bitterness, young.

Santa Ynez Valley Winery

From Santa Ynez Valley Winery, Santa Ynez:

Cabernet Sauvignon, Santa Ynez Valley, 1980, $5.
Vegetal herbal style.
Sight: clear, deep dark ruby.
Nose: vegetal, herbaceous.
Taste: dry, full body, tart, fruity, vegetal, herbaceous, soft, lingering finish.

Santino

From Santino Wines, Plymouth:

Cabernet Sauvignon, El Dorado County, 1980, $8.
Tastes more like Zinfandel; very nice though.
Sight: clear, medium garnet.
Nose: a bit herbal, earthy.
Taste: dry, lots of berries, full body, fruity, good acid, woody, balanced.

August Sebastiani

From Sebastiani Vineyards, Sonoma:

Country Cabernet Sauvignon, California, NV, $6.89 per magnum.
Solid table wine.
Sight: clear, medium-to-deep ruby.

Nose: clean, light fruit.
Taste: dry, medium body, tannic, some fruit, balanced, long finish.

Sequoia Grove

From The Allen Family, Rutherford:

Cabernet Sauvignon, Napa Valley, 1981, $12.
Huge and assertive, jammy fruit, different style of Cabernet, try a bottle first.
Sight: clear, dark purple-ruby.
Nose: Zinfandel and Petite Sirah aromas, jammy.
Taste: dry, big, tannic, woody, tastes like Petite Sirah, hard and awkward, needs time, long alcoholic finish.

Cabernet Sauvignon, Napa Valley, Cask 2, 1980, $12.
Stylistic and priced a bit high.
Sight: clear, deep ruby.
Nose: earthy, vegetal.
Taste: dry, medium body, very tannic, some fruit, earthy flavors, balanced, long full finish.

Shafer Vineyards

From Shafer Vineyards, Napa:

Cabernet Sauvignon, Napa Valley, 1980, $11.
Price and nose hurt this wine.
Sight: clear, deep ruby.
Nose: rubbery, woody aromas.
Taste: dry, intense rich fruit, moderate tannin, balance, long finish.

Sierra Vista

From Sierra Vista Winery, Placerville:

Cabernet Sauvignon, El Dorado County, Estate Bottled, 1980, $8.
Tastes a bit more like Zinfandel, but is still pleasant.
Sight: clear, deep purple.
Nose: spicy, berries, a bit like Zinfandel.
Taste: dry, tannic, full body, good fruit, clean, slightly herbal.

Silverado Vineyards

From Silverado Vineyards, Napa:

Cabernet Sauvignon, Napa Valley, 1981, $11.
Big Cabernet that needs time to round out its rough edges.

Sight: clear, deep ruby-purple.
Nose: complex bell pepper, rich and jammy aromas.
Taste: dry, full body, soft fruit, firm structure, hard now, woody and tannic, long finish, some bitterness.

Silver Oak Cellars

From Silver Oak Cellars, Oakville:

Cabernet Sauvignon, Alexander Valley, 1979, $16.
Drinks well now—the price is a bit high.
Sight: clear, deep garnet.
Nose: woody, cedary, closed.
Taste: dry, full body, very woody, a bit soft, rich in fruit, balanced, long finish.

Cabernet Sauvignon, Napa Valley, Bonny's Vineyard, 1979, $32.
Price is high for wine that seems pretty simple.
Sight: clear, deep ruby-garnet.
Nose: deep, spicy, bit of oxidation.
Taste: dry, lots of wood, has good structure, clean, grapy, not dusty, lacks complexity.

Simi

From Simi Winery, Healdsburg:

Cabernet Sauvignon, Alexander Valley, 1978, $9.50.
Drinking well now—round full flavor.
Sight: clear, medium ruby, garnet edge.
Nose: closed, bit woody.
Taste: dry, full body, rich fruit, full Cabernet flavors, good acid and balanced tannin, long finish.

Cabernet Sauvignon, Alexander Valley, 1980, $10.
Good balance of flavors, but lots of harsh tannin now.

Sight: medium deep ruby-red.
Nose: clear, jammy, piney, sage.
Taste: dry, full body, good ripe fruit, but has gritty texture, lots of tannin, tannic finish, needs time.

Smith & Hook

From Smith & Hook, Soledad:
Cabernet Sauvignon, Monterey County, 1980, $9.50.
For lovers of that vegetal character.
Sight: clear, medium ruby, garnet edge.
Nose: vegetal, pepper, very intense.
Taste: dry, full body, fruit, vegetal character comes through, tangy finish, stylistic.

Smith-Madrone

From Smith-Madrone, St. Helena:
Cabernet Sauvignon, Napa Valley, Estate Bottled, 1980, $12.50.
Big, young Cabernet.
Sight: clear, deep ruby color.
Nose: closed aromas.
Taste: dry, full body, closed but fruity, good structure, woody, long finish.

Smothers

From Vine Hill Wines, Santa Cruz:
Cabernet Sauvignon, Alexander Valley, 1979, $12.50.
May need too much time. Fruit may fade before tannins reach a moderate level.
Sight: clear, deep ruby.
Nose: tobacco, woody, complex, interesting.
Taste: dry, full, big, lots of fruit, tannic, big style, long finish.

Souverain

From Souverain Cellars, Geyserville:
Cabernet Sauvignon, North Coast, 1979, $7.50.
For current drinking; good value.
Sight: clear, deep garnet.

Nose: deep anise, licorice, perfumed.
Taste: dry, nice fruit, medium body, clean, balanced, good structure, long finish.

Spring Mountain

From Spring Mountain Vineyards, St. Helena:
Cabernet Sauvignon, Napa Valley, 1980, $13.
Tannin and alcohol may need too much time; fruit may not last.
Sight: clear, deep ruby.
Nose: closed, wood.
Taste: dry, full body, tannic, huge, hot, fruit is closed, lots of wood on finish.

Stephens Winery

From Stephens Winery, Oakville:
Cabernet Sauvignon, Napa Valley, 1981, $8.
Has structure of a big wine but lacks full flavor.
Sight: medium ruby.
Nose: fruit, some alcohol.
Taste: dry, medium fruit, good balance, simple style, a bit hot, finish falls off.

Sterling

From Sterling Vineyards, Calistoga:
Cabernet Sauvignon, Napa Valley, 1980, $12.50.
Simple but delicious.
Sight: clear, deep, dark, ruby red.
Nose: floral, violets.
Taste: dry, full body, a bit of heat from alcohol, grapy, good acid, moderate tannin, long finish.
Cabernet Sauvignon, Napa Valley, Reserve, 1979, $27.50.
Distinctive style, very assertive and drinkable Cabernet.
Sight: clear, deep, red ruby.
Nose: deep, complex, cassis, eucalyptus.
Taste: dry, full body, very clean, excellent balance, spicy cherry fruit, ripe, mouth-filling, long finish.

Stevenot Winery

From Stevenot Winery, Murphys:
Cabernet Sauvignon, Calaveras County, 1980, $8.
Needs time.
Sight: clear, deep purple.
Nose: closed, varietal.
Taste: dry, full body, tannic, some fruit, moderate acid, very closed, hard to evaluate.

Stone Creek

From Stone Creek Cellars, Healdsburg:
Cabernet Sauvignon, Sonoma County, Dry Creek Valley, 1981, $6.
Grapy, fruity Cabernet.
Sight: clear, deep purple.
Nose: grapy, Gamay-like.
Taste: dry, fruity, medium body, lighter style, short finish, not a lot of wood.

Stonegate

From Stonegate Winery, Calistoga:
Cabernet Sauvignon, Napa Valley, 1979, $12.
Solid Cabernet, needs some age.
Sight: clear, deep ruby.
Nose: herbal, tobacco, lots of wood.
Taste: dry, big, tannic, lots of extract, chocolate and cranberry flavor, balanced, full, long finish.

Rodney Strong

From Sonoma Vineyards, Windsor:
Cabernet Sauvignon, Alexander Valley, Alexander's Crown Vineyard, 1978, $12.
Mature, woody style.
Sight: clear, medium-deep garnet.
Nose: mature, woody, full aromas.
Taste: dry, full body, tannic, pruney, woody, mature, long finish.
Cabernet Sauvignon, Alexander Valley, Alexander's Crown Vineyard, 1979, $12.
Distinct style, good dose of tannin.
Sight: medium garnet.
Nose: coffee, smoky, tea.

Taste: dry, full body, tannic, coffee flavor, balanced, woody finish.

Susiné

From Susiné Cellars, Suisun City:
Cabernet Sauvignon, Suisun Valley, 1981, $5.50.
Young, big style.
Sight: clean, deep ruby-purple.
Nose: clear, anise.
Taste: dry, full body, big, ripe, woody, lots of fruit flavor, spicy, long finish.

Sycamore Creek

From Sycamore Creek Vineyards, Morgan Hill:
Cabernet Sauvignon, Central Coast, 1981, $20.
A lot of money for a wine style that seems to be passé.
Sight: clear, deep purple.
Nose: very ripe fruit, lots of wood, alcoholic.
Taste: dry, very tannic, has very ripe fruit, not very rich, big style, awkward, alcoholic. Will it last?

Johnson Turnbull

From Johnson Turnbull Vineyards, Oakville:
Cabernet Sauvignon, Napa Valley, 1981, $12.
Tannic, thick and jammy now, needs cellaring.
Sight: brilliant, deep purple.
Nose: clean, anise, tropical fruit, minty.
Taste: dry, very tannic, but sweet fruit character underneath, good balance but young now, tannic finish.

Vichon

From Vichon Winery, Oakville:
Cabernet Sauvignon, Napa Valley, 1981, $13.
Full, intense Cabernet; some jammy flavors; this wine needs time.
Sight: clear, deep garnet.
Nose: lots of spice and pepper, jammy.
Taste: dry, full body, lots of fruit, Zinfandel character, good acid and wood, balanced, jammy, berry, peppery, long finish.

Cabernet Sauvignon, Napa Valley, Fay Vineyard, 1980, $16.
Great structure, needs some time.
Sight: clear, deep purple-ruby.
Nose: closed, hints of anise, lots of depth.
Taste: dry, full body, lots of wood, full fruit, hard, closed flavors, good acid, long finish.
Cabernet Sauvignon, Napa Valley, Volker Eisele Vineyard, 1980, $16.
A more accessible Cab than the Fay Vineyard above.
Sight: clear, medium purple.
Nose: deep, forward, anise, assertive.
Taste: dry, full body, good fruit, tart, assertive flavors, anise, wood flavors, balanced.

Villa Mt. Eden

From Villa Mt. Eden Winery, Oakville:
Cabernet Sauvignon, Napa Valley, 1980, $12.
Needs a lot of time; very woody.
Sight: clear, deep dark ruby.
Nose: very woody.
Taste: dry, very young, bitter and woody, some fruit underneath, lingering finish.

Vose Vineyards

From Vose Vineyards, Napa:
Cabernet Sauvignon, Napa–Mt. Veeder, 1979, $12.50.
Needs time, all components are here.
Sight: clear, deep purple.
Nose: rich, deep jammy.
Taste: dry, full body, tannic, good fruit and acid, varietal, cassis, intense flavors, somewhat balanced, long finish.

Cabernet Sauvignon, Napa Valley, Special Reserve, 1978, $10.
For those who like woody, mature Cabernet.
Sight: clear, deep purple.
Nose: oaky, berries, herbal.
Taste: dry, fruity, full body, mature, clean, lots of wood flavor, slight bitterness and wood on finish.

William Wheeler

From Wheeler Vineyards, Healdsburg:
Cabernet Sauvignon, Sonoma County, Dry Creek Valley, 1980, $9.
Needs time to soften.
Sight: clear, deep ruby.
Nose: weedy, herbal.
Taste: dry, full body, lots of fruit and tannin, full Cabernet character, hard finish.

Whitehall Lane

From Whitehall Lane Winery, St. Helena:

Cabernet Sauvignon, Napa Valley, 1981, $12.
Excellent fruit; tannic now.
Sight: very dark, opaque ruby edge.
Nose: clean, varietal flavors.
Taste: dry, full body, tannic, intense fruit, balanced, but closed, long finish.

Wine Discovery

From Wine Discovery, Healdsburg:
Cabernet Sauvignon, Sonoma County, 1980, $3.89.
Good price for an easy-to-drink Cabernet.
Sight: clear, medium deep garnet.
Nose: perfumed, wood, bell pepper.
Taste: dry, full body, clean, ripe fruit, bitter toward end, simple and short, balanced finish.

Woltner

From Woltner Cellars, Healdsburg:
Cabernet Sauvignon, North Coast, 1979, $3.50.
A very light style of Cabernet for a reasonable price.
Sight: clear, medium brick color.
Nose: light varietal aromas.
Taste: dry, light body, some varietal character, soft fruit flavors, moderate acidity, flavors and finish fall off.

Zaca Mesa

From Zaca Mesa Winery, Los Olivos:
Cabernet Sauvignon, Santa Barbara County, 1981, $8.
Soft, old California style.
Sight: clear, medium-to-deep garnet.

Nose: a bit cooked, vegetal aroma.
Taste: dry, medium body, lots of fruit, rich, ripe, slightly bitter from tannin or wood, slightly cooked, long finish.

ZD Wines

From ZD Wines, Napa:
Cabernet Sauvignon, California, 1980, $12.
Nice for current drinking, will age well.
Sight: clear, deep inky purple.
Nose: earthy, woody, closed.
Taste: dry, woody, full body, tannic, lots of fruit, good acid, lots of varietal character, balanced, long finish.

CHARDONNAY

Spectator Selections

Chateau Bouchaine

From Chateau Bouchaine, Los Carneros:
Chardonnay, Napa Valley, 1982, $14.50.
Classic Napa Valley Chardonnay with great character.
Sight: brilliant, deep yellow-gold.
Nose: clean, tropical fruit, figs, guava.
Taste: dry, full body, well-defined fruit, intense and rich, good

acid and balance, great structure and finish.

Matanzas Creek Winery

From Matanzas Creek Winery, Santa Rosa:
Chardonnay, Sonoma Valley, Estate Bottled, 1982, $18.
Big rich Chardonnay with good wood backbone.
Sight: brilliant, yellow-gold.
Nose: perfumed, toasty, figs.
Taste: rich, lush, but delicate figs and Chardonnay fruit and good acid structure, lots of wood and acid on finish.

Robert Mondavi Winery

From Robert Mondavi Winery, Oakville:

Chardonnay, Napa Valley, Reserve, 1981, $20.
One of the best Chardonnays we've tasted to date.
Sight: brilliant, medium green-gold.
Nose: toasty, oak, some fruit.
Taste: dry, full body, rich, lots of complexity, great Chardonnay fruit, woody, very well balanced, complex long finish.

Pine Ridge

From Pine Ridge Winery, Yountville:
Chardonnay, Napa Valley, Oak Knoll, Cuvée, 1982, $13.
A big gutsy Chardonnay with a great future.
Sight: clear, medium green-gold.
Nose: closed, peppermint, cloves, oak.

Taste: dry, ripe flavors, full body, slightly rough, buttery, firm acid, young flavors, balanced, long finish.

Raymond

From Raymond Vineyard & Cellar, St. Helena:
Chardonnay, Napa Valley, 1981, $12.
This wine is a bargain at $12.

Sight: medium-to-deep gold.
Nose: clean, a bit of vanilla, somewhat closed.
Taste: dry, full body, rich fruit, soft and drinkable, viscous, oily, well balanced, long finish.

Best Buys

Acacia

From Acacia Winery, Napa:
Chardonnay, Napa Valley, Vin de Lies, 1982, $7.50.
Tremendous value in Chardonnay.
Sight: brilliant, medium gold.
Nose: closed, bit of wood, trace of fruit.
Taste: dry, tart, full body, good fruit and acid, balanced, clean, some bitterness on finish, overall pleasant on palate.

Adelaída

From Adelaída Cellars, Paso Robles:
Chardonnay, Paso Robles, 1982, $7.75.
Excellent Chardonnay for the price.
Sight: brilliant, medium greengold.
Nose: Chardonnay, vanilla, oak.
Taste: dry, medium body, good simple Chardonnay fruit, pineapple, balanced.

Fetzer

From Fetzer Vineyards, Redwood Valley:

Sundial Chardonnay, Mendocino, 1983, $6.50
Great fruity, crisp and clean style.
Sight: clear, light gold.
Nose: light, clean, fruity.
Taste: dry, clean, and fruity, good varietal fruity Chardonnay, rich clean finish.

Kendall-Jackson

From Kendall-Jackson Vineyards & Winery, Lakeport:
Chardonnay, California, 1982, $8.
Great debut for this winery.
Sight: clear, medium gold.
Nose: toasty, lemony fruit.
Taste: dry, rich clean fruit, citric, complex flavors, good balanced acid and oak, long finish.

Landmark

From Landmark Vineyards, Windsor:
Chardonnay, Sonoma County, 1981, $9.
Good value in high-quality Chardonnay.
Sight: clear, light gold.
Nose: clean, semi-closed, fruity.
Taste: dry, full body, good fruit and acid balance, fruity style.

Mirassou

From Mirassou Vineyards, San Jose:
Chardonnay, Monterey County, 1982, $7.50.
Nice Chardonnay at a good price.
Sight: clear, light gold.
Nose: clean, appley, spicy, some wood.
Taste: dry, clean, full body, good appley flavors, well structured, long finish.

J. Pedroncelli

From J. Pedroncelli Winery, Geyserville:
Chardonnay, Sonoma County, 1982, $7.75.
Great value in current drinking Chardonnay.
Sight: medium gold.
Nose: clean, varietal, some oak.
Taste: dry, clean fruit, lots of wood but balanced, good acid, elegant, long clean finish.

River Oaks Vineyards

From River Oaks Vineyards, Healdsburg:

Chardonnay, Alexander Valley, 1983, $6.
Generous fruit in a clean and crisp style.
Sight: light gold.
Nose: appley, grassy.
Taste: nice, rich appley butter flavor, oily texture, some melon, good acid and structure, some heat on finish.

Round Hill

From Round Hill Vineyards, St. Helena:
"House" Chardonnay, California, NV, $4.50.
This would be a value at twice the price.
Sight: brilliant, medium gold.
Nose: nice varietal, lemony, slight oak.
Taste: dry, medium body, simple varietal flavors, lively acidity, tart, well balanced, lingering finish.

Stratford

From Cartlidge, Moser & Forsyth, St. Helena:
Chardonnay, California, 1982, $8.50.
Excellent fruity style.
Sight: clear, medium straw-gold.

Nose: perfumy, fruity, light.
Taste: dry, intense fruit, medium body, tart fruit, balanced, light wood.

Tijsseling Family Vineyards

From Tijsseling Vineyards, Ukiah:
Chardonnay, Mendocino County, 1982, $11.75.
A good value; drink or cellar.
Sight: brilliant, medium gold.
Nose: appley, oaky, banana aromas.
Taste: dry, good fruit, tart, medium body, crisp, appley, young, balanced flavors, long finish.

Trois Freres

From Lakespring Winery, Napa:
Chardonnay, Napa Valley, 1982, $6.
Good balance and texture.
Sight: light gold.
Nose: clove, spice, fruit, oak.
Taste: dry, rich silky texture, full body, good fruit, varietal, balanced, some wood on finish.

White Oak Vineyards

From White Oak Vineyards, Healdsburg:
Chardonnay, Sonoma County, 1982, $10.
Elegant wine with depth and character.
Sight: dull, medium gold.
Nose: wood, cloves, pineapple.
Taste: dry, full body, rich, apple and pineapple fruit, great structure and balance, full long finish.

WHITE OAK
VINEYARDS
CHARDONNAY
SONOMA COUNTY
VINTAGE 1982
Produced and bottled by
White Oak Vineyards at Healdsburg
in Sonoma County, California.
Alcohol 13.5% by Volume

Highly Recommended

Alexander Valley Vineyards

From Alexander Valley Winery Co., Healdsburg:

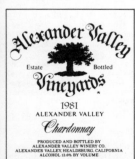

Estate   Bottled
Vineyards
1981
ALEXANDER VALLEY
Chardonnay
PRODUCED AND BOTTLED BY
ALEXANDER VALLEY WINERY CO.
ALEXANDER VALLEY, HEALDSBURG, CALIFORNIA
ALCOHOL 13.6% BY VOLUME

Chardonnay, Alexander Valley, 1981, $10.
Clean, complex wine with a good life ahead.
Sight: brilliant, medium gold.
Nose: clean, citric, pineapple.
Taste: dry, medium body, clean, good oak flavor, crisp, complex, good fruit and acid, balanced.

Boeger

From Boeger Winery, Placerville:
Chardonnay, El Dorado, 1982, $9.
A very fine Chardonnay from an unexpected area.
Sight: clear, medium gold.
Nose: delicate aroma, mature, some wood.

Taste: dry, very clean, slight residual sugar adds complexity, subtle, delicious oak flavors.

Davis Bynum

From Davis Bynum Winery, Healdsburg:
Chardonnay, Sonoma County, Allen Hafner Reserve, 1981, $9.50.
A very reasonable price for a high-quality Chardonnay.
Sight: clear, medium gold.
Nose: subtle, citric, good fruit and oak aromas.
Taste: dry, clean, full body, very fruity, crisp, lively acid, subtle oak, balanced, long finish.

Chateau Montelena

From Chateau Montelena Winery, Calistoga:

Chardonnay, Alexander Valley, 1982, $14.
Elegant, in balance, polished Chardonnay.
Sight: clear, medium gold.
Nose: lightly fruity and oaky, complex, tightly knit.
Taste: dry, medium body, green apples, good fruit, complex, tart, light wood, balanced, will age, silky feel.

Clos du Bois

From Clos du Bois Winery, Healdsburg:

Chardonnay, Alexander Valley, Calcaire Vineyard, 1982, $11.25.
A Chardonnay with finesse, one of the best from 1982 we've tasted.
Sight: clear, medium gold.
Nose: flinty, oak bouquet.
Taste: dry, nice fruit, flavor, clean, good acid, well structured, finesse, light pineapple.

Guenoc

From Guenoc Winery, Middletown:

Chardonnay, Lake County 40 percent, Sonoma County 34 percent, Mendocino County 26 percent, 1981, $8.50.
Needs time—a great value.
Sight: brilliant, deep gold.
Nose: ripe, rich, pineappley, clean.
Taste: dry, medium-full body, lots of extract, clean, good acid and fruit, well balanced, lots of pineapple character, balanced.

Haywood

From Haywood Winery, Sonoma:

Chardonnay, Sonoma County, 1981, $9.75.
Great value in distinctive Chardonnay.
Sight: light green-gold.
Nose: clean, varietal fruit.
Taste: dry, medium body, clean ripe fruit, complex, well balanced, strong structure, crisp, long, clean finish.

Jekel Vineyard

From Jekel Vineyard, Greenfield:

Chardonnay, Monterey County, Home Vineyard, Private Reserve, 1981, $14.50.
Outstanding example of balanced Chardonnay.
Sight: brilliant, medium gold.
Nose: rich oak, pineapple aromas.
Taste: dry, rich, tart, medium body, clean fruit flavors, moderate oak, well balanced, long finish.

Kenwood

From Kenwood Vineyards, Kenwood:

Chardonnay, Sonoma Valley, 1982, $11.
Very fine structure, will age without getting fat.
Sight: light yellow-gold.
Nose: clean, some fruit, young, appley.
Taste: dry, crisp, appley, good tart fruit, crisp acidity, good structure, fresh, lean, well balanced.

Laurent Perrier

From Caves Laurent-Perrier, San Jose:

Chardonnay, Blanc de Blancs, California, 1982, $9.50.
A lean, crisp style of Chardonnay that will reward those who wait.
Sight: brilliant, pale straw.
Nose: minty, leafy, apples.
Taste: dry, full body, taut, tart, leafy, appley fruit character, good citric acid, clean appley finish.

Matanzas Creek Winery

From Matanzas Creek Winery, Santa Rosa:

Chardonnay, Sonoma County, 1981, $14.
A serious contender for any Chardonnay lover.
Sight: brilliant, medium-to-deep lemony gold.
Nose: rich, very ripe and complex, woody.
Taste: dry, big and ripe, full body, viscous, fat, lots of oak in balance, good structure, balanced, long full finish.

Chardonnay, Sonoma County, 1982, $15.
Classic Chardonnay with the wood to match.
Sight: brilliant, yellow-gold.
Nose: figs and fruit, nice clean oak.
Taste: a big wine with lots of ripe Chardonnay fruit, good acid, balanced with oak, flavors just coming together.

Morgan Winery

From Morgan Winery, Salinas:

Chardonnay, Monterey County, 1982, $12.
Beautifully structured Chardonnay.
Sight: brilliant, medium gold.
Nose: clean, oaky, tropical fruit aromas.
Taste: dry, full body, round full flavors, good acid, complex, slight heat, balanced, long finish.

Mountain House

From Mountain House Winery, Cloverdale:

Chardonnay, Sonoma County, 1981, $11.
Great fruit and wood balance—tremendous potential.
Sight: clear, medium yellow-gold.
Nose: ripe, toasty oak and fruit aromas.
Taste: dry, full body, aggressive oak flavors, vanillin, strong fruit and acid, balanced, round flavors, long finish.

Simi

From Simi Winery, Healdsburg:
Chardonnay, Mendocino

County, Reserve, 1980, $20.
Outstanding Chardonnay.
Sight: yellow-green.

Nose: complex, rich, toasty, pineapple.
Taste: dry, very full body, rich and complex fruit, toasty, good acid and fruit balance, long clean finish.

Sonoma-Cutrer

From Sonoma-Cutrer Vineyards, Windsor:
Chardonnay, Russian River Valley, Estate Bottled, 1981, $9.50.
Complex Chardonnay at the right price.
Sight: brilliant, deep greenish gold.
Nose: clean, closed, ripe fruit.

Taste: dry, full body, rich, spicy fruit, lively acidity, toasty wood flavors, long finish.

Rodney Strong

From Sonoma Vineyards, Windsor:
Chardonnay, Russian River Valley, River West Vineyard, 1981, $10.
Very clean, tart style.
Sight: clear, light-to-medium gold.
Nose: fruity, fig aromas.
Taste: dry, full body, fruity, tart, citric flavors, moderate wood in background, well balanced, long finish.

Recommended

Acacia

From Acacia Winery, Napa:
Chardonnay, Napa Valley, 1982, $12.50.
Needs more time in the bottle.
Sight: brilliant, medium gold.
Nose: closed, wood, some fruit, pineapple.
Taste: dry, clean, full body, woody, closed, lots of acid, awkward.
Chardonnay, Napa Valley, Carneros District, Marina Vineyard, 1982, $16.
Very stylish.
Sight: brilliant, medium gold.
Nose: complex, pineapple, clean aromas.
Taste: dry, full body, complex flavors, clean, balanced, good acid, long finish.
Chardonnay, Napa Valley, Carneros District, Winery Lake Vineyard, 1982, $14.
Needs time.
Sight: brilliant, medium gold.
Nose: fruity, low wood, Chardonnay fruit.
Taste: dry, very tart, clean, lemony, woody, clove flavor, balanced.

Ahern

From Ahern Winery Ltd., San Fernando:
Chardonnay, Edna Valley,

MacGregor Vineyard, 1982, $12.
Solid Chardonnay.
Sight: clear, medium greengold.
Nose: toasty, vegetal, herbal aromas.
Taste: dry, medium body, toasty ripe fruit, some citric and vegetal flavors, balanced, long clean finish.
Chardonnay, Edna Valley, Paragon Vineyard, 1982, $10.
Big style of Chardonnay—needs time and food.
Sight: brilliant, yellow gold.
Nose: clean, spicy, cloves, Chardonnay.
Taste: dry, full body, lots of extract and good acidity, firm structure, intense and assertive flavor, long finish.

Alexander Valley Vineyards

From Alexander Valley Winery Co., Healdsburg:
Chardonnay, Alexander Valley, 1982, $10.
Great value in drinkable Chardonnay.
Sight: brilliant, medium gold.
Nose: spices, cloves, Chardonnay fruit.

Taste: dry, full body, good balanced fruit, some complexity, forward, long lingering finish.

Bacigalupi

From Belvedere Wine Co., Healdsburg:
Chardonnay, Sonoma County, 1981, $12.
Oaky style.
Sight: brilliant, medium gold.
Nose: toasty, ripe fruit.
Taste: dry, good full fruit, medium body, lots of wood, young, well balanced, woody finish.

Ballard Canyon

From Ballard Canyon Winery, Solvang:
Chardonnay, Santa Barbara County, 1982, $13.
Nice Chardonnay.
Sight: brilliant, medium gold.
Nose: melons, low intensity.
Taste: dry, appley, clean, full body, good fruit, balanced, young.

Balverne

From Balverne, Windsor:
Chardonnay, Sonoma County, 1980, $12.
Needs time; will improve.
Sight: brilliant, medium gold.
Nose: wood and fruit aromas.

Taste: dry, young, full body, strong fruit and acid, lots of wood, young and awkward.

Bandiera

From Bandiera Winery, Cloverdale:

Chardonnay, Mendocino County, 1982, $6.
Clean and simple Chardonnay—an honest value.
Sight: brilliant, medium straw.
Nose: appley, pineapple aromas.
Taste: dry, medium body, good fruit, just a bit thin, apple flavors, simple, balanced.

Bargetto

From Bargetto's Winery, Soquel:

Chardonnay, Santa Barbara County, 1981, $9.50.
Woody style.
Sight: brilliant, deep gold.
Nose: herbal, woody, perfumy.
Taste: dry, tart, medium body, some heat, chalky, lots of wood, sweet-sour finish.

Cypress Chardonnay, California, 1982, $8.
Very fruity style of Chardonnay.
Sight: clear, medium straw.
Nose: floral, some fruit, slightly tanky.
Taste: dry, almost sweet impression though, intense fruit, rich, moderate acid, balanced, pleasant lingering finish.

Belli & Sauret Vineyards

From HMR Ltd., Paso Robles:

Chardonnay, Paso Robles, 1982, $7.50.
Reminds us of Sauvignon Blanc; a nice wine.
Sight: brilliant, medium gold.
Nose: herbal, citric.
Taste: dry, tart, herbal, good acid, medium body, balanced, lingering finish.

Beringer

From Beringer Vineyards, St. Helena:

Chardonnay, Napa Valley, 1982, $9.75.

Woody wine but not ponderous.
Sight: brilliant, yellow-gold.
Nose: resinous, appley.
Taste: dry, medium body, some appley fruit, rough and woody, some bitterness, woody finish.

Chardonnay, Napa Valley, Private Reserve, 1981, $15.
Another winner in this series; needs age.
Sight: clear, light gold.
Nose: closed, citrusy, appley aromas.
Taste: dry, full body, closed, rich, spicy fruit, good structure, balanced, long finish.

David Bruce

From David Bruce, Los Gatos:

Chardonnay, California, 1981, $10.
Full Chardonnay in Bruce's style.
Sight: clear, medium gold.
Nose: very ripe, pineapple aromas.
Taste: dry, a bit hot, big, full body, good character, tart acidity, woody long finish.

Chardonnay, Santa Cruz Mountains, 1981, $18.
Oaky style, high in price.
Sight: brilliant, medium gold.
Nose: citric, lots of wood.
Taste: dry, good fruit, full body, high extract, lots of varietal character, big, buttery finish, balanced.

Chardonnay, Sonoma County, Wasson Vineyard, 1981, $12.
Soft, round style, very drinkable.
Sight: clear, medium-to-deep gold.
Nose: citric, light intensity.
Taste: dry, tart, medium body, some fruit, a bit thin in middle, oak in finish, long finish.

Burgess

From Burgess Cellars, St. Helena:

Chardonnay, Napa Valley, 1981, $12.50.
Well made, though a bit hot.
Sight: brilliant, medium gold.
Nose: clean, appley, light oak.
Taste: dry, slightly hot, medium body, appley, tart, crisp, good balance.

Davis Bynum

From Davis Bynum Winery, Healdsburg:

Chardonnay, Sonoma County, Reserve Bottling, 1982, $10.
Needs some age.
Sight: clear, light gold.
Nose: fresh, apples, assertive.
Taste: dry, medium body, very fruity, moderate woodiness, awkward at this time, slightly bitter finish.

Calera

From Calera Wine Co., Hollister:

Chardonnay, Santa Barbara County, 1982, $9.75.
Will benefit from a bit more age.
Sight: clear, light gold.
Nose: oak, figs, fruity.
Taste: dry, full body, toasty, lots of fruity flavors, balanced, good acid, long finish.

1982

CALERA
Chardonnay

SANTA BARBARA COUNTY

PRODUCED & BOTTLED BY
CALERA WINE COMPANY
HOLLISTER CALIFORNIA

Grapes from the Los Alamos Vineyard, Santa Barbara County, California Alcohol 13.9 percent by volume

Callaway

From Callaway Vineyard &
Winery, Temecula:
**Chardonnay, Temecula,
California, 1982, $8.50.**
Clean wine for seafood.
Sight: brilliant, medium straw-
gold.
Nose: closed.
Taste: dry, medium body, tart,
clean, good varietal character,
appley, well balanced.

Cambiaso

From Cambiaso Vineyards,
Healdsburg:
**Chardonnay, Sonoma
County, 1982, $7.67.**
Some off-flavors detract from
fruit flavor.
Sight: clear, light straw.
Nose: perfumed, some melon
fruit.
Taste: dry, medium body,
some odd flavors, fruity, bal-
anced, some bitterness on finish.

J. Carey

From J. Carey Vineyards &
Winery, Solvang:
**Chardonnay, Santa Ynez
Valley, Adobe Canyon Vine-
yard, 1983, $12.**

Young, fruity Chardonnay; a
well-structured wine.
Sight: clear, light gold.
Nose: fruity, definite wood
aromas.
Taste: dry, clean fruit, medium
body, has an off-flavor, good
structure, lingering finish.

Carneros Creek Winery

From Carneros Creek Winery,
Napa:
**Chardonnay, Napa Valley,
1981, $10.**
Still young and awkward.
Sight: clear, medium yellow-
gold.
Nose: closed, spicy-citric,
oaky.
Taste: dry, full body, closed
but good, fruit, balanced, young
and awkward, lingering finish.
**Chardonnay, Sonoma
County, 1981, $10.**
Pricey, bitter finish detracts.
Sight: clear, medium gold.
Nose: pineapple, oak, closed.
Taste: dry, medium body,
woody and closed, wood domi-
nates now, fruit may come
through, seems tired.

Chalk Hill Winery

From Chalk Hill Winery,
Healdsburg:
**Chardonnay, Chalk Hill
Vineyard, 1982, $6.**
Cellar; needs time.
Sight: brilliant, medium-to-
deep gold.
Nose: closed, oaky, some
fruit.
Taste: dry, full body, intense
fruit, high acid, woody, dumb.

Chateau Bouchaine

From Chateau Bouchaine, Los
Carneros:
**Chardonnay, Alexander
Valley, 1982, $14.**
Has great potential as rough
edges smooth out.

Sight: brilliant, medium gold.
Nose: rich, ripe figs, pineapple.
Taste: dry, full body, rich ripe
fruit, firm structure, loads of
acid, Chardonnay fruit, finish falls
off.

Chateau Chevalier

From Chateau Chevalier
Winery, St. Helena:
**Chardonnay, California,
1982, $12.50.**
Needs time to come together.
Sight: clear, medium straw.
Nose: clean, closed, some oak.
Taste: dry, medium body, in-
tense apple fruit, a bit hard, still
developing, good balance, hot
and toasty finish.

Chateau De Leu

From Chateau De Leu Winery,
Suisun:
**Chardonnay, Green Val-
ley, Solano County, 1982,
$6.95.**
Odd and out of the ordinary
style.
Sight: clear, medium gold.
Nose: rich, slight pineapples.
Taste: dry, bit hot, exotic fla-
vor, mouth-filling, leafy, minty
character.

Chateau Montelena

From Chateau Montelena
Winery, Calistoga:
**Chardonnay, Napa Valley,
1981, $16.**
Fruity, toasty style.
Sight: brilliant, medium gold-
green.
Nose: woody, nutty, fruit un-
derneath.
Taste: dry, good fruit, full
body, big style, toasty, oaky, bal-
anced, fruity finish.

Chateau St. Jean

From Chateau St. Jean,
Kenwood:
**Chardonnay, Alexander
Valley, Belle Terre Vine-
yards, 1981, $15.**
Less oaky, more refreshing
than other St. Jean Chardonnays.
Sight: brilliant, medium straw
green-gold.

Nose: clean, appley, some toastiness.

Taste: dry, medium body, clean, appley, good acid, complex wood, crisp, well balanced, long finish.

Chardonnay, Alexander Valley, Belle Terre Vineyards, 1982, $15.50.

This wine will grow on you.

Sight: brilliant, light straw.

Nose: peaches, spicy, oak.

Taste: dry, full body, balanced, good fruit flavors, subtle and complex, mile-long finish.

Chardonnay, Alexander Valley, Jimtown Ranch, 1981, $14.75.

Another feather in an already full cap.

Sight: brilliant, medium gold.

Nose: clean, closed, citrusy.

Taste: dry, clean, medium body, citrusy quality, good acid, nice wood overtones, well balanced.

Chardonnay, Alexander Valley, Robert Young Vineyards, 1982, $18.

Young and assertive Chardonnay, great backbone.

Sight: clear, medium gold.

Nose: light, figs and vanilla, varietal.

Taste: dry, full body, lots of ripe citric fruit, good acid, balanced, young and assertive, lingering finish.

Chardonnay, Sonoma County, Frank Johnson Vineyard, 1981, $14.75.

Has a long life ahead.

Sight: brilliant, light gold.

Nose: rich, buttery fruit.

Taste: dry, full body, rich, toasty, good acid, complex and young, excellent balance, full, lingering finish.

Chardonnay, Sonoma Val-

ley, McCrea Vineyard, 1981, $14.95.

Austere style.

Sight: clear, pale gold.

Nose: clean, closed, some apple fruit.

Taste: dry, full body, clean, great fruit and acid, balanced, toasty oak, long finish.

Cilurzo

From Cilurzo Vineyard & Winery, Temecula:

Chardonnay, Temecula, 1982, $7.

Clean Chardonnay without wood flavor.

Sight: clear, light gold.

Nose: clean, appley, fruity aromas.

Taste: dry, crisp, medium body, appley, good balance, lingering finish.

Clos du Bois

From Clos du Bois Winery, Healdsburg:

Chardonnay, Alexander Valley, Barrel Fermented, 1982, $9.

Fruity style.

Sight: brilliant, medium gold.

Nose: nice apples, fruit.

Taste: dry, clean, good fruit, well balanced, nice fruity finish.

Chardonnay, Dry Creek Valley, Flintwood Vineyard, 1982, $11.25.

Nice flavors, but short on acid and finish.

Sight: clear, medium gold.

Nose: tasty, grapefruit on nose.

Taste: dry, bit soft on palate, nice fruit flavors, could use more acid, bit short on finish.

Clos Du Val

From Clos Du Val Wine Co., Napa:

Chardonnay, California, 1982, $12.50.

High priced for what you get.

Sight: brilliant, light straw.

Nose: clean, closed, light fruit.

Taste: dry, medium body, good simple flavors, appley fruit, short on finish.

Concannon

From Concannon Vineyard, Livermore:

Chardonnay, Monterey County, 1981, $8.

Simple style.

Sight: clear, light gold.

Nose: closed, candied, melons.

Taste: dry, medium body, appley, tart, crisp flavors, some wood, lingering finish.

Chardonnay, Santa Maria Valley, 1982, $8.

Assertive lemony flavor, high in acid.

Sight: straw.

Nose: toasty, apples.

Taste: dry, full body, lemony, chalky, very high in acid, a bit simple in middle, tart finish.

Conn Creek

From Conn Creek Winery, St. Helena:

Chardonnay, North Coast, Chateau Maja, 1982, $6.50.

Unusual and quite appealing style.

Sight: brilliant, light gold.

Nose: appley, floral botrytis character.

Taste: dry, raw, woody Chardonnay, simple flavors, strong fruit, finish falls off.

Cosentino Select

From Cosentino Wines, Modesto:

Chardonnay, California, "The Sculptor," 1983, $8.

Needs time to come together—has some potential.

Sight: clear, medium gold.

Nose: appley, clean, varietal flavors.

Taste: dry, medium body, good balance, simple and slightly coarse flavors, appley, crisp, short on finish.

Crystal Valley

From Crystal Valley Cellars, Modesto:

Chardonnay, California, Deer Creek Vineyards, 1982, $5.50.

Simple style for a reasonable price.

Sight: clear, medium gold.
Nose: bit stinky, light in character.
Taste: dry, light body, tart, simple, soft, fruit and acid in balance, short finish.

De Loach Vineyards

From De Loach Vineyards, Santa Rosa:

Chardonnay, Russian River Valley, 1982, $12.

Needs time, has potential.

Sight: clear, medium gold.
Nose: closed, austere.
Taste: dry, good fruit, closed, young, good acid, clean, awkward.

Domaine Laurier

From Domaine Laurier, Forestville:

Chardonnay, Sonoma County, 1982, $13.

Fine Chardonnay with good fruit and some complexity.

Sight: brilliant, yellow-gold.
Nose: pineapple, citric, toasty.
Taste: dry, full body, great lemon, pineapple fruit, subtle and balanced, good acid, toasty, clean finish.

Donna Maria Vineyards

From Donna Maria Vineyards, Healdsburg:

Chardonnay, Chalk Hill Vineyard, 1982, $10.

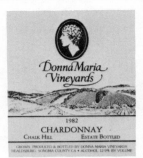

Balanced woody style.

Sight: brilliant, medium gold.
Nose: big assertive nose, lots of fruit.
Taste: dry, great tart flavor, full body, crisp, lots of acid, full wood flavors, balanced.

J. Patrick Doré Selections

From Coastal Wines Ltd., Sausalito:

Chardonnay, Santa Maria Valley, 1982, $5.50.

Different Chardonnay style.

Sight: clear, deep gold.
Nose: perfumy, ripe, botrytis.
Taste: dry, full body, low fruit, some oxidation, woody, tart, some bitterness.

Dry Creek Vineyard

From Dry Creek Vineyard, Healdsburg:

Chardonnay, Sonoma County, 1982, $10.

Another winner from Dry Creek.

Sight: brilliant, light gold.
Nose: toasty, apples, very clean.
Taste: dry, full body, good fruit and acid, balanced, delicate and elegant, good structure, lingering finish.

Chardonnay, Sonoma County, Vintner's Reserve, 1981, $14.

Very stylish and complex: will reward a year of bottle age.

Sight: clear, medium gold.
Nose: closed, good fruit and wood.

Taste: dry, tart, medium body, very clean and slightly hot, oaky, balanced, slightly hot lingering finish.

Eaglepoint

From Scharffenberger Cellars, Ukiah:

Chardonnay, Mendocino County, 1982, $9.50.

Whole lot of wood in this wine.

Sight: brilliant, medium straw.
Nose: light perfumed, wood and fruit.
Taste: dry, full body, very ripe hard fruit and lots of fruit and wood, woody finish.

Estrella

From Estrella River Winery, Paso Robles:

Chardonnay, San Luis Obispo County, NV, $4.50.

Good value for a non-complex Chardonnay.

Sight: brilliant, medium gold.
Nose: varietal, somewhat musty.
Taste: dry, medium body, a bit hot, lots of extract, well made with good acid, balanced.

Fetzer

From Fetzer Vineyards, Redwood Valley:

Chardonnay, California, Special Reserve, 1982, $10.

Very drinkable Chardonnay with promise.

Sight: brilliant, medium gold.
Nose: clean, lemony, apples.
Taste: dry, medium body, ripe fruit, good acid, a bit awkward now, some bitterness, long clean finish, some heat.

Chardonnay, Mendocino County, Barrel Select, 1982, $8.50.

Good value in clean Chardonnay.

Sight: clear, medium gold.
Nose: clean, lemony, apples.
Taste: dry, tart, medium body, good acid, balanced, medium fruit, long finish.

Sundial Chardonnay, Mendocino County, 1982, $6.50.

Big style of Chardonnay.

Sight: brilliant, medium straw.
Nose: fruity, some wood, sulfur aromas.

Taste: dry, medium-to-full body, good fruit, appley, a bit hot and bitter, long finish.

Fisher Vineyards

From Fisher Vineyards, Santa Rosa:
Chardonnay Sonoma County, 1981, $14.
Lots of potential, needs about a year.
Sight: brilliant, medium gold.
Nose: closed, fruity and spicy, wood aromas.
Taste: dry, full, slight sweet flavor, rich fruit, lots of acid, oak in balance, long finish.
Chardonnay, Sonoma County, 1982, $14.
Has volatile component on nose and palate, pricey.
Sight: brilliant, medium green-gold.
Nose: pineapple, trace of nail polish, resin.
Taste: dry, full body, ripe Chardonnay fruit, good acid, butter, pineapple, some volatile flavors on finish.

Louis J. Foppiano

From Louis J. Foppiano Winery, Healdsburg:
Chardonnay, Sonoma County, 1981, $8.75.
If you like a balanced oaky style, try this.
Sight: brilliant, medium gold.
Nose: woody, fruit, balanced aroma.
Taste: dry, medium body, good fruit, new flavors, young, good balance.
Chardonnay, Sonoma County, 1982, $9.25.
Has an herbal character we usually associate with Sauvignon Blanc.
Sight: brilliant, pale gold.
Nose: clean, herbal like Sauvignon Blanc.
Taste: dry, full body, grassy, toasty, charred character, good acid and balance, long finish.

Franciscan Vineyards

From Franciscan Vineyards, Rutherford:
Chardonnay, Napa Valley, 1981, $9.50.

Nice fruity, simple style.
Sight: brilliant, medium gold.
Nose: light intensity, fruity aroma.
Taste: dry, clean, medium-to-full body, simple fruity style, tart, good acid, wood in background, balanced.

Fritz

From Fritz Cellars, Cloverdale:
Chardonnay, Sonoma County, 1982, $9.
Big, oaky style, not very subtle.
Sight: brilliant, medium gold.
Nose: oaky, toasty, citric grapefruity, bit of green apple, clove.
Taste: full-bodied, spicy-oaky, slightly sour aftertaste, oily texture but lots of raw wood flavor.

Geyser Peak

From Geyser Peak Winery, Healdsburg:
Chardonnay, Sonoma County, 1981, $6.75.
Clean, woody Chardonnay.
Sight: brilliant, medium gold.
Nose: spicy, cloves.
Taste: dry, lots of wood, high extract, good acid, medium body, fruity and clean finish.

Girard

From Girard Winery, Oakville:
Chardonnay, Napa Valley, 1981, $12.50.
Young wine in an oaky style.
Sight: brilliant, medium gold.
Nose: very fruity, oaky.
Taste: dry, tart, medium body, very young flavors, strong oak, clean, crisp, long finish.

Glen Ellen

From Glen Ellen Winery, Glen Ellen:
Chardonnay, Sonoma Valley, Les Pierres, 1982, $10.
Not overly varietal, but a pleasant wine.
Sight: clear, medium straw.
Nose: woody, herbal, closed.
Taste: dry, medium body, good fruit, balanced, pleasant flavor, woody finish.

Grgich Hills

From Grgich Hills Cellar, Rutherford:
Chardonnay, Napa Valley, 1980, $16.75.
Big and elegant.
Sight: clear, lemon yellow.
Nose: fruity, oaky, perfumy.
Taste: dry, full body, big, rich, full and complex, nice fruit, moderate oak, very well balanced, long stylish finish.
Chardonnay, Napa Valley, 1981, $17.
Nicely made; pricey though.
Sight: clear, light-to-medium gold.
Nose: clean, woody, fruity.
Taste: dry, medium body, good fruit and acid, simple flavors, moderate wood, long finish.

Groth

From Groth Vineyards and Cellars, Napa:
Chardonnay, Napa Valley, 1982, $13.
Everything's here but finesse.
Sight: clear, medium gold.
Nose: lemony, citric fruit, some oak.
Taste: dry, full body, ripe, raw pineapple fruit, very flavorful, clean finish.

Guenoc

From Guenoc Winery, Middletown:
Chardonnay, Lake County 67 percent, Mendocino County 33 percent, 1982, $9.
Not very varietal, but a sturdy dinner wine.
Sight: medium gold.
Nose: honeyed, woody floral.

Taste: soft, slightly sweet, silky texture, medium body, slightly harsh finish.

Hacienda Wine Cellars

From Hacienda Wine Cellars, Sonoma:

Chardonnay, Sonoma County, Selected Reserve, 1981, $15.
Rich pineapple flavors.
Sight: brilliant, medium gold.
Nose: closed, pineapple, woody.
Taste: dry, full body, lots of assertive pineapple fruit, balanced, good acid, complex, woody finish.
Chardonnay, Sonoma Valley, "Clair de Lune," 1982, $9.
An unusual style, has lots of mint in nose and palate.
Sight: pale gold.
Nose: peppermint.
Taste: dry, very woody, peppermint on palate, structure is fine.

Handley

From Handley Cellars, Philo:
Chardonnay, North Coast, 1982, $12.
Nice varietal flavors, bit short on finish.
Sight: brilliant, medium gold.
Nose: toasty oak, some fruit.
Taste: dry, rich ripe fruit, buttery, good acid, balance, nice flavors, finish falls off a bit.

Haywood

From Haywood Winery, Sonoma:

Chardonnay, Sonoma Valley, 1982, $10.
Good acidity suggests a wine that will develop well.
Sight: brilliant, deep straw.
Nose: green apple, slightly spicy, vanilla edge.
Taste: tart apple flavors, simple, a bit watery in the middle, sharp finish.

Husch Vineyards

From H.A. Oswald Family, Philo:
Chardonnay, La Ribera Ranch, Mendocino, 1982, $9.
Good food wine.
Sight: clear, light gold, green.
Nose: vinous, fruit.
Taste: dry, medium body, tart, crisp, clean, balanced, lingering finish.
Chardonnay, Monterey, 1982, $10.
Big Chardonnay; needs cellaring.
Sight: clear, medium gold.
Nose: pine, pineapples.
Taste: dry, full body, rich, complex, tropical fruit, good acid and oak balance, a bit chalky on finish.

Johnson's Alexander Valley

From Johnson's Alexander Valley, Healdsburg:
Chardonnay, Alexander Valley, NV, $6.50.
Nice, lighter-bodied Chardonnay.
Sight: brilliant, medium gold.
Nose: light, perfumy, clean.

Taste: dry, very tart, clean, good fruit, medium body, moderate wood, balanced, long finish.

Jordan

From Jordan Vineyard and Winery, Healdsburg:
Chardonnay, Alexander Valley, 1981, $15.75.
Big blockbuster Chardonnay.
Sight: brilliant, yellow-gold.
Nose: oaky, buttery.
Taste: dry, full body, rich, ripe pineapple, very good acid and balance and structure, maybe a touch too much wood, some bitterness on finish.

Lakespring

From Lakespring Winery, Napa:
Chardonnay, Napa Valley, 1981, $10.
Big flavorful style.
Sight: clear, medium straw-gold.
Nose: clean, light aromas.
Taste: dry, big, hot, fruity, some wood, slightly bitter on finish.

Landmark

From Landmark Vineyards, Windsor:
Chardonnay, Alexander Valley, 1981, $9.
Young; reasonable price.
Sight: clear, medium green-gold.
Nose: varietal, oaky.
Taste: dry, medium-to-full body, viscous, clean, lots of oak flavors, slightly bitter, good character, long finish.

Chardonnay, Alexander Valley, Proprietor Grown, 1982, $10.
Some fruit, much wood, long finish.
Sight: brilliant, bright yellow.
Nose: very woody, floral edge.
Taste: woody, some fresh tropical fruit flavors, but a very woody style, very long woody finish.

Chardonnay, Sonoma County, 1982, $9.
Good Chardonnay character for the price.
Sight: brilliant, light gold.
Nose: toasty, spicy, fresh apple, vanilla.
Taste: toasty-fruity flavor, a bit alcoholic, silky-smooth feel; not too long, alcoholic finish.

Leeward

From Leeward Winery, Oxnard:
Chardonnay, Central Coast, 1982, $9.75.
Still too young.
Sight: clear, medium gold.
Nose: spicy, cloves, closed.
Taste: dry, good clean fruit, good balance, good structure.

Chardonnay, Edna Valley, 1982, $14.
Has potential, needs time.
Sight: clear, medium yellow-gold.
Nose: woody, closed.
Taste: dry, full body, lots of extract, fruit, woody, awkward now but should come around.

Chardonnay, Monterey County, Ventana Vineyard, 1982, $15.
Young, needs cellaring.
Sight: brilliant, medium gold.
Nose: clean, fruity, oak, pineapples.
Taste: dry, full body, flavorful, pineapple flavor, tart, citric, balanced.

Chardonnay, Santa Maria Valley, Bien Nacido Vineyard, 1982, $12.
Will blow a Chardonnay lover's mind.
Sight: clear, light gold.
Nose: rich, pineappley, bubble-gum aromas.
Taste: dry, full body, rich, complex fruit, pineapples, great structure, balanced, super-long finish.

Charles Lefranc

From Charles Lefranc Cellars, San Jose:
Chardonnay, San Benito County, 1981, $7.65.
Stylish, woody, but not heavy.
Sight: brilliant, medium gold.
Nose: appley, new-wood aromas.
Taste: dry, medium body, apples, crisp, high in acid, lots of wood, a bit hard on finish.

Liberty School

From Caymus Vineyards, Rutherford:
Chardonnay, Napa Valley, Lot 3, NV, $6.
Chardonnay fruit, balanced, some odd flavors detract.
Sight: medium gold.
Nose: varietal, sawdust/woody aromas.
Taste: dry, full body, lots of Chardonnay fruit, balanced, some odd flavors detract.

J. Lohr

From Turgeon & Lohr Winery, San Jose:
Chardonnay, Monterey County, Reserve 1981, $14.
Seems a bit high-priced—needs time.
Sight: brilliant, medium gold.
Nose: appley, fragrant.
Taste: dry, crisp, medium body, tart flavors, well balanced, young, long finish.

Richard Longoria

From J. Carey Vineyards, Solvang:
Chardonnay, Santa Maria Valley, 1983, $11.
Apples-and-spice style of Chardonnay.
Sight: brilliant, pale straw.
Nose: spicy, a bit of wood, mostly fruit.
Taste: dry, tart, nice fruit, clean, closed, young and spicy, appley.

Longoria Wine Cellars

From Longoria Wine Cellars, Buellton:

Chardonnay, Santa Maria Valley, 1982, $8.75.
Crisp style that needs time.
Sight: brilliant, medium gold.
Nose: apples, rich fruit.
Taste: dry, full, crisp, nice oak, balanced, good acid, slightly bitter on finish.

Maddalena Vineyard

From San Antonio Winery, Los Angeles:
Chardonnay, San Luis Obispo County, 1982, $5.95.
Simple, buttery, slightly vegetal Chardonnay.
Sight: brilliant, greenish gold.
Nose: buttery, slightly vegetal, cooked apple, slightly spicy.
Taste: ripe, flavors carry through from the nose, soft, not much acid.

Manzanita Cellars

From Manzanita Cellars, Napa:
Chardonnay, Napa Valley, 1982, $14.
Rough going now, but lots of nice flavors.
Sight: brilliant, medium gold.
Nose: clean, ripe apple aromas.
Taste: dry, full body, big and muscular, woody, good appley fruit, balanced, lingering finish.

M. Marion

From M. Marion, Los Gatos:
Chardonnay, California, 1982, $4.50.
Solid wine for the price.
Sight: clear, yellow-gold.
Nose: slight botrytis, apples, fruity.
Taste: dry, medium body, spicy and lemony fruit, a bit short in the middle, balanced, lingering finish, simple wine.

Louis M. Martini

From Louis M. Martini, St. Helena:
Chardonnay, California, 1982, $7.
Although this wine has some flaws, it might have appeal to some.
Sight: clear, medium straw.
Nose: oxidized, mercaptin aromas, some fruit under.

Taste: dry, medium body, good structure, good fruit, bitter, some moldy flavors, bitter on finish.

Paul Masson

From Paul Masson, Saratoga:
Chardonnay, Monterey, 1981, $8.50.
Pleasant drink despite its faults.
Sight: brilliant, yellow-green.
Nose: butter, pineapple, honey.
Taste: dry, rich, buttery fruit, seems flabby and chalky on palate, chalky on finish.

McDowell Valley Vineyards

From McDowell Valley Vineyards, Hopland:
Chardonnay, McDowell Valley, Estate Bottled, 1981, $9.50.
Lighter style of Chardonnay.
Sight: brilliant, medium yellow.
Nose: fruity, touch of sulfur.
Taste: dry, tart, fruity, lacks complexity and finesse, young flavors, some wood in background, short on finish.

Robert Mondavi Winery

From Robert Mondavi Winery, Oakville:
Chardonnay, Napa Valley, 1981, $10.
Drinking well now.
Sight: brilliant, full gold.
Nose: closed, mostly fruit aromas present.
Taste: dry, good fruit, full body, moderate wood and acid, balanced, round flavors.

The Monterey Vineyard

From The Monterey Vineyard, Gonzales:
Chardonnay, California, 1981, $5.99.
Good value.
Sight: brilliant, light gold.
Nose: woody, a bit of fruit.
Taste: dry, light fruit, light wood, medium body, simple, short finish.

Monticello Cellars

Monticello Cellars, Yountville:
Chardonnay, Napa Valley, 1981, $11.50.
Needs time to round off.
Sight: brilliant, pale straw-gold.
Nose: fruity, some sulfur.
Taste: dry, full body, woody, clean, good flavor and acid, balanced, long finish.
Chadonnay, Napa Valley, Barrel Fermented, 1982, $18.
Intense barrel-fermented flavors, needs more time.
Sight: deep gold, green hue.
Nose: toasty, vanilla, apples.
Taste: lots of vanilla, apple and fruit flavors, balanced with good acid, good structure but a lot of wood.

Mountain View

From Mountain View Vintners, Napa:
Chardonnay, Napa Valley, Special Selection, 1982, $7.50.
Bit high in acid, otherwise an OK Chardonnay.
Sight: clear, medium gold, green tint.
Nose: clean, simple apple aromas.
Taste: dry, medium body, clean crisp appley, lemony flavors, unbalanced forward acidity, high fruit extract.
Chardonnay, Sonoma County, 1982, $5.99.
Simple, fruity and pleasant.
Sight: brilliant, yellow-green.
Nose: musty, some fruit, grassy.
Taste: dry, medium body, some simple raw fruit, good acid, and balanced raw finish.

Mount Eden Vineyards

From Mount Eden Vineyards, Saratoga:
Chardonnay, Monterey County, 1982, $12.50.
Woody style with good fruit and texture.
Sight: brilliant, green-gold.
Nose: toasty, vanilla, citric.
Taste: dry, full body, rich and oily, good acid but lots of wood, raw and simple.

Napa Cellars

From Napa Cellars, Oakville:
Chardonnay, Alexander Valley, Black Mountain Vineyard, 1981, $11.50.
Needs time to round off the edges.
Sight: brilliant, medium-to-deep gold.
Nose: fruity, some wood.
Taste: dry, full body, clean, good varietal character, buttery, some heat and bitterness, long finish.

Parducci

From Parducci Wine Cellars, Ukiah:
Chardonnay, Mendocino County, 1982, $7.50.
Some weird flavors, but OK at the price.
Sight: medium straw, green edge.
Nose: figs, varietal.
Taste: dry, full body, balanced, good but simple Chardonnay, some liniment and heat on finish.

Pendleton

From Pendleton Winery, Santa Clara:
Chardonnay, Monterey County, Private Reserve, 1981, $12.
Big rich style.
Sight: brilliant, deep gold.

Nose: spicy, buttery, rich ripe fruit.

Taste: dry full body, complex, hints of botrytis, rich fruit, complex long finish.

Robert Pepi

From Robert Pepi Winery, Oakville:

Chardonnay, Napa Valley, 1981, $11.
Big style; needs time.
Sight: brilliant, medium gold, green tint.
Nose: closed, some fruit in background.
Taste: dry, full body, slightly hot, viscous, clean, lots of wood flavors, long finish.
Chardonnay, Napa Valley, 1982, $11.
Bit low in fruity character, good oak flavors.
Sight: clear, medium gold.
Nose: wood, not much Chardonnay, toasty.
Taste: dry, medium body, very woody, high in acid, has some fruit, oaky feel on finish.

Joseph Phelps Vineyards

From Joseph Phelps Vineyards, St. Helena:

Chardonnay, Napa Valley, 1981, $12.75.
Well done in the oaky style.
Sight: brilliant, light gold.
Nose: clean, oaky, fruity.

Taste: dry, clean, full-bodied, good fruit, buttery flavors, balanced, long finish.

Chardonnay, Sonoma County, Schellville, 1981, $14.
Big hard wine, needs additional bottle age.
Sight: clear, deep gold.
Nose: full, rich, oaky.
Taste: dry, hot, somewhat bitter, good acid, lots of oak, full body, balanced, some bitterness on finish.

Chardonnay Sonoma Sangiacomo Vineyard, 1982, $14.
A high price for a very, very oaky style.
Sight: brilliant, medium yellow-gold.
Nose: oaky, lemony aromas.
Taste: dry, full body, oak flavor dominates fruit, fruit underneath, good structure and balance, a bit flabby, woody finish, some heat.

Pine Ridge

From Pine Ridge Winery, Yountville:

Chardonnay, Napa Valley, Stag's Leap District, 1981, $13.50.
Well made in the buttery, big style.
Sight: clear, medium-deep gold.
Nose: ripe, rich, pineappley.
Taste: dry, full body, buttery, big, lots of extract, full fruit, good acid balance, long full finish.

Poplar

From Poplar Vineyards, Napa:
Chardonnay, Napa County, 1982, $7.50.
Young now, needs time.
Sight: brilliant, medium gold.
Nose: odd aroma, some fruit.
Taste: dry, tangy, medium body, apples, citric, balanced, clean finish.
Chardonnay, Sonoma County, 1981, $7.50.
A bit pricey, simple style.
Sight: clear, pale straw.
Nose: oaky, some fruit.
Taste: dry, clean, fruity, some wood, simple, short woody finish.

Quail Ridge

From Quail Ridge Winery, Napa:
Chardonnay, Napa Valley, 1981, $16.
A young wine that needs some time.
Sight: brilliant, medium gold.
Nose: oaky, some fruit, light intensity.
Taste: dry, good fruit, tart, strong acid, new wood flavors, citrusy, rich in extract—long finish.
Chardonnay, Napa Valley, 1982, $14.
Subtle and understated.
Sight: clear, medium gold.
Nose: a bit unclean, opens up a bit.
Taste: dry, medium body, subtle complexity, good structure, slight bitterness.
Chardonnay, Sonoma County, 1982, $9.
Lighter style of Chardonnay, very drinkable, without being simple.
Sight: clear, pale green-gold.
Nose: woody, citrusy, complex.
Taste: dry, medium body, grapefruity, vanilla flavors, good acid, balanced long finish.

Raymond Vineyard

From Raymond Vineyard and Cellar, St. Helena:
Chardonnay, Napa Valley, 1982, $13.
Wood dominates, has richness and viscosity.
Sight: clear, medium gold.
Nose: woody, clean pineapple, ripe.
Taste: dry, oily, viscous, good, appley Chardonnay character, lots of wood, full style, clean.

Rutherford Hill

From Rutherford Hill Winery, Rutherford:
Chardonnay, Napa Valley, Jaeger Vineyards, 1981, $11.50.
Good for current drinking.
Sight: clear, medium gold.
Nose: woody, simple fruit.
Taste: dry, full body, nice clean fruit, good acid, balanced, some heat, long finish.

RUTHERFORD HILL

1980
Napa Valley
CHARDONNAY
Jaeger Vineyards

PRODUCED AND BOTTLED BY RUTHERFORD HILL WINERY
RUTHERFORD, CALIF., USA • ALCOHOL 12.4% BY VOLUME

Chardonnay, Napa Valley, Jaeger Vineyards, Cellar Reserve, 1980, $16.
Oaky pineapple style.
Sight: brilliant, medium to deep gold.
Nose: very woody, intense aroma.
Taste: dry, full body, fruity, balanced, oaky, deep, pineapple, long finish.

St. Francis

From St. Francis Winery, Kenwood:
Chardonnay, Napa Valley, Carneros District, Jacobs Vineyard, 1982, $14.
A long life ahead.
Sight: brilliant, light gold.
Nose: fruity, spicy, oaky.
Taste: dry, deep, citric fruit, full body, high in acid, young, oaky, balanced, oaky finish.
Chardonnay, North Coast, 1982, $9.
Very floral style of Chardonnay.
Sight: clear, medium-to-deep gold.
Nose: floral, very ripe fruit.
Taste: dry, ripe, full body, Riesling-like, good fruit and acid, balanced understated oak, clean finish.
Chardonnay, Sonoma Valley, 1981, $10.75.
Lay this one away.
Sight: brilliant, light gold.
Nose: clean, pineapples, somewhat closed.
Taste: dry, medium body, good tart fruit, oaky, a bit closed, balanced, lingering finish.

Saintsbury

From Saintsbury, St. Helena:
Chardonnay, Sonoma County, 1982, $11.
Lots of wood, some sour flavors detract.
Sight: clear, green straw.
Nose: clean oak, pineappley aromas.
Taste: dry, ripe Chardonnay fruit, good wood, some slightly sour flavors, good structure, long, lingering finish.

Sanford

From Sanford Winery, San Luis Obispo:
Chardonnay, Santa Maria Valley, 1982, $12.
Oaky, very young style.
Sight: brilliant, green-gold.
Nose: closed, toasty, woody.
Taste: dry, fruity, woody, full body, fruit understated, closed, slightly bitter finish.

San Martín

From San Martin Winery, San Martin:
Chardonnay, San Luis Obispo County, 1981, $7.15.
Stylistic and austere.
Sight: brilliant, medium gold.
Nose: very oaky, light fruit.
Taste: dry, medium body, very woody, tart, lots of acid, short on finish.

Santa Ynez Valley Winery

From Santa Ynez Valley Winery, Santa Ynez:
Chardonnay, Santa Ynez Valley, 1982, $8.
Good value: will appreciate in quality and value in the cellar.
Sight: clear, light gold.
Nose: toasty, some fruit, closed.
Taste: dry, medium body, some wood, tart young flavors, citric, good acid, long finish.

August Sebastiani

From Sebastiani Vineyards, Sonoma:
Country Chardonnay, California, 1982, $6.89/1.5 liter
Solid value-priced wine.

Sight: clear, light-medium gold.
Nose: a bit appley.
Taste: dry, bit chalky, medium body, light apple fruit, not assertive.

Sequoia Grove

From The Allen Family, Rutherford:
Chardonnay, Napa Valley, Estate Bottled, 1981, $12.
Intense pineapple style.
Sight: brilliant, medium gold.
Nose: woody, closed, pineapple, complex.
Taste: dry, full body, ripe, rich, good fruit and acid, good structure, some wood, lingering finish.
Chardonnay, Sonoma-Cutrer Vineyards, 1981, $10.50
Lots of potential here—be patient.
Sight: brilliant, medium gold.
Nose: varietal, closed, some wood.
Taste: dry, tart, medium body, a bit hard and hot, closed flavors, lots of fruit and wood in background.

Silverado Vineyards

From Silverado Vineyards, Napa:
Chardonnay, Napa Valley, 1982, $10.
Young now, but has the structure and potential to last.
Sight: brilliant, green-gold.
Nose: appley, minty, vanilla oak.
Taste: dry, full body, rich, spicy, oaky fruit, oaky, a bit rough on palate now, long finish.

Simi

From Simi Winery, Healdsburg:
Chardonnay, Mendocino County, 1981, $11.
Falls off on finish, pleasant.
Sight: clear, light gold.
Nose: clean, complex pineapples/oak.
Taste: dry, full body, good fruit, complex, a bit chalky, slightly short finish.

Smothers

From Vine Hill Wines, Santa Cruz:

Chardonnay, California, 1982, $11.
Try it if you prefer a woody style.
Sight: clear, light gold.
Nose: toasty, oaky, some fruit.
Taste: dry, full body, simple fruit, very woody on palate and in finish.

Chardonnay, Sonoma County, 1982, $12.50.
Pricey.
Sight: clear, medium-deep gold.
Nose: candied, woody, rich, Chardonnay.
Taste: dry, very ripe, full body, candied flavors, pineapple, woody, long finish.

Sonoma-Cutrer

From Sonoma-Cutrer Vineyards, Windsor:

Chardonnay, Russian River Valley, Cutrer Vineyard, 1981, $12.75.
Big woody style, but plenty of fruit behind it.
Sight: brilliant, medium yellow-gold.
Nose: very woody, cedary, some fruit.
Taste: dry, full body, taste follows nose, hard, ripe fruit, good acid, good long finish.

Stag's Leap Wine Cellars

From Stag's Leap Wine Cellars, Napa:

Chardonnay, Napa Valley, 1982, $13.50.
Heat and harshness detract from an otherwise nice wine.
Sight: brilliant, green straw.
Nose: buttery, vanilla, spice.
Taste: dry, medium body, simple, spicy fruit, balanced, short, clean finish, some heat.

Stevenot Winery

From Stevenot Winery, Murphys:

Chardonnay, Mendocino County, 1981, $9.
Stylish fruity Chardonnay.
Sight: clear, medium gold.

Nose: light, some wood and fruit.
Taste: dry, full body, woody, good fruit and acid, clean, citric, grapefruit, balanced though hot.

Chardonnay, Sonoma County, 1981, $8.50.
Good value.
Sight: brilliant, medium straw-gold.
Nose: clean, moderate, oaky aromas.
Taste: dry, medium body, good acid, lots of varietal fruit, citric, balanced wood flavors, long finish.

Stone Creek

From Stone Creek Cellars, Healdsburg:

Chardonnay, Alexander Valley, Special Selection, 1982, $6.
High alcohol hurts this otherwise fine wine.
Sight: clear, light-to-medium gold.
Nose: apples, citrus fruit aromas.
Taste: dry, good fruit, medium body, moderate oak, balanced except for high alcohol, long finish.

Stonegate

From Stonegate Winery, Calistoga:

Chardonnay, Alexander Valley, 1982, $9.
Good with balanced fruit, simple Chardonnay.
Sight: medium straw-green.
Nose: green peaches and grapefruit.
Taste: dry, full-bodied, raw, woody, green-peach flavors, good acid, good structure, long clean finish.

Chardonnay, Napa Valley, Spaulding Vineyard, 1981, $15.
Rambunctious, pricey.
Sight: brilliant, yellow-gold.
Nose: assertive pineapple, bubblegum.
Taste: dry, full body, intense, aggressive flavors, pineapple, big and rough, raw flavors.

Chardonnay, Sonoma County, 1981, $9.

Well balanced by fruit and wood.
Sight: clear, medium-deep gold.
Nose: understated, oaky, vanillin.
Taste: dry, sweetish flavors, lots of fruit, ripe, lots of oak, acid in balance, lingering finish.

Rodney Strong

From Sonoma Vineyards, Windsor:

Chardonnay, Sonoma County, Chalk Hill Vineyard, 1982, $9.95.
Ripe Chardonnay with lots of fruit.
Sight: clear, green-gold.
Nose: clean, botrytis, apples, pears.
Taste: dry, full-body, tart, clean, ripe fruit, good acid and balance, wood flavors.

Chardonnay, Sonoma County, Chalk Hill Vineyard, 1981, $10.
Clean, mature, oaky style of Chardonnay.
Sight: clear, medium gold.
Nose: mature, woody, seems a bit closed.
Taste: dry, full body, nice fruit, good acid, sweet oaky flavor, rich, balanced, long oaky finish.

Vichon

From Vichon Winery, Oakville:

Chardonnay, Napa Valley, 1981, $15.
Very stylish and young Chardonnay.
Sight: brilliant, medium straw-gold.
Nose: varietal, bit of oak.
Taste: dry, clean, woody, medium body, restrained and a bit closed on palate, balanced, crisp finish.

Chardonnay, Napa Valley, 1982, $15.
Excellent achievement in a difficult vintage for white wines.
Sight: brilliant, medium gold.
Nose: nice oak and Chardonnay.
Taste: dry, full body, rich, intense, lush and full, great acid and backbone, buttery and appley.

Villa Mt. Eden

From Villa Mt. Eden Winery, Oakville:

Chardonnay, Napa Valley, Estate Bottled, 1981, $13.

A wine that will reward bottle age.

Sight: brilliant, medium-deep gold.

Nose: rich, very clean, pineappley.

Taste: dry, clean, citric, full body, a bit high in alcohol, young, good fruit flavors, woody, long, hot finish.

Mark West Vineyards

From Mark West Vineyards, Forestville:

Chardonnay, Russian River Valley, Estate Bottled, 1981, $9.

Pineappley flavor.

Sight: clear, medium gold.

Nose: some fruit, a bit of wood.

Taste: dry, good fruit, medium body, light wood, simple, pineapples, lingering tart finish.

Wine Discovery

From Wine Discovery, Healdsburg:

Chardonnay, Santa Barbara County, 1982, $3.99.

Very tart, light-style Chardonnay.

Sight: clear, medium gold.

Nose: oaky, varietal, appley.

Taste: dry, medium body, intense tart fruit, high in acid, short on middle and finish.

Woltner

From Woltner Cellars, Healdsburg:

Chardonnay, Central Coast, Cask 631, 1982, $5.

Good varietal Chardonnay for the money.

Sight: clear, medium green-gold.

Nose: vanilla, fruity, honey aromas.

Taste: dry, full body, good acidic fruit up front, one-dimensional, some good wood, lingering finish.

Zaca Mesa

From Zaca Mesa Winery, Los Olivos:

Toyon Chardonnay, Santa Barbara County, 1982, $6.

Rubber aromas detract.

Sight: brilliant, medium gold.

Nose: tar aromas, fruit, rubbery.

Taste: dry, very tart, woody, low fruit, herbal.

ZD Wines

From ZD Wines, Napa:

Chardonnay, California, 1981, $12.95.

A very big, stylish Chardonnay.

Sight: brilliant, deep yellow-gold.

Nose: floral, oaky, varietal.

Taste: dry, very ripe fruit, medium body, oily, nice acid, lots of oak, balanced, very long-lasting finish.

Stephen Zellerbach Vineyard

From Stephen Zellerbach Cellars, Healdsburg:

Chardonnay, Alexander Valley, Warnecke Sonoma Vineyard, 1982, $10.49.

Good food wine.

Sight: clear, medium straw.

Nose: clean, citric, fruity.

Taste: dry, medium body, simple but clean fruit, balanced, some wood on finish.

CHENIN BLANC

Best Buy

Lakespring

From Lakespring Winery, Napa:

Chenin Blanc, Napa Valley, 1983, $6.

Generous fruit in a dry Chenin Blanc.

Sight: light straw.

Nose: intensely floral, pippin apple-fresh, honey on the edge.

Taste: dry, clean, crisp, lean, well-defined fruit, finishes with good acid bite, lemony.

Highly Recommended

Almadén

From Almadén Vineyards, San Jose:

Chenin Blanc, California, 1982, $3.55.

Good value in a very fruity style of Chenin.

Sight: brilliant, pale straw.
Nose: assertive, apples, melons.
Taste: off-dry, assertive, medium body, apple flavors, clean, very well balanced.

Concannon

From Concannon Vineyards, Livermore:

Chenin Blanc, California, Noble Vineyards, 1982, $4.75.

Worth seeking out.

Sight: clear, pale straw.
Nose: clean, citric, grapefruit.
Taste: dry, medium body, good fruit and wood, complex flavors, balanced.

Grand Cru Vineyards

From Grand Cru Vineyards, Glen Ellen:

Dry Chenin Blanc, Clarksburg, 1983, $6.50.

Very clean, off-dry Chenin Blanc with lots of varietal flavor.

Sight: brilliant, straw.
Nose: clean, fresh, yeasty, grassy.
Taste: off-dry, full body, clean, lots of ripe assertive varietal fruit, melons, touch citric, tart clean finish.

Hacienda Wine Cellars

From Hacienda Wine Cellars, Sonoma:

Dry Chenin Blanc, California, 1983, $5.50.

Just what you want in a Chenin Blanc.

Sight: brilliant, pale straw.
Nose: clean varietal fruit, melons.
Taste: off-dry, full body, good, tart, spicy, melony fruit, good balance, long clean finish.

Parducci

From Parducci Wine Cellars, Ukiah:

Chenin Blanc, Mendocino County, 1982, $4.50.

A wine for summer quaffing.

Sight: brilliant, pale gold.
Nose: clean, melony.
Taste: off-dry, clean, light body, full melon fruit, nice acid, well balanced.

Pine Ridge

From Pine Ridge Winery, Yountville:

Chenin Blanc, Napa Valley, Yountville District, 1983, $6.50.

Textbook, off-dry Chenin Blanc.

Sight: brilliant, pale straw.
Nose: clean, steely Chenin Blanc character.
Taste: off-dry, crisp, fresh, good lemony Chenin Blanc, apply fruit, great acid and balance.

San Martín

From San Martin Winery, San Martin:

Soft Chenin Blanc, California, 1982, $4.99.

A simple, straightforward sipping wine.

Sight: brilliant, light straw.
Nose: varietal, melon, fruit aromas.
Taste: sweet, very soft and light, great fruit, good varietal character, low acid, balanced, short finish.

Simi

From Simi Winery, Healdsburg:

Chenin Blanc, Mendocino County, 1983, $6.50.

More complexity than one would expect from a Chenin Blanc.

Sight: brilliant, pale straw.
Nose: intensely fruity, honeydew melon.
Taste: honey-like, soft, slightly spicy orangey flavors, good acid backbone carries a complex honey-citrus finish.

Recommended

Bel Arbres Vineyards

from Bel Arbres Vineyards,
Redwood Valley:

Chenin Blanc, California, 1982, $5.75.

Distinctive Chenin flavors—very pleasant to drink.

Sight: brilliant, light straw.

Nose: clean, melons, classic Chenin aromas.

Taste: off-dry, clean, grapefruit, medium body, fruity flavors, good acid, well balanced.

Boeger

From Boeger Winery,
Placerville:

Chenin Blanc, El Dorado, 1983, $5.50.

Soft, slightly syrupy sipping wine.

Sight: brilliant, straw, greenish.

Nose: slightly grassy, moldy or green fruit.

Taste: off-dry, fairly rich, silky texture, decadent fruit flavors, not heavy, soft balance of fruit and acid.

Callaway

From Callaway Vineyard & Winery, Temecula:

Chenin Blanc-Dry, Temecula, 1982, $6.

Great flavors, somewhat short on finish.

Sight: brilliant, medium yellow-gold.

Nose: light, balanced fruit aromas.

Taste: dry, simple flavors, light body, clean fruit, slightly low in acid, short on finish.

Cassayre-Forni Cellars

From Cassayre-Forni Cellars, Rutherford:

Dry Chenin Blanc, Napa Valley, Lot 1, 1982, $6.

A different style; not the melony style.

Sight: clear, light gold.

Nose: piney, resinous, some fruit.

Taste: dry, light body, tart, woody, piney, resinous flavor, balanced, good acid, short finish.

Chappellet

From Chappellet Vineyard, St. Helena:

Chenin Blanc, Napa Valley, 1982, $7.50.

Clean, dry Chenin.

Sight: brilliant, pale-to-light gold.

Nose: clean, melons.

Taste: dry, medium body, melons, good balance, excellent character.

Cilurzo

From Cilurzo Vineyard & Winery, Temecula:

Chenin Blanc, Temecula, 1982, $5.

Easy to drink, good value.

Sight: brilliant, pale straw.

Nose: bit fruity, light intensity.

Taste: off-dry, fruity, clean, light body, balanced, short finish.

Congress Springs

From Congress Springs Vineyards, Saratoga:

Chenin Blanc, Santa Cruz Mountains, 1983, $7.

Unusual style for a California Chenin Blanc, rich in texture but not opulent in fruit.

Sight: medium yellow.

Nose: toasty, lemony, austere.

Taste: Slightly sweet, with sufficient acid to balance, a fairly rich wine with lemon-apple fruit, buttery, slightly toasty aftertaste.

Dry Creek Vineyard

From Dry Creek Vineyard, Healdsburg:

Dry Chenin Blanc, California, 1983, $6.

A very clean and crisp Chenin Blanc.

Sight: brilliant, pale straw.

Nose: melons, citrus, apples.

Taste: dry, melons, honeydew, lemony, pleasant and crisp, lingering finish.

Estrella

From Estrella River Winery,
Paso Robles:

Chenin Blanc, Paso Robles, 1982, $5.

Soft, easy to drink.

Sight: brilliant, pale gold.

Nose: fruity, clean, honey aromas.

Taste: off-dry, light-to-medium body, clean, honey, soft flavors.

Fetzer

From Fetzer Vineyards,
Redwood Valley:

Chenin Blanc, North Coast, 1982, $5.50.

Lots of melony flavors—a good buy.

Sight: brilliant, pale straw.

Nose: light, melons, clean.

Taste: off-dry, clean, crisp, light body, tart flavors, easy short finish.

Chenin Blanc, North Coast, 1983, $5.50.

Simple, light and clean quaffing wine.

Sight: brilliant, light gold.

Nose: grassy, melons, fruity.

Taste: dry, medium body, clean fruit, melons, good balance, firm acidity, lingering finish.

Geyser Peak

From Geyser Peak Winery,
Geyserville:

Soft Chenin Blanc, Alexander Valley, Nervo Ranch, 1982, $5.

Easy sipping Chenin.

Sight: brilliant, pale straw.

Nose: clean, appley, fresh.

Taste: medium, sweet, light body, clean, good fruit, soft acid, balanced, clean finish.

Grand Cru Vineyards

From Grand Cru Vineyards,
Glen Ellen:

Dry Chenin Blanc, Clarksburg, 1982, $6.50.

Great flavors, clean dry style.

Sight: brilliant, pale straw.

Nose: fruity, melons, clean.

Taste: dry, light body, clean,

fresh, melons, crisp, good acid, tart flavors, balanced, lingering finish.

Guenoc

From Guenoc Winery, Middletown:
Chenin Blanc, Guenoc Valley, 1982, $5.
Almost too dry.
Sight: brilliant, pale straw-gold.
Nose: light, some melons.
Taste: dry, slightly bitter, good fruit and acid, melony character, some bitterness on finish.
Chenin Blanc, Guenoc Valley, 1983, $5.
A lot of character for Chenin Blanc; a good balance of fruit and acid.
Sight: medium gold.
Nose: clean, apples, melon, Chenin Blanc.
Taste: dry, full body, soft and clean, good fruit, palate follows nose, long, clean finish.

Hacienda Wine Cellars

From Hacienda Wine Cellars, Sonoma:
Dry Chenin Blanc, Sonoma County, 1982, $5.50.
Dry Chenin without the bitterness.
Sight: clear, pale straw.
Nose: dry, clean, medium body, varietal, melony flavors, good acid, balanced.

Kenwood

From Kenwood Vineyards, Kenwood:
Dry Chenin Blanc, California, 1982, $6.
Clean; pricey.
Sight: brilliant, light gold, some spritz.
Nose: floral, clean, low intensity.
Taste: off-dry, medium body, fruity, clean, tart, tangy, short finish.
Dry Chenin Blanc, California, 1983, $6.
Ripe, tart fruit, but not dry.
Sight: brilliant, pale straw.

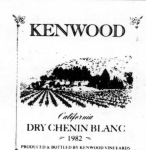

California
DRY CHENIN BLANC
~ 1982 ~
PRODUCED & BOTTLED BY KENWOOD VINEYARDS
KENWOOD, CALIFORNIA
ALCOHOL 11.9% BY VOLUME

Nose: some varietal character, sweaty.
Taste: off-dry, full body, good acid, balanced, tart lean fruit, clean fruit.

Lakespring

From Lakespring Winery, Napa:
Chenin Blanc, Napa Valley, 1981, $6.50.
Good for food though pricey.
Sight: clear, pale straw.
Nose: crisp, fruity.
Taste: dry, medium body, some bitterness, fruity, good acid, balanced, lingering finish.

The Monterey Vineyard

From The Monterey Vineyard, Gonzales:
Chenin Blanc, Monterey County, 1982, $3.99.
Needs food.
Sight: clear, light straw.
Nose: sulfur, some fruit.
Taste: dry, medium body, good fruit, simple style, balanced, a bit short on acid, short finish.

J. Pedroncelli

From J. Pedroncelli Winery, Geyserville:
Chenin Blanc, Sonoma County, 1982, $4.50.
For warm-weather consumption.
Sight: brilliant, spritzy, medium straw.
Nose: fresh, fruity.
Taste: off-dry, clean, good fruit and acid, spritzy on palate, well balanced.

R. H. Phillips Vineyard

From R. H. Phillips Vineyard, Camino:
Chenin Blanc, Yolo County, Dunnigan Hills, 1983, $4.49.
Clean, pleasant sipping wine. Varietally true.
Sight: pale straw.
Nose: cantaloupe, slightly grassy, burnt match on the edge.
Taste: soft, grapy fruit, short, slightly chalky on finish.

August Sebastiani

From Sebastiani Vineyards, Sonoma:
Country Chenin Blanc, NV, $6 per 1.5 liter.
Clean party quaff.
Sight: brilliant, medium straw.
Nose: good fruit, slight sulfur.
Taste: off-dry, very ripe fruit, light body, a bit low in acid, tart finish.

Simi

From Simi Winery, Healdsburg:
Chenin Blanc, North Coast, 1982, $6.50.
Clean and varietal.
Sight: brilliant, pale straw.
Nose: clean varietal.
Taste: dry, light body, good character and fruit, well balanced, clean finish.

Souverain

From Souverain Cellars, Geyserville:
Chenin Blanc, North Coast, 1982, $5.
Clean, light quaff.
Sight: clear, light straw.

Nose: clear, spicy, cloves.
Taste: dry, medium body, good fruit, balanced, full flavors, fruit drops off, short finish.

Stevenot Winery

From Stevenot Winery, Murphys:

Chenin Blanc Dry, El Dorado County, 1981, $4.95.
Woody, heavy-handed style.
Sight: clear, medium-to-deep gold.

Nose: intense aroma, woody.
Taste: dry, woody, fruity, varietal, medium body, some bitterness on middle and finish.

Chenin Blanc Dry, El Dorado County, 1982, $4.95.
A clean Chenin with body.
Sight: clear, medium straw.
Nose: some fruit, floral, melons.
Taste: dry, tart, clean, spicy, good fruit, good acid, balanced.

GAMAY/GAMAY BEAUJOLAIS

Spectator Selection

J. Lohr

From Turgeon & Lohr Winery, San Jose:

Monterery Gamay, Monterey County, 1982, $4.50.
A winner for the second straight year.
Sight: clear, light ruby.
Nose: very clean, fresh, Gamay aromas.
Taste: dry, very clean, grapy, good fruit, nice lively acid, very well balanced.

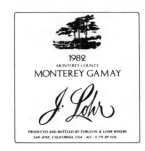

Recommended

Almadén

From Almadén Vineyards, San Jose:

Gamay Beaujolais, San Benito County, 1983, $5.85.
Needs to be chilled; not much fruit for this type.
Sight: magenta-cranberry.
Nose: spicy, slightly rubbery, earthy.
Taste: dry, slightly bitter, spicy but not very fruity.

Cilurzo

From Cilurzo Vineyard & Winery, Temecula:

Gamay Beaujolais, Temecula, 1981, $5.
Intense woody style.
Sight: clear, deep garnet.
Nose: woody, some fruit.
Taste: dry, medium body, some grapy fruit, earthy-woody, bitter finish.

Falcon Crest

From Spring Mountain Vineyards, St. Helena:

Gamay Beaujolais, Napa Valley, 1981, $6.50.
Light red wine for food.
Sight: clear, medium-to-deep ruby.
Nose: spicy, Pinot Noir aromas.
Taste: dry, medium body, very earthy, good acid, tart flavors, balanced.

Fetzer

From Fetzer Vineyards,
Redwood Valley:

Gamay Beaujolais, Mendocino, 1983, $4.25.
Tastes like a raspberry sour,
serve chilled.
Sight: clear, medium violet.
Nose: clean, raspberry candy.
Taste: dry, medium body, very
tart and clean, hard fruit, good
acid, balanced, tangy-clean finish.

Mill Creek Vineyards

From Mill Creek Vineyards,
Healdsburg:

**Gamay Beaujolais,
Sonoma County, 1982, $5.**
Clean, easy to drink.
Sight: bright, medium ruby-purple.
Nose: clean Gamay, grapy aromas.
Taste: dry, simple, fruity, medium body, good acid, balanced,
earthy fruit, lingering finish.

Parducci

From Parducci Wine Cellars,
Ukiah:

Gamay Beaujolais, Mendocino County, 1981, $4.25.
A lighter style of Gamay—for
current drinking.
Sight: clear, light-to-medium
red.
Nose: earthy, berries, grapy.
Taste: dry, good fruit, light
body, clean, varietal, good acid,
balanced, lingering finish.

Robert Pecota

From Robert Pecota Winery,
Calistoga:

**Gamay Beaujolais, Napa
Valley, 1983, $5.25.**
Heavy-handed, lacking assertive fruit.
Sight: brilliant, bright purple.
Nose: light, grapy, cherries.
Taste: dry, slightly low in fruit,
moderate bitterness, some alcohol and heavy on finish.

Preston

From Preston Vineyards &
Winery, Healdsburg:

**Gamay Beaujolais, Dry
Creek Valley, 1983, $4.50.**
Has a pleasant fruity flavor;
serve slightly chilled.
Sight: brilliant, bright purple-ruby color.
Nose: acetone, banana-like
aromas.
Taste: dry, good fruit, clean,
light body, crisp, balanced.

A. Rafanelli

From A. Rafanelli, Healdsburg:

**Gamay Beaujolais,
Sonoma County, Unfiltered,
1980, $4.25.**
A Gamay Beaujolais for those
who like a fuller style.
Sight: clear, medium ruby.
Nose: rich, fruity, varietal.
Taste: dry, clean, medium
body, rich, full fruit, good acid,
tannin, balanced.
**Gamay, Napa Valley,
1982, $4.99.**
A good, light, red food wine.
Sight: clear, medium ruby.
Nose: complex, earthy, grapy.
Taste: dry, medium body, assertive fruit, complex, tart, good
structure, balanced.

Charles F. Shaw

From Charles F. Shaw
Vineyards & Winery, St.
Helena:

**Gamay, Napa Valley, Domaine Elucia Reserve, 1981,
$5.99.**
Can take a few years of age,
but why wait?
Sight: brilliant, medium purple.
Nose: berries, complex aromas, clean.

Taste: dry, big, complex,
earthy flavors, good structure,
varietal, balanced, lingering finish.

Souverain

From Souverain Cellars,
Geyserville:

**Gamay Beaujolais, North
Coast, 1982, $4.75.**
Serve slightly chilled—a nice
quaff.
Sight: brilliant, medium red-ruby.
Nose: grapy, Gamay, earthy,
stemmy.
Taste: dry, tart, some bitterness, light body, a bit of tannin,
good grapy Gamay character,
balanced.

Wente Bros.

From Wente Bros., Livermore:

Gamay Beaujolais, California, 1981, $4.17.
Serve chilled.
Sight: clear, light orange-ruby.
Nose: earthy, stemmy, mature.
Taste: dry, medium body,
fruity, tangy, bitter on finish,
slight tannin.

GEWÜRZTRAMINER

Best Buys

Round Hill

From Round Hill Vineyards, St. Helena:

Gewürztraminer, Napa Valley, 1983, $5.

A bit soft in finish, otherwise very nice.

Sight: clear, light straw, green tint.

Nose: clean, spicy, grapefruit, rose petals.

Taste: clean, off-dry, very nice fruit, a bit soft, nicely balanced, clean finish.

St. Francis

From St. Francis Winery, Kenwood:

Gewürztraminer, Sonoma Valley, 1982, $6.40.

Textbook Gewürztraminer; light and spicy.

Sight: brilliant, light gold.

Nose: light, spicy, varietal.

Taste: off-dry, light body, nice fruit, spicy, grapefruit, good acid, tart flavors, balanced, lingering finish.

Highly Recommended

Chateau St. Jean

From Chateau St. Jean, Kenwood:

Gewürztraminer, Alexander Valley, Robert Young

Vineyards, 1982, $18/ 375ml.

Dessert in a glass; needs no food accompaniment.

Sight: clear, deep gold.

Nose: floral, honey, botrytis.

Taste: sweet, viscous, very rich fruit, floral, lots of complexity, honey flavor on finish.

Clos du Bois

From Clos du Bois, Healdsburg:

Gewürztraminer, Alexander Valley, Early Harvest, 1983, $7.50.

An outstanding Gewürztraminer; has the structure

and character most never achieve.

Sight: brilliant, medium straw.

Nose: clean, floral, spicy, intense varietal character.

Taste: dry, medium body, clean, very spicy assertive fruit, ripe flavors, fine acidity, very well balanced, refreshing, lingering finish.

Villa Mt. Eden

From Villa Mt. Eden Winery, Oakville:

Gewürztraminer, Napa Valley, Late Harvest, 1983, $12.

Beautiful, spicy, firm flavors.
Sight: brilliant, deep gold color.
Nose: botrytis, apples aroma.
Taste: sweet, full body, viscous, lots of character, good structure, complex, young, long finish.

Recommended

Davis Bynum

From Davis Bynum Winery, Healdsburg:

Gewürztraminer, Sonoma County, Westside Road, 1983, $5.50.
Clean varietal; could be nicer if drier.
Sight: clear, slightly spritzy, brassy color.
Nose: rose petals.
Taste: off-dry, floral, clean, slightly citric, rose-petal character, a bit too tart.

J. Carey

From J. Carey Vineyards & Winery, Solvang:

Gewürztraminer, Santa Maria Valley, 1982, $6.75.
Slightly sweet and very fruity.
Sight: clear, pale straw.
Nose: light, grapefruit, varietal.
Taste: off-dry, tart, fruity, light body, very clean, good acid, balanced with a lingering finish.

Gewürztraminer, Alexander Valley, 1983, $8.
Good wine with food, has good balance.
Sight: brilliant, pale straw-green.
Nose: light aroma, some spice.
Taste: dry, tart, good varietal character, nice acid, citric on finish.

Gewürztraminer, Alexander Valley, Belle Terre Vineyards, Selected Late Harvest, 1981, $13/375ml.

Special wine for a special occasion.
Sight: clear, deep yellow-gold.
Nose: slightly lemony, botrytis aromas.
Taste: sweet, intense, full body, viscous, syrupy fruit, honey, botrytis, moderate acid, balanced, long finish.

Clos du Bois

From Clos du Bois, Healdsburg:
Gewürztraminer, Early Harvest, Alexander Valley, 1982, $7.50.
Simple, varietal wine for the price.
Sight: clear, pale straw.
Nose: clean, grapy, some varietal.
Taste: off-dry, light body, simple, direct spicy flavors, short finish.

Donna Maria Vineyards

From Donna Maria Vineyards, Healdsburg:
Gewürztraminer, Chalk Hill Vineyards, 1982, $6.
Stylish, very clean Gewürztraminer.
Sight: brilliant, pale straw.
Nose: piney, spicy, varietal.
Taste: off-dry, clean, light body, spicy character, moderate acid, long finish.

Fetzer

From Fetzer Vineyards, Redwood Valley:
Gewürztraminer, North Coast, 1982, $6.
Easy sipping.
Sight: brilliant, light-medium gold.
Nose: floral, lightly varietal.
Taste: off-dry, fruity, clean, good acid, pleasant flavors, touch of spritz on the palate, very well balanced.

Gewürztraminer, North Coast, 1983, $6.
Pleasant drink, but ends abruptly.
Sight: brilliant, medium gold.
Nose: full, heavy, botrytis Gewürztraminer.
Taste: dry, very full body, good honey—botrytis, Gewürztraminer flavor, then a bit soapy and fat, short finish.

Grand Cru Vineyards

From Grand Cru Vineyards, Glen Ellen:
Gewürztraminer, Alexander Valley, 1982, $8.50.
Intensely varietal.
Sight: brilliant, light-to-medium gold.
Nose: slight spice and botrytis.
Taste: off-dry, intense spicy fruit, clean, good acid, very varietal, balanced, full finish.

Hacienda

From Hacienda Wine Cellars, Sonoma:

Gewürztraminer—Dry, Sonoma County, 1983, $6.75.
Lots of potential in this Gewürztraminer.
Sight: pale gold.
Nose: perfumed, spicy, varietal.
Taste: off-dry, full body, good lush fruit, balanced, clean spicy finish.

Hop Kiln Winery

From Hop Kiln Winery, Healdsburg:

Gewürztraminer, Russian River Valley, 1983, $7.50.
Has a coarse character; nice style though.
Sight: clear, light gold.
Nose: spicy, grapefruit.
Taste: dry, light body, hard, not much fruit, a bit coarse, lingering finish.

Husch Vineyards

From H.A. Oswald Family, Philo:

Gewürztraminer, Anderson Valley, 1982, $6.25.
Will go well with fruit or light food.
Sight: brilliant, pale green gold.
Nose: clean, spicy, good varietal character.
Taste: off-dry, good fruit, clean, medium body, balanced, lots of grapefruit flavors, short on finish.

Gewürztraminer, Anderson Valley, Late Harvest, 1982, $9.50.
Limited availability; try as an aperitif.
Sight: clear, medium gold.
Nose: peaches, light, clean.
Taste: sweet, full body, botrytis, lots of apricots, well balanced, lingering sweet finish.

Kenwood

From Kenwood Vineyards, Kenwood:

Gewürztraminer, Sonoma Valley, 1983, $6.50.
Has clean, although light, va-

KENWOOD
Sonoma Valley
GEWÜRZTRAMINER
1983
PRODUCED & BOTTLED BY KENWOOD VINEYARDS
KENWOOD, CALIFORNIA
ALCOHOL 11.5% BY VOLUME

rietal character and is best served chilled.
Sight: light straw.
Nose: ripe, spicy varietal aromas.
Taste: off-dry, full body, soft, sweet, spicy Gewürztraminer fruit, balanced, but cloying on the finish.

Paul Masson

From Paul Masson Vineyards, Saratoga:

Gewürztraminer, Monterey, 1982, $4.20.
Nose is very clean, great flavors.
Sight: brilliant, light straw.
Nose: fine varietal nose.
Taste: off-dry, a bit flabby and cloying, nice varietal flavors, clean finish.

Matrose

From Matrose Wines, Cloverdale:

Traminer, Alexander Valley, 1983, $7.
Tastes like Gewürztraminer, feels like Gewürztraminer, needs time to develop.
Sight: brilliant, pale-to-medium straw.
Nose: grapefruit, slightly spicy.
Taste: allspice, citrus flavors, soft on palate but rich enough to stand up to food, slightly bitter on finish but balanced with fruit.

The Monterey Vineyard

From The Monterey Vineyard, Gonzales:

Gewürztraminer, Monterey County, 1982, $4.99.
Nice sipping wine for the price—not textbook Gewürztraminer.
Sight: brilliant, light straw.
Nose: light, rose petals, some grapefruit.
Taste: off-dry, tart, balanced, simple, pleasant, not particularly varietal.

Monticello Cellars

From Monticello Cellars, Napa:

Gewürz Traminer, Napa Valley, 1982, $6.50.
Assertive, but slight bitterness detracts.
Sight: clear, light straw gold.
Nose: light, varietal aromas.
Taste: dry, some bitterness, full fruit flavors, spicy, melons, tart flavors, good balance.

J. Pedroncelli

From J. Pedroncelli Winery, Geyserville:

Gewürztraminer, Sonoma County, 1983, $5.25.

J. PEDRONCELLI
SONOMA COUNTY
GEWÜRZTRAMINER
1983

Simple, pleasant sipper.
Sight: brilliant, medium straw.
Nose: floral-carnation, rosy and citrusy.
Taste: soft, simple, slightly lemony and spicy, soft finish, sweetness covers a slight bitterness.

Round Hill

From Round Hill Vineyards, St. Helena:

Gewürztraminer, North Coast, 1982, $4.50.
Would be good with light foods.
Sight: brilliant, light-to-medium gold.
Nose: light, some varietal character and spice.
Taste: off-dry, tart, good character, light body, balanced fruit and acid, short finish.

Rutherford Hill

From Rutherford Hill Winery, Rutherford:

Gewürztraminer, Napa Valley, 1982, $5.75.
Serve very chilled or wine will be bitter.
Sight: clear, greenish straw.
Nose: varietal, spicy, rose petals.
Taste: off-dry, clean, good varietal, light residual sugar helps, bittersweet finish, seems slightly out of balance, lacks acid.

St. Francis

From St. Francis Winery, Kenwood:

Gewürztraminer, Sonoma Valley, 1983, $6.50.
Heavy; nice flavors, has fine character.
Sight: clear, pale, almost colorless.
Nose: has Muscat spiciness.
Taste: sweet, grapy flavor, a bit heavy, very clean and fruity, viscous.

Sebastiani

From Sebastiani Vineyards, Sonoma:

Gewürztraminer, Sonoma Valley, 1982, $5.75.
Reasonably priced.
Sight: brilliant, light gold.
Nose: spicy, grapefruit.
Taste: dry, light body, fruity, clean, good acid, spicy grapefruit flavors, slightly soapy finish.

Smothers

From Smothers–Vine Hill Wines, Santa Cruz:

Gewürztraminer, Alexander Valley, 1981, $9.75.
Serve chilled with light fruits.
Sight: brilliant, medium gold.
Nose: honey, a bit closed.
Taste: sweet, full body, a bit cloying, clean fruit flavors, lacks some acid, balanced, long finish.

Susiné

From Susiné Cellars, Suisun City:

Gewürztraminer, Napa Valley, 1983, $5.50.
OK, simple Gewürztraminer, but short on finish.

Sight: medium gold.
Nose: light, grapefruit, appley.
Taste: dry, full body, heavy on palate, simple, appley fruit, some bitterness on finish.

Vose Vineyards

From Vose Vineyards, Napa:

Gewürztraminer, Napa Valley, 1982, $7.50.
Should be served with food.
Sight: brilliant, light yellow.
Nose: floral, spicy, perfume.
Taste: dry, good varietal flavors, medium body, balanced, crisp acidity, lingering finish.

Mark West Vineyards

From Mark West Vineyards, Forestville:

Gewürztraminer, Russian River Valley, 1983, $6.95.
Short on finish.
Sight: clear, pale straw-gold.
Nose: light varietal, pine aromas.
Taste: off-dry, light body, nice flavors, clean, slightly bitter though short.

Wine Discovery

From Wine Discovery, Healdsburg:

Gewürztraminer, Napa Valley, 1982, $4.75.
Not a spicy Gewürz, but varietal in all other ways.
Sight: clear, pale straw.
Nose: light varietal, some grapefruit aromas.
Taste: dry, medium body, light fruit, some grapefruit character, tart and clean through finish.

MERLOT

Best Buy

Santa Ynez Valley Winery

From Santa Ynez Valley Winery, Santa Ynez:

Merlot l'Enfant, Santa Ynez Valley, 1983, $4.25.

Light and fruity, nouveau style, better than most California Gamay Beaujolais.
Sight: medium ruby.
Nose: tar, berries, fermentation aromas.

Taste: dry, medium body, some good berry and other flavors, tart and clean, good acid and balance.

Highly Recommended

Caparone Winery

From Caparone Winery, Paso Robles:

Merlot, Santa Maria Valley, Tepusquet Vineyard, Unfined and Unfiltered, 1981, $10.

Has rough edges now, but given some time this should be an excellent Merlot.

Sight: clear, deep purple-ruby.

Nose: rich, perfumed, olives, herbal.

Taste: dry, full body, tannic, rich fruit, chocolaty flavors, good balance, firm structure, long finish.

Rutherford Hill

From Rutherford Hill Winery, Rutherford:

Merlot, Napa Valley, 1980, $10.

Excellent wine for the cellar.

Sight: clear, red ruby.

Nose: clean, herbal, olives, dill.

Taste: dry, full body, great fruit, balanced, very complex, long finish.

St. Francis

From St. Francis Winery, Kenwood:

Merlot, Sonoma Valley, Estate Bottled, 1981, $10.75.

Great structure.

Sight: brilliant, ruby red.

Nose: intense, herbal, olive, dill.

Taste: dry, medium body, rich, complex fruit, woody, balanced acid and tannin, long finish.

Recommended

Bel Arbres Vineyards

From Bel Arbres Vineyards, Redwood Valley:

Merlot, Sonoma, 1981, $7.

Sound varietal Merlot for the price.

Sight: clear, medium ruby.

Nose: light fruit, low intensity.

Taste: dry, a bit light in body, some fruit, not complex, no defects, sound wine.

Boeger

From Boeger Winery, Placerville:

Merlot, El Dorado, Estate Bottled, 1981, $9.

Great potential.

Sight: clear-to-medium ruby.

Nose: closed, coffee aromas.

Taste: dry, soft, closed, some fruit showing, full body, balanced, needs time.

Clos du Bois

From Clos du Bois Winery, Healdsburg:

Merlot, Alexander Valley, 80 percent Merlot, 20 percent Cabernet Sauvignon, 1981, $8.50.

Big style Merlot, well priced.

Sight: clear, medium ruby garnet.

Nose: clean, simple spicy, fruity.

Taste: dry, full body, soft, good spicy fruit, tannic, balanced acid, tannic fruit.

Clos Du Val

From Clos du Val Wine Co., Napa:

Merlot, Napa Valley, 1981, $13.50.

Pure Merlot, elegant and firmly balanced.

Sight: clear, medium ruby-red.

Nose: intense cherry, herbal, Merlot.

Taste: dry, good Merlot flavor and character, warm, soft, good acid and tannin, young and with lots of potential.

Crystal Valley

From Crystal Valley Cellars, Modesto:

Merlot, California, Limited Reserve, 1980, $7.

Simple, fruity Merlot.
Sight: clear, medium ruby.
Nose: herbal, bell pepper, vegetal.
Taste: dry, full body, soft, balanced, good fruit, pleasant flavors.

Diablo Vista

From Diablo Vista Winery, Benicia:

Merlot, Sonoma County, Dry Creek Valley, 1981, $7.50.

In a world of $12 Merlots this has a lot of character for the price.
Sight: clear, deep ruby-purple.
Nose: earthy, spicy.
Taste: dry, good fruit, full body, good balance and structure, cherry, herbal, a bit hot, long finish.

J. Patrick Doré Selections

From Coastal Wines Ltd., Sausalito:

Merlot, Napa Valley, 1980, $4.50.

Simple table wine at a market-conscious price.
Sight: clear, medium garnet.
Nose: woody, minty, some dill.
Taste: dry, medium body, soft flavors, fruity, good varietal character, balanced, soft lingering finish.

Farview Farm Vineyard

From Farview Farm Vineyard, Soledad:

Merlot, Templeton, 1980, $6.50.

Drinking well now; fruit seems to be thinning out a bit.
Sight: clear, medium brick-garnet.
Nose: olives, oxidized, caramel, minty.
Taste: dry, full body, cooked-vegetable flavors, soft fruit, tannin balanced, moderate Merlot character.

Fenestra

From Fenestra Winery, Livermore:

Merlot, Napa Valley, 1982, $11.

Soft, elegant, drinkable Merlot.
Sight: medium garnet.
Nose: herbal, tobacco, cedar and olives.
Taste: soft, elegant varietal fruit with clean herbal/tobacco notes, medium body, clean fruit.

Lakespring

From Lakespring Winery, Napa:

Merlot, Napa Valley, 1981, $10.

Merlot with a lot of backbone and rich flavors.
Sight: clear, deep garnet.
Nose: clean, minty, some wood, dill.
Taste: dry, very rich, chocolaty, herbaceous, woody, soft tannin, lingering finish.

Louis M. Martini

From Louis M. Martini, St. Helena:

Merlot, North Coast, 1980, $5.05.

Almost too soft.
Sight: clear, medium red-ruby.
Nose: pleasant, very soft and fruity.
Taste: dry, pleasant, fruity, medium body, some varietal character, balanced.

Matanzas Creek Winery

From Matanzas Creek Winery, Santa Rosa:

Merlot, Sonoma County, 1980, $12.50.

Needs lots of time.
Sight: clear, deep purple ruby.
Nose: nice fruit, herbal, dill aromas, closed.
Taste: dry, full body, good fruit and acid, surprisingly balanced for youthful feel, varietal, long finish.

Merlot, Sonoma Valley, 1981, $12.50.

High-priced for alcoholic Merlot.
Sight: clear ruby.

MATANZAS CREEK WINERY

1980

SONOMA VALLEY
MERLOT

Nose: alcohol and plum aromas.
Taste: dry, full body, tart, soft but ripe fruit, tannic and raw, some heat on finish.

Mill Creek Vineyards

From Mill Creek Vineyards, Healdsburg:

Merlot, Sonoma County, 1980, $8.50.

Needs time, but a well-structured Merlot.
Sight: clear, medium-to-deep ruby.
Nose: woody, some perfume, rubbery aromas.
Taste: dry, good varietal, medium-to-full body, soft fruit, well balanced, lingering finish.

Mill Creek Vineyards
1981
SONOMA COUNTY
Merlot

Merlot, Sonoma County, 1981, $9.

Good for current drinking.
Sight: clear, medium red-ruby.
Nose: pleasant, herbal, woody, olives.

Taste: dry, full body, olives, herbal, good balance, woody finish.

Pine Ridge

From Pine Ridge Winery, Yountville:

Merlot, Napa Valley, Selected Cuvée, 1981, $12.50.
Simple but very tasty Merlot.
Sight: clear, deep ruby.
Nose: clean, spicy, oaky aromas.
Taste: dry, full body, simple but elegant, good structure, floral character, a bit short on finish.

Stag's Leap Wine Cellars

From Stag's Leap Wine Cellars, Napa:

Merlot, Napa Valley, 1981, $13.50.
Needs time to develop further complexity.
Sight: clear, medium-deep ruby.
Nose: clean, berries, green olives.
Taste: dry, full body, good fruit flavors, balanced, good structure but hot on finish.

Sterling Vineyards

From Sterling Vineyards, Calistoga:

Merlot, Napa Valley, 1981, $11.
Has good potential, though seems one-dimensional now.
Sight: clear, nice red-ruby color.
Nose: soft, ripe, closed.

Taste: dry, full body, beautiful ripe fruit, drinkable, clean, good acid, balanced, lingering flavors and finish.

Stephen Zellerbach Vineyard

From Stephen Zellerbach Cellars, Healdsburg:

Merlot, Alexander Valley, 1980, $8.50.
Ordinary wine, has off-character on nose.
Sight: clear, deep ruby.
Nose: rubbery, a bit ripe, burnt.
Taste: dry, a bit tannic, full body, tobacco and cherry flavors, short finish.

PETITE SIRAH/PETITE SYRAH

Recommended

Bogle Vineyards

From Bogle Vineyards, Clarksburg:

Petite Sirah, Clarksburg, NV, $3.75.
Stylish, huge, and grapy.
Sight: clear, deep purple-ruby.
Nose: berries, low on pepper.
Taste: dry, full body, intense, grapy, berry flavors, assertive, light overripe, long finish.

Cilurzo

From Cilurzo Vineyard and Winery, Temecula:

Petite Sirah, Temecula, 1980, $7.
Overwhelming style; very stemmy.
Sight: clear, deep purple-ruby.
Nose: jammy, grapy, very stemmy.
Taste: dry, medium body, overwhelmingly stemmy quality, big, fruity and woody, lots of wood on finish.

Concannon

From Concannon Vineyard, Livermore:

Petite Sirah, California, 1979, $5.75.
Great value that needs a lot of time.
Sight: clear, very deep purple.
Nose: clean, anise, ground pepper.
Taste: dry, full body, very young, clean, huge, full varietal, woody, long finish.

Fawn's Glen

From William Baccala Winery, Ukiah:

Petite Sirah, Mendocino County, 1981, $6.
Good value.
Sight: clear, deep purple.
Nose: fruity, pepper underneath.
Taste: dry, tannic, full body, moderate tart fruit, ground pepper, young, long full finish.

FAWN'S GLEN

1981
Mendocino County
PETITE SIRAH

BOTTLED FOR WILLIAM BACCALA BY PARSONS CREEK WINERY, UKIAH, CA · ALCOHOL 12.9% BY VOLUME

Fetzer

From Fetzer Vineyards, Redwood Valley:

Petite Syrah, Mendocino County, 1981, $5.50.
Needs eons.

Sight: clear, deep purple.
Nose: a bit closed, ground pepper.
Taste: dry, full body, huge, tannic, ground pepper, fruit is there somewhere, unending finish.

Guenoc

From Guenoc Winery, Middletown:
Petite Sirah, 68 percent Lake County, 32 percent Napa County, 1980, $6.
Needs eons; well worth the price.
Sight: clear, deep, very inky purple.
Nose: closed, spicy, good varietal character.

Taste: dry, full body, good fruit and tannin, tart, well structured, balanced though big, long finish.

Parducci

From Parducci Wine Cellars, Ukiah:
Petite Sirah, Mendocino County, 1979, $5.
Needs much more time to open up.
Sight: clear, dark purple.
Nose: closed, very low intensity.
Taste: dry, closed, full body, subdued fruit, good acid, long finish.

Ridge

From Ridge Vineyards, Cupertino:

Petite Sirah, York Creek, 1981, $8.50.
Tremendous fruit, assertive tannin. A stylish, likable wine.
Sight: very deep purple.
Nose: floral, spicy, woody fruit.
Taste: dry, very tannic but balanced with peppery Petite Sirah fruit, long finish, needs time.
Petite Sirah, York Creek, Devil's Hill, 1980, $9.
Needs a lot of time; hard to taste at current stage.
Sight: clear, deep, purple-black.
Nose: fruity, closed, ground pepper.
Taste: dry, very tannic, puckery, full body, lots of extract, fruity, ground pepper, unending finish.

PINOT NOIR

Best Buy

J. Pedroncelli

From J. Pedroncelli Winery, Geyserville:
Pinot Noir, Sonoma County, 1980, $4.50.

Excellent value in a surprisingly complex wine.
Sight: clear, medium-deep garnet.
Nose: leathery, cherries, good fruit.

Taste: dry, very nice fruit, herbal, cherries, leathery, well balanced, long finish.

Highly Recommended

Acacia

From Acacia Winery, Napa:
Pinot Noir, Napa Valley,

Carneros District, lund Vineyard, 1981, $15.
Drinks well, but has a long life ahead.
Sight: clear, deep ruby color.
Nose: lots of cherries and spice, clean.
Taste: dry, clean, lots of fruit, full body, varietal, young, complex, well balanced, long finish.
Pinot Noir, Napa Valley, Winery Lake Vineyards, 1981, $17.50.
A great Pinot—this one's for the cellar.

Sight: clear, medium ruby.
Nose: deep, spicy, clean aromas.
Taste: dry, clean, full body, tart fruit, lots of cherries, tannic, leathery, very well balanced, long full finish.

Buena Vista

From Buena Vista Winery, Sonoma:
Pinot Noir, Sonoma Valley, Carneros, Special Selection, 1981, $12.

Uncommon character for a California Pinot Noir.
Sight: purple-ruby.
Nose: spicy, cherry aromas.
Taste: dry, full body, good clean Pinot Noir character, good depth and structure, tannin and acid, uncommon character, clean finish.

Davis Bynum

From Davis Bynum Winery, Healdsburg:
Pinot Noir, Russian River Valley, 1980, $8.
Needs time—well worth the price.
Sight: clear, medium-to-deep ruby.
Nose: deep, rich, spicy aroma.
Taste: dry, good fruit, medium body, clean, very nice Pinot Noir flavors, tannic, balanced.

Carneros Creek Winery

From Carneros Creek Winery, Napa:
Pinot Noir, Napa Valley, Carneros District, 1981, $16.
Classic fruity style.
Sight: clear, medium ruby.
Nose: closed, bit spicy, wood.
Taste: dry, good fruit flavor, clean, tannic, closed on palate, good wood.

Napa Sun Winery

From Napa Sun Winery, Napa:
Pinot Noir, Napa Valley, 1981, $5.50.
Fine value in ready-to-drink Pinot—this wine will take some age.
Sight: clear, medium-to-deep garnet.
Nose: plummy, clean Pinot aromas.
Taste: dry, medium body, soft fruit, clean, very silky texture, plummy, good acid, lingering finish.

Sanford

From Sanford Winery, San Luis Obispo:
Pinot Noir, Santa Maria Valley, 1981, $10.50.
Great value in Pinot Noir.
Sight: clear, medium-to-deep ruby.

Nose: leathery, woody, spicy.
Taste: dry, tart, clean fruit, good acid, woody, spicy, balanced, long finish.

Winery Lake

From Winery Lake Vineyards/Belvedere Winery, Healdsburg:
Pinot Noir, Los Carneros, 1981, $12.
A classically proportioned Pinot Noir; structure will keep it fit for years.
Sight: clear, medium red-garnet.
Nose: spicy, woody, black cherry aromas.
Taste: dry, very spicy flavors, full body, clean fruit, black cherries, woody, rich, some rough edges, firm acidity.

Recommended

Acacia

From Acacia Winery, Napa:
Pinot Noir, Carneros District, Lee Vineyard, 1981, $15.
Drinks well now.
Sight: clear, medium red-ruby.
Nose: cloves, spicy, some leathery aromas.
Taste: dry, good fruit, medium body, clean cherry flavors, full, round, balanced, long finish.
Pinot Noir, Carneros District, Madonna Vineyard, 1981, $15.

Spicy, fruity style.
Sight: clear, medium ruby.
Nose: light wood, very spicy.
Taste: dry, tart, clean, very young and awkward, medium body, closed flavors, great Pinot character.
Pinot Noir, Carneros District, St. Clair Vineyard, 1981, $15.
Needs lots of time.
Sight: clear, deep ruby.
Nose: closed, cherries, clean, some leathery aromas.
Taste: dry, full body, clean,

tart, very young, very closed, has the structure to age well, long finish.
Pinot Noir, Napa Valley–Carneros, Lee Vineyard, 1982, $15.
Shows great promise, but needs time to come together.
Sight: clear, medium garnet.
Nose: cherry, toasty, vanilla, good depth.
Taste: tart, moderately tannic, intense spice and fruit, lots of wood.
Pinot Noir, Napa Valley–

Carneros, St. Clair Vineyard, 1982, $15.
Young, awkward, tannic, like a barrel sample now. Almost too young to assess—don't expect to drink it on the same night you buy it.
Sight: very deep purple.
Nose: grape-cherry, menthol edge.
Taste: grapy, tannic, intensely fruity, floral and spicy, long finish.

Pinot Noir, Napa Valley–Carneros, Winery Lake Vineyard, 1982, $15.
Complex nose, forward fruit and flavors make this an enjoyable wine already.
Sight: clear, red-garnet.
Nose: cherry, floral, tobacco edge, cedary, toasty, coffee.
Taste: satiny texture, plummy, coffee-like, some tannin, coffee flavors on finish.

Almadén

From Almadén Vineyards, San Jose:
Pinot Noir, San Benito County, 1982, $5.85.
Ripe, woody style but not alcoholic; not an ager.
Sight: deep red-garnet.
Nose: rich, ripe, raisiny, clovey spice.
Taste: ripe, almost cooked flavors, more wood than fruit.

Beringer Vineyards

From Beringer Vineyards, St. Helena:
Pinot Noir, Sonoma County, Estate Bottled, Small Lot, Knights Valley Vineyard, 1980, $10.
Simple style of Pinot Noir.
Sight: clear, medium ruby, garnet edge.
Nose: closed, woody, slight volatile acidity.
Taste: dry, medium body, fruit, tannin, good acid, tobacco, cherry fruit, long lingering finish.

David Bruce

From David Bruce, Los Gatos:
Pinot Noir, Santa Cruz Mountains, 1980, $12.
Very big, complex wine in the David Bruce style.

Sight: clear, medium garnet.
Nose: rich Pinot aromas, very clean.
Taste: dry, tart, ripe, full body, hot, stylistic, lots of complexity, oaky, balanced, long finish.

Buena Vista

From Buena Vista Winery, Sonoma:
Pinot Noir, Sonoma Valley, Carneros, 1980, $7.
Wine is at its peak, drink now.
Sight: clear, medium garnet.
Nose: some spice and oak.
Taste: dry, full body, good fruit, but dried out and showing its age, a bit dry and bitter on finish.

Davis Bynum

From Davis Bynum Winery, Healdsburg:
Pinot Noir, Sonoma County, Reserve, 1980, $10.50.
Complex, developed Pinot Noir.
Sight: clear, medium ruby, garnet edge.
Nose: fruity, woody, spicy.
Taste: dry, full body, soft, balanced fruit and acid, intense fruit under wood, long full finish.

Calera

From Calera Wine Co., Hollister:
Pinot Noir, California, Jensen Vineyard, 1981, $18.
Most drinkable of the three Caleras here, still needs time.

CALERA
JENSEN
California Pinot Noir Table Wine
1981
PRODUCED & BOTTLED BY
CALERA WINE COMPANY
HOLLISTER CALIFORNIA

Sight: clear, light-to-medium garnet.
Nose: closed, leathery, cherry fruit.
Taste: dry, full body, fruity, complex oak flavor, fruit is somewhat hidden under wood, good acid, lingering finish.

Pinot Noir, California, Reed Vineyard, 1981, $18.
Has a lot of potential; will be very complex.
Sight: clear, deep garnet.
Nose: closed, some depth of wood and spice.
Taste: dry, closed flavors, full body, high acid, woody, complexity has not yet developed.

Pinot Noir, California, Selleck Vineyard, 1981, $18.
Sight: clear light garnet, tawny on edge.
Nose: spicy, closed aromas.
Taste: dry, medium body, tart fruit, closed flavors, strong acid, good structure, spicy, balanced, lingering finish.

Caymus Vineyards

From Caymus Vineyards, Rutherford:
Pinot Noir, Napa Valley, 1980, $6.50.
A young Pinot with lots of potential.
Sight: clear, medium garnet.
Nose: clean, fruity, cherries, slight mint aromas.

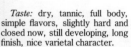

Taste: dry, tannic, full body, simple flavors, slightly hard and closed now, still developing, long finish, nice varietal character.

Pinot Noir, Napa Valley, Special Selection, 1981, $12.50.
Very tannic, seems low on fruit.
Sight: clear, deep garnet.
Nose: fruity, sweet cherry aroma.
Taste: dry, full body, clean fruit, nice balance, tannic, needs time.

Chateau Chevalier

From Chateau Chevalier Winery, St. Helena:
Pinot Noir, Napa Valley, 1980, $11.75.
Soft, drinkable, and relatively high priced.
Sight: clear, medium ruby.
Nose: closed, some wood and fruit.
Taste: dry, tart fruit, medium body, not much tannin, a bit low in acid, short on finish, pleasant flavors.

Clos du Bois

From Clos du Bois Winery, Healdsburg:
Pinot Noir, Alexander Valley, 1980, $6.
Good value.
Sight: clear, medium garnet.
Nose: oaky, earthy, cherries.
Taste: dry, good fruit, clean, tannic, very woody, a bit short, balanced.

Pinot Noir, Dry Creek Valley, Proprietor's Reserve, 1980, $10.75.
With evidence of substantial barrel aging, this is a wine to lay down. It's only beginning to come together.
Sight: clear, deep ruby.
Nose: plummy, floral, concentrated fruit and light spice.
Taste: creamy texture, grapy, plummy, more than moderate tannin, substantial oak, raw finish.

Clos Du Val

From Clos Du Val Wine Co., Napa:
Pinot Noir, Napa Valley, 1981, $9.75.
Very light in style.
Sight: clear, light-to-medium garnet.
Nose: light perfumed nose.
Taste: dry, thin, light body, some fruit, moderate varietal character, short on finish.

Dehlinger Winery

From Dehlinger Winery, Sebastopol:
Pinot Noir, Sonoma County, 1980, $10.
Needs aging, very complex and pleasant wine.
Sight: clear, deep ruby.
Nose: spicy, floral, young Pinot Noir aromas.
Taste: dry, good fruit, earthy, medium body, tannic, complex oak flavors, well balanced.

De Loach Vineyards

From De Loach Vineyards, Santa Rosa:
Pinot Noir, Sonoma County, Estate Bottled, 1981, $9.
For current drinking.
Sight: clear, medium ruby.
Nose: spicy, violets, some fruit.
Taste: dry, clean, soft fruit, good flavor, cherries, medium body, good acid, balanced.

Fetzer

From Fetzer Vineyards, Redwood Valley:
Pinot Noir, California, Special Reserve, 1980, $10.
Big style Pinot Noir.
Sight: clear, medium garnet.
Nose: clean Pinot, smoky, tarry.
Taste: dry, full body, good acid and Pinot character but fruit seems a bit sluggish, tannic finish, some heat.

Pinot Noir, Mendocino, 1981, $5.50.
Attractive but lots of wood. Definitely needs food. Try it with brie.
Sight: clear, medium garnet.
Nose: wood and cherries, Pinot Noir.
Taste: dry, medium body, lots of wood, not much fruit, bitter, woody finish.

Fritz

From Fritz Cellars, Cloverdale:
Pinot Noir, Sonoma County, Dry Creek Valley, 1981, $4.50.
A Pinot for current drinking.
Sight: brilliant, medium purple-ruby.
Nose: a bit of sulfur, fruit and Pinot character underneath.
Taste: dry, good fruit, medium-full body, tart, nice Pinot flavors, a touch of oak, well balanced.

Geyser Peak

From Geyser Peak Winery, Healdsburg:
Pinot Noir, Sonoma County, Kiser Ranch, Estate Bottled, 1978, $5.85.

Pinot for current consumption.
Sight: clear, medium garnet, mature color.
Nose: fruity, woody, leathery.
Taste: dry, very soft, clean, medium body, good varietal character, lots of wood, balanced.

Gundlach-Bundschu

From Gundlach-Bundschu Winery, Vineburg:
Pinot Noir, Sonoma Valley, Rhinefarm Vineyards, 1982, $9.25.
A lack of acid keeps us from getting more excited.
Sight: clear, deep ruby.
Nose: deep, concentrated fruit and wood, smoky.
Taste: dry, clean, berries, a bit low in acid causing imbalance, otherwise complex.

Hacienda

From Hacienda Wine Cellars, Sonoma:
Pinot Noir, Sonoma Valley, 1981, $12.
Well made, worth the price.
Sight: clear, medium ruby.
Nose: clean, varietal, coffee, tobacco, leather, spicy.
Taste: dry, full body, good balance, lots of fruit, good tannin, well structured, some heat on finish.

Husch Vineyards

From Husch Vineyards, Philo:
Pinot Noir, Anderson Valley, 1981, $9.
Young, needs time.
Sight: clear, deep ruby-purple.
Nose: berries, rich fruit.
Taste: dry, full body, some fruit, balanced, clean, good varietal character.

Inglenook Vineyards

From Inglenook Vineyards, Rutherford:
Pinot Noir, Napa Valley, 1980, $6.
Strong and coarse Pinot Noir—has a ripe, valley flavor.
Sight: clear, rich, medium garnet.
Nose: fruity, spicy, slightly cooked character.
Taste: dry, full body, nice fruit,

shows some maturity, pleasant to drink, full, lingering finish.

Johnson's Alexander Valley

From Johnson's Alexander Valley Wines, Healdsburg:
Pinot Noir, Alexander Valley, 1979, $8.
Mature, showing oxidation, may be on the down side, but drinkable still.
Sight: deep mahogany.
Nose: older, "wet wood," leathery.
Taste: spicy Pinot Noir fruit and plenty of wood, leafy aftertaste.

Louis M. Martini

From Louis Martini Winery, St. Helena:
Pinot Noir, Napa Valley, $5.
This wine is a bargain for drink-now Pinot Noir.
Sight: clear, medium garnet.
Nose: nice, fruity, soft, lots of complex Pinot aromas.
Taste: dry, medium-full body, soft, good full Pinot character, leathery, complex, fresh fruit, very well balanced.

Matanzas Creek Winery

From Matanzas Creek Winery, Santa Rosa:
Pinot Noir, Sonoma County, Quail Hill Ranch, 1980, $9.50.
Young Pinot Noir that shows signs of future complexity.
Sight: medium garnet.

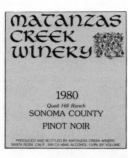

MATANZAS CREEK WINERY

1980
Quail Hill Ranch
SONOMA COUNTY
PINOT NOIR

PRODUCED AND BOTTLED BY MATANZAS CREEK WINERY, SANTA ROSA, CALIF. BW-CA 4846. ALCOHOL 13.9% BY VOLUME

Nose: woody, sweaty, smoky, some fruit underneath, perfumed.
Taste: dry, medium body, hard but supple fruit, smoky, balanced, lots of wood, good tannin, young finish.

Mill Creek Vineyards

From Mill Creek Vineyards, Healdsburg:
Pinot Noir, Sonoma County, 1981, $7.
Drink now, good value.
Sight: clear, light to medium garnet.
Nose: woody, spicy, some cherry fruit.
Taste: dry, light to medium body, woody flavor, lacks fruit, some heat and bitterness on finish.

Robert Mondavi Winery

From Robert Mondavi Winery, Oakville:
Pinot Noir, Napa Valley, 1980, $7.50.
Well-made California Pinot.
Sight: clear, medium-to-deep garnet.
Nose: pleasant, complex, leathery.
Taste: dry, nice fruit, woody but balanced, complex, needs time, long finish.

Mont St. John

From Mont St. John Cellars, Napa:
Pinot Noir, Napa Valley, Carneros, 1981, $9.75.
Pricey for wine that is already showing its age.
Sight: cloudy, medium mahogany.
Nose: leather, oxidized.
Taste: dry, medium body, leathery flavors, good acid, but seems sluggish, finish falls off.

Ross-Kellerei

From Ross-Kellerei, Buellton:
Pinot Noir, Santa Barbara County, 1980, $6.
Fair price for a wine that seems a bit soft.
Sight: clear, deep garnet.

Nose: raisiny, some Pinot character.

Taste: dry, tart, soft flavors, woody, some tobacco and leather flavors, short finish.

Roudon Smith Vineyards

From Roudon-Smith Vineyards, Santa Cruz:

Pinot Noir, Edna Valley, 1981, $14.

Has potential, needs age to develop further.

Sight: clear, medium-to-deep garnet.

Nose: spicy, berries, reminds us of Zinfandel.

Taste: dry, clean, good fruit, full body, berries, rich, balanced, long finish.

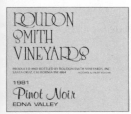

Rutherford Hill

From Rutherford Hill Winery, Rutherford:

Pinot Noir, Napa Valley, 1979, $7.50.

Great Pinot for current drinking.

Sight: clear, medium-deep garnet.

Nose: spicy, leathery.

Taste: dry, clean, full body, good Pinot Noir character, leathery, a bit of cherry fruit, good acid, well balanced.

St. Francis

From St. Francis Winery, Kenwood:

Pinot Noir, Sonoma Valley, 1981, $10.75.

High in acid, needs time.

Sight: clear, light-to-medium garnet.

Nose: woody, cedary, fruity, cherries, cranberries.

Taste: dry, tangy, medium body, tart fruit, high in acid, closed, seems dumb at this time.

Saintsbury

From Saintsbury, St. Helena:

Pinot Noir, Sonoma Valley, 1982, $8.

Everything there but the finish. Shows promise.

Sight: clear, light garnet-brick.

Nose: clean, lively, floral, spicy Pinot.

Taste: dry, full body, clean spicy flavor, good acid, balanced tannin and fruit, clean finish.

Santa Lucia Cellars

From Santa Lucia Cellars, Paso Robles:

Pinot Noir, Paso Robles, 1982, $4.95.

A Beaujolais style.

Sight: clear, has sediment, brick.

Nose: bubblegum aromas, some fruit.

Taste: dry, very fruity, lots of strawberry fruit flavors, simple, a bit hot on palate.

Sea Ridge

From Sea Ridge Winery, Cazadero:

Pinot Noir, Sonoma County, 1981, $9.75.

Simple, pricey.

Sight: clear, light-to-medium garnet.

Nose: earthy, stemmy, young.

Taste: dry, medium body, good fruit, not complex, low tannin, good acid.

August Sebastiani

From Sebastiani Vineyards, Sonoma:

Country Pinot Noir, California, NV, $5.50 per magnum.

Needs food.

Sight: clear, medium garnet.

Nose: clean, varietal, spicy.

Taste: dry, medium body, some fruit, slight sourness, woody finish.

Sebastiani

From Sebastiani Vineyards, Sonoma:

Pinot Noir, Tres Rouge, Sonoma Valley, 1979, $4.85.

Very woody style.

Sight: clear-to-medium-deep garnet.

Nose: woody, earthy, some fruit.

Taste: dry, thin, shallow fruit, lots of wood and tannin, bitter, short finish.

Smith-Madrone

From Smith-Madrone, St. Helena:

Pinot Noir, Napa Valley, Estate Bottled, 1981, $10.

Very nice varietal flavor; a good value.

Sight: clear, light-to-medium garnet.

Nose: rich fruit, assertive, leathery.

Taste: dry, medium body, intense fruit, balanced, woody, leathery, long finish.

Stone Creek

From Stone Creek Cellars, Healdsburg:

Pinot Noir, Napa Valley, Special Selection, 1979, $4.

Good value. It's simple but tastes as Pinot Noir should.

Sight: medium-light ruby-garnet.

Nose: cherries, tobacco, Pinot.

Taste: dry, medium body, coarse but good varietal character, tarry, some bitterness on finish.

Rodney Strong

From Sonoma Vineyards, Windsor:

Pinot Noir, Russian River Valley, River East Vineyard, 1980, $10.
Simple, drinkable Pinot Noir.
Sight: clear, medium garnet, some brick.
Nose: slightly minty, a bit smoky.
Taste: dry, nice fruit, simple, is drinkable. Bit short on finish.

Taft Street

From Taft Street Winery, Forestville:

Pinot Noir, Monterey County, 1982, $7.50.
Value in simple Pinot Noir.
Sight: clear, medium-deep red garnet.
Nose: good varietal character, slight sweaty edge, cooked celery.
Taste: dry, fruity, simple, clean, medium body, moderate tannin and structure, not heavy.

Trefethen Vineyards

From Trefethen Vineyards, Napa:

Pinot Noir, Napa Valley, 1980, $8.

Trefethen VINEYARDS

NAPA VALLEY 1980
PINOT NOIR

GROWN, PRODUCED & BOTTLED BY
TREFETHEN VINEYARDS
NAPA, CALIFORNIA, U.S.A.

ALCOHOL 12.7% BY VOLUME

Well-structured Pinot Noir.
Sight: clear, medium garnet.
Nose: very earthy and cooked, good fruit.
Taste: dry, a bit hot, full body, clean, fruity, earthy character, balanced, long finish.

Villa Mt. Eden

From Villa Mt. Eden Winery, Oakville:

Pinot Noir, Napa Valley, 1980, $9.
Clean Pinot in the style of Burgundy.
Sight: clear, medium garnet.

Nose: clean, woody, complex, varietal.
Taste: dry, complex, full body, leathery, earthy, lots of Pinot Noir character, well balanced.

William Wheeler

From William Wheeler Vineyards, Healdsburg:

Pinot Noir, Sonoma County, Bacigalupi Vineyard, 1981, $8.
Varietal Pinot Noir that is closed now.
Sight: clear, medium-deep ruby.
Nose: fruity, slightly stinky.
Taste: dry, one-dimensional, full body, clean, young flavors, good acid, balanced.

ZD Wines

From ZD Wines, Napa:

Pinot Noir, Napa Valley–Carneros, 1980, $12.
Still needs time—will reward age.
Sight: clear, deep ruby.
Nose: spicy, deep woody aromas.
Taste: dry, full body, spicy, tannic, woody flavors, deep and a bit closed, soft, round feel, balanced.

RIESLING

Best Buys

Ballard Canyon

From Ballard Canyon Winery, Solvang:

Johannisberg Riesling, Santa Ynez Valley, Reserve, 1982, $8.75.
Serve with fruits or light food.
Sight: spritzy, clear, light yellow gold.
Nose: floral, melons.
Taste: off-dry, good character, medium body, clean, assertive, lots of apricot fruit, balanced, lingering finish.

Caymus Vineyards

From Caymus Vineyards, Rutherford:

Johannisberg Riesling, Napa Valley, Late Harvest Special Selection, 1983, $9.
Complex and young, much potential for improvement.
Sight: clear, medium gold.
Nose: pineapple, honey.
Taste: sweet, full body, honey, clean, lots of lemon flavor, great acid, nice long finish.

Special 1982 Selection

CAYMUS VINEYARDS

NAPA VALLEY
Johannisberg Riesling
LATE HARVEST

Produced from selectively picked grapes at 29% sugar by weight.
This bottled wine retains 7% residual sugar by weight.

Grown, Produced and Bottled by Caymus Vineyards
Rutherford, Napa Valley, California
Alcohol 10.8% by volume

Maddalena Vineyard

From San Antonio Winery, Los Angeles:

Johannisberg Riesling, California, 1983, $4.35.
Serve nice and cold.
Sight: a bit spritzy, light gold.
Nose: fruity, clean, floral.
Taste: off-dry, nectarines, intense without being heavy, delicate, lingering finish.

Raymond

From Raymond Vineyard & Cellar, St. Helena:

Johannisberg Riesling, Napa Valley, Late Harvest, 1982, $8.50.
A bargain in dessert Riesling.
Sight: brilliant, medium gold.
Nose: clean, spicy, apricots, varietal.
Taste: sweet, medium-to-full body, clean, moderate botrytis character, assertive apricot flavors, balanced, strong acid, long finish.

Highly Recommended

Estrella

From Estrella River Winery, Paso Robles:

Johannisberg Riesling, Paso Robles, Estate Bottled, 1982, $6.
A pleasure to drink for a very reasonable price.
Sight: clear, medium gold.
Nose: fresh, clean, lots of apricots.
Taste: off-dry, medium body, very tart, good apricot flavors, crisp, lively acid, well balanced, lingering finish.

Grgich Hills

From Grgich Hills Cellar, Rutherford:

Johannisberg Riesling, Napa Valley, 1983, $7.50.
Distinctive style of Riesling.
Sight: clear, pale straw-gold.
Nose: piney, good fruit, floral.
Taste: dry, medium body, tangerine-like fruit, good balance, ripe flavor, a bit short on finish, honeysuckle aftertaste.

Jekel Vineyard

From Jekel Vineyard, Greenfield:

Johannisberg Riesling, Monterey County, Arroyo Seco, 1982, $6.50.
Intense flavor and delicacy—better than just a good buy.
Sight: clear, medium gold.
Nose: apricots, honey aromas.
Taste: sweet, medium body, full fruit, apricots and honey flavors abound, delicate, good balance, crisp, lingering finish.

Joseph Phelps Vineyards

From Joseph Phelps Vineyards, St. Helena:

Johannisberg Riesling, Napa Valley, Selected Late Harvest, 1980, $15/375ml.
Strong acid and balance suggest that this will be a long-lived dessert wine.
Sight: clear, deep gold.
Nose: nutty, honey, botrytis.
Taste: sweet, full body, good varietal Riesling character, honey, apricots, good acid, very well balanced, long finish.

Johannisberg Riesling, Napa Valley, Special Select Late Harvest, 1982, $22.50/375ml.
Tremendously rich and complex without the heavy feel.
Sight: brilliant, deep green-gold.
Nose: intense, botrytis, pineapple aromas.

Taste: sweet, medium body, pineapple, honey flavors, light yet viscous and thick, great complexity, balance, luscious.

Rodney Strong

From Sonoma Vineyards, Windsor:

Johannisberg Riesling, Russian River Valley, Le Baron Vineyard, 1983, $7.25.
Tremendous fruit complexity in a clean, balanced wine.
Sight: medium straw.
Nose: piney, orange cream.
Taste: slightly sweet with a lemony acid structure and sweet orange and tropical fruit flavors.

Mark West Vineyards

From Mark West Vineyards, Forestville:

Johannisberg Riesling, Russian River Valley, Late Harvest, 1982, $12.50/375ml.
For very special occasions.
Sight: brilliant, deep gold.
Nose: developed, deep botrytis.
Taste: sweet, good acid, full body, viscous, intense fruit, clean, floral apricot flavors, very well balanced, long finish.

Recommended

Ballard Canyon

From Ballard Canyon Winery, Solvang:

Johannisberg Riesling, Santa Ynez Valley, 1982, $7.
Nice for sipping.
Sight: clear, medium yellow-straw.
Nose: floral, pine tar, resinous.
Taste: off-dry, clean, light body, tart fruit, lots of Riesling character, a bit short on finish.

Johannisberg Riesling, Santa Ynez Valley, Reserve, 1982, $8.75.
For fruits or light food.
Sight: brilliant, light · yellow-gold.
Nose: floral, melons.
Taste: off dry, good character, medium body, clean, assertive, well balanced.

Bargetto

From Bargetto Winery, Soquel:

Johannisberg Riesling, California, 1982, $6.
Solid Riesling.
Sight: brilliant, medium gold.
Nose: light, spicy, apples.
Taste: sweet, clean, medium body, lots of apricots, floral, good acid, short finish.

Johannisberg Riesling, California, Late Harvest, 1982, $9.
Needs more acid.
Sight: brilliant, deep gold.
Nose: botrytis, apricots.
Taste: sweet, full body, thick, viscous, slightly low in acid, definite botrytis character, balanced.

Callaway

From Callaway Vineyards and Winery, Temecula:

White Riesling, Temecula, California, 1983, $5.25.
Astringent flavors, appley style for Riesling.
Sight: clear, pale gold.
Nose: appley.
Taste: off-dry, medium body, good fruit, appley, astringent, flavor of skins, lingering finish.

Chappellet

From Chappellet Vineyard, St. Helena:

Johannisberg Riesling, Napa Valley, 1982, $7.50.
Crisp, clean Riesling.
Sight: brilliant, pale straw.
Nose: clean, fruity.
Taste: dry, good fruit, light body, melon flavors, crisp acid, balanced.

CHAPPELLET
1982
Napa Valley
JOHANNISBERG RIESLING

Chateau St. Jean

From Chateau St. Jean, Kenwood:

Johannisberg Riesling, Alexander Valley, Robert Young Vineyards, 1983, $8.
Has grapefruit character, delicate fruit.
Sight: brilliant, medium straw.
Nose: clean, floral, some grapefruit.
Taste: dry, clean, good fruit character, nice acid, floral, grapefruit, balanced, lingering finish.

Johannisberg Riesling, Sonoma County, 1983, $8.
Clean, tart, citric style.
Sight: clear, light gold.
Nose: floral, fruity, grapefruit.
Taste: dry, lots of tart grapefruit, clean fruit, balanced, clean finish.

Clos du Bois

From Clos du Bois Winery, Healdsburg:

Johannisberg Riesling, Alexander Valley, Early Harvest, 1982, $6.50.
Pleasant dry-style Riesling.
Sight: brilliant, light, straw-gold.
Nose: floral, fruity.
Taste: dry, light body, floral, fruity, some apricots, tart fruit, good acid, well balanced.

Concannon

From Concannon Vineyard, Livermore:

Johannisberg Riesling, Livermore Valley, Late Harvest "Botrytised," 1982, $16/375 ml.
Distinctive dessert wine.
Sight: brilliant, deep gold.
Nose: orange peels, heavy botrytis, apricots.
Taste: sweet, thick, full body, lots of apricot flavors, moderate botyrtis character, short finish.

SINCE 1883
Concannon
1982
LIVERMORE VALLEY
LIVERMORE–RIESLING

Estrella River Winery

From Estrella River Winery, Paso Robles:

Johannisberg Riesling, Paso Robles, Estate Bottled, 1983, $6.
Great burst of fruit but lacks finesse.
Sight: brilliant, medium-pale straw.
Nose: clean, floral, pineapple, pleasant.
Taste: off-dry, medium body, lots of nice piney-lemony-appley flavors, good high acid, heavy clean finish.

Fetzer

From Fetzer Vineyards,
Redwood Valley:
**Johannisberg Riesling,
Mendocino, 1983, $6.**
Complex style, definite pine
resin character.
Sight: clear, light-to-medium
old.
Nose: spicy, pine resin aro-
mas.
Taste: off-dry, soft, spicy, cin-
amon, complex, lingering finish.

Franciscan Vineyards

From Franciscan Vineyards,
Rutherford:
**Johannisberg Riesling,
Napa Valley, Select Late
Harvest, 1982, $25.**
Worth waiting for; super des-
ert wine.
Sight: brilliant, deep gold.
Nose: young, apricot aromas,
botrytis, honey.
Taste: sweet, complex, young,
full body, viscous, lots of botry-
s, dumb and awkward, acid
seems low, intense fruit on fin-
h.

Freemark Abbey

From Freemark Abbey Winery,
St. Helena:
**Johannisberg Riesling,
Napa Valley, 1983, $6.75.**
Green now, but may develop
cely.
Sight: clean, light yellow-
green.
Nose: grapefruit and peaches.

Taste: off-dry, good acid and
balance, tart peach-grapefruit flavor, trace of sour bitterness on
finish.
**Johannisberg Riesling,
Napa Valley, Edelwein Gold,
1982, $17.50/350 ml.**
Very complex dessert Riesling.
Sight: clear, light straw.
Nose: pine resin, botrytis,
complex aromas.
Taste: sweet, full body, intense, rich, powerful, complex
fruit, balanced, lingering finish.

Gabrielle y Caroline

From Gabrielle y Caroline,
Soledad:
**Riesling, Monterey
County, Late Harvest, 1982,
$13.85/350 ml.**
A delightful and unique Ries-
ling dessert wine—worth the
price.
Sight: brilliant, deep gold.
Nose: deep, botrytis, apricot,
complex, spicy.
Taste: sweet, full body, clean
fruit, complex botrytis, oily, vis-
cous feel, lots of apricots, very
well balanced, long full finish.

Hagafen

From Hagafen Cellars, Napa:
**Johannisberg Riesling,
Napa Valley, Winery Lake
Vineyard, 1983, $8.75.**
A bit pricey, but a clean Ries-
ling.
Sight: clear, medium gold.
Nose: piney, resin aromas.
Taste: off-dry, floral, piney,

balanced, a bit viscous, lingering
finish.

Haywood

From Haywood Winery,
Sonoma:
**White Riesling, Sonoma
Valley, 1983, $7.**
Pleasant flavor to roll around
on your tongue.
Sight: clear, spritzy, straw.
Nose: clean, spicy, rose petal.
Taste: off-dry, medium body,
spritzy, good acid and balance,
palate follows nose with rose-
petal flavors, long clean finish.
**White Riesling, Sonoma
Valley, Early Harvest, 1982,
$6.75.**
This is a dry and assertive
Riesling—it would be best
served with food.
Sight: clear, medium yellow-
gold.
Nose: fruity, pear aromas.
Taste: dry, medium body,
moderate-to-high acidity, pear
flavors, slight bitterness on fin-
ish.

Kendall-Jackson Vineyards

From Kendall-Jackson Vineyards
& Winery, Lakeport:
**Johannisberg Riesling,
Clear Lake, 1982, $6.**
Simple, sweet style of sipping
wine.
Sight: brilliant, medium-to-
deep green-gold.
Nose: not assertive, grapefruit
aromas.

Taste: sweet, soft, almost cloying on palate, fruity, a bit low in acid, simple flavors, short finish.

Konocti

From Konocti Winery, Kelseyville:
White Riesling, Lake County, 1982, $4.50.
Lots of Riesling character, great buy.
Sight: clean, light yellow-gold.
Nose: clean, botrytis, honey, floral fruit.
Taste: off-dry, full body, good acid and fruit, botrytis, fruit comes through & blends with grapefruity sweet aftertaste.

Mirassou

From Mirassou Vineyards, San Jose:
Johannisberg Riesling, Monterey County, 1982, $8.50.
Super dessert Riesling.
Sight: brilliant, medium gold.
Nose: sweet, ripe flavors, full body, clean floral flavors, honey, a bit low in acid, balanced, long finish.

Robert Mondavi Winery

From Robert Mondavi Winery, Oakville:
Johannisberg Riesling, Napa Valley, 1982, $6.75.
Light sipping Riesling.
Sight: brilliant, light-to-medium gold.
Nose: very light, floral.
Taste: dry, nice fruit and acid, medium body, balanced, floral character, very clean finish.
Johannisberg Riesling, Napa Valley, Special Selection, 1982, $8.

1982
Napa Valley
JOHANNISBERG RIESLING
ALCOHOL 11.7% BY VOLUME
PRODUCED AND BOTTLED BY
ROBERT MONDAVI WINERY
OAKVILLE, CALIFORNIA

A relatively inexpensive dessert Riesling.
Sight: brilliant, medium straw-gold.
Nose: apricots, floral aromas.
Taste: off-dry, light, apricots, candy, clean, good acid, very well balanced.

The Monterey Vineyard

From The Monterey Vineyard, Gonzales:
Johannisberg Riesling, Monterey County, 1982, $6.50.
Clean sipping wine.
Sight: clear, light straw.
Nose: floral, fruity.
Taste: dry, light-to-medium body, tart fruit, strong acid, a bit soapy on finish.

Napa Sun Winery

From Napa Sun Winery, Napa:
Johannisberg Riesling, Napa Valley, 1982, $3.99.
Sweet and simple Riesling.
Sight: clear, light straw-gold.
Nose: clean, rose petals, floral.
Taste: off-dry, medium body, rich, ripe fruit, a bit cloying and fat, lingering sweet finish.

Newlan

From Newlan Vineyards & Winery, Napa:
Johannisberg Riesling, Napa Valley, Late Harvest Berry Selected 1981, $18/ 375 ml.
Nice first release of dessert wine.
Sight: brilliant, deep gold.
Nose: subdued botrytis, more fruity.
Taste: sweet, fruity, apricots, thick, very viscous, good acid, balanced.

Obester

From Obester Winery, Half Moon Bay:
Johannisberg Riesling, Monterey County, 1983, $7.25.
Simple, sweet, pleasant to sip.
Sight: light gold.
Nose: floral, peachy, edge of burnt matches.

Taste: sweet, rich, bananas, peaches and slightly spicy, not cloying but definitely sweet.

J. Pedroncelli

From J. Pedroncelli Winery, Geyserville:
Johannisberg Riesling Sonoma County, 1983, $4.
Pleasant to drink and affordable.
Sight: clean, light bronze.
Nose: intensely fruity, kerosene-like but not floral.
Taste: just barely off-dry, tart tangy, peach-citrus flavor, good finish.

Joseph Phelps Vineyard

From Joseph Phelps Vineyard, St. Helena:
Johannisberg Riesling Napa Valley, Early Harvest 1983, $7.50.
Everything is here for a great Riesling—very complex flavors.
Sight: brilliant, pale straw.
Nose: clean, floral, peaches, apricots, complex.
Taste: dry, tart, medium body, clean, good acid, rich fruit, balanced, complex flavors, clean finish.
Johannisberg Riesling Napa Valley, Late Harvest 1982, $11.25.
A good value in a light dessert wine.
Sight: brilliant, medium gold.
Nose: floral, some botrytis.
Taste: sweet, good floral honey flavors, rich, medium body, spicy, clean, well balanced long finish.
Johannisberg Riesling, Napa Valley, Selected Late Harvest, 1980, $11.25/375 ml.
Excellent dessert wine.
Sight: clear, deep gold.
Nose: nutty, honey, botrytis.
Taste: sweet, good character, full body, viscous, honey, apricots, good acid, long finish, excellent balance.
Johannisberg Riesling, Napa Valley, Selected Late Harvest, 1981, $25/375 ml.
This is Phelps's forte.

Sight: brilliant, deep gold.
Nose: complex, young, floral, honey.
Taste: sweet, viscous, full body, good apricot flavors, nice acid, very well balanced, though still very young.

Raymond

From Raymond Vineyard & Cellar, St. Helena:
Johannisberg Riesling, Napa Valley, 1983, $6.50.
Young wine that needs some age.
Sight: clear, straw.
Nose: clean, melony.
Taste: off-dry, full body, balanced acid and fruit, lots of Chenin Blanc–like fruit, some apples, some bitterness on finish.

Round Hill

From Round Hill Vineyards, St. Helena:
Johannisberg Riesling, Napa Valley, 1983, $5.50.
Clean, appley flavors, not very varietal.
Sight: clear, pale straw.
Nose: floral, appley.
Taste: off-dry, very tart, clean, spicy, not too varietal, clean on finish.

ROUND HILL

JOHANNISBERG RIESLING

NAPA VALLEY
1983

CELLARED & BOTTLED BY ROUND HILL VINEYARDS
ST. HELENA, CALIFORNIA, ALCOHOL 11.5% BY VOLUME

St. Francis

From St. Francis Winery, Kenwood:
Johannisberg Riesling, Sonoma Valley, 1982, $5.40.
Aroma is very attractive, falls off a bit on the palate.

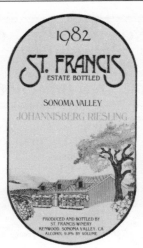

1982

ST. FRANCIS
ESTATE BOTTLED

SONOMA VALLEY

JOHANNISBERG RIESLING

PRODUCED AND BOTTLED BY
ST. FRANCIS WINERY
KENWOOD, SONOMA VALLEY, CA
ALCOHOL 9.8% BY VOLUME

Sight: brilliant, pale straw-gold.
Nose: floral, a bit spicy.
Taste: off-dry, tart, fruity, light body, lemony fruit, floral, balanced, though a bit short.

San Martín

From San Martin Winery, San Martin:
Soft Johannisberg Riesling, California, 1982, $5.99.
A pleasant sweet quaff.
Sight: brilliant, medium gold.
Nose: spicy, floral.
Taste: sweet, light, fruity, low acid, a bit cloying, easy to drink, short finish.

Susiné

From Susiné Cellars, Suisun City:
Johannisberg Riesling, El Dorado, Special Select Late Harvest, 1982, $10.
A very sweet and thick dessert wine.
Sight: clear, medium-deep gold.
Nose: a bit stinky, honey, botrytis.
Taste: very sweet, nice fruit flavors, complex, honey, caramel, pineapple, very viscous, luscious finish.

Trefethen Vineyards

From Trefethen Vineyards, Napa:
White Riesling, Napa Valley, 1982, $6.75.
Clean and well priced.
Sight: brilliant, light pale straw.
Nose: floral, clean.
Taste: dry, light body, slightly bitter, nice floral Riesling, good acid, lingering finish.

Mark West Vineyards

From Mark West Vineyards, Forestville:
Johannisberg Riesling, Russian River Valley, 1982, $6.95.
Needs to be served with light foods.
Sight: brilliant, light straw.
Nose: light, floral, resin aromas.
Taste: dry, spicy, light body, floral, slight bitterness, good acid, balanced, lingering finish.

Zaca Mesa

From Zaca Mesa Winery, Los Olivos:
Johannisberg Riesling, Santa Barbara County, 1982, $8.
Well-made Riesling for light foods or drinking by itself.
Sight: brilliant, medium straw.
Nose: floral, slightly candied aromas.
Taste: off-dry, light body, tart, spicy character, floral fruit, good acid, well balanced, lingering finish.

SAUVIGNON BLANC/FUMÉ BLANC

Spectator Selections

Chateau St. Jean

From Chateau St. Jean, Kenwood:

Fumé Blanc, Sonoma County, 1983, $9.75.
Delicacy and finesse without sacrifice of varietal character.
Sight: pale straw.
Nose: delicate and fruity.
Taste: dry, clean, assertive, delicate fig fruit, herbal, balanced, long lingering finish, lots of finesse.

Fumé Blanc, Sonoma Valley, St. Jean Vineyards, 1982, $10.50.
Worth every penny.
Sight: clear, pale gold.
Nose: complex, fruity, citric.
Taste: dry, full body, deep complex fruit, perfect balance, great crisp acid, very long lingering finish.

Kenwood

From Kenwood Vineyards, Kenwood:

Sauvignon Blanc, Sonoma County, 1982, $8.50.
A convincing argument for Sauvignon Blanc's taking over the top white-wine spot in California.
Sight: clear, light-to-medium straw-gold.
Nose: very assertive grassy aromas.
Taste: dry, rich clean fruit, varietal, grassy, medium body, tart acidity, very well balanced, lingering finish.

Best Buys

Fetzer

From Fetzer Vineyards, Redwood Valley:

Fumé Blanc, Mendocino County, 1982, $7.
Great value in stylish Fumé.
Sight: clear, light gold.
Nose: assertive, grassy, herbal, varietal.
Taste: dry, clean, herbal, full body, tart, full flavors, balanced.

Stag's Leap Wine Cellars

From Stag's Leap Wine Cellars, Napa:

Sauvignon Blanc, Napa Valley, 1982, $9.
Austere food wine; classic in the Graves style.

Sight: brilliant, clear, light gold.
Nose: clean, closed, herbal.
Taste: dry, complex, austere, tart, full body, fresh fruit, good herbal character.

Susiné

From Susiné Cellars, Suisun City:

Sauvignon Blanc, Suisun Valley, Brown Vineyard, 1983, $5.75.
Remarkably complex Sauvignon Blanc.
Sight: brilliant, medium gold.
Nose: very fruity, rose petals, grapefruit, melons.
Taste: dry, full body, ripe, complex, grapefruit, melon flavors, great balance, some Gewürztraminer character, clean flavors, finish lingers.

Highly Recommended

Chateau Bouchaine

From Chateau Bouchaine, Los Carneros:

Sauvignon Blanc, Sonoma County, 1982, $8.50.
Understated but assertive enough for food.
Sight: brilliant, light straw.
Nose: clean, herbal, fruity.
Taste: dry, full body, crisp, austere, balanced, excellent acid, fruity, long finish.

Chateau St. Jean

From Chateau St. Jean, Kenwood:

Fumé Blanc, Sonoma County, Forrest Crimmons Ranch, 1982, $10.25.
Another winner from St. Jean; grassy style.
Sight: brilliant, pale gold.
Nose: grassy, herbal, fruity.
Taste: dry, tart, grassy style, lingering crisp acidity, balanced, lots of fruit, herbal finish.

Fumé Blanc, Sonoma County, La Petite Etoile, 1983, $10.50.
Great Sauvignon Blanc, structured for a long life.
Sight: brilliant, light straw.
Nose: perfumed, floral, herbal.
Taste: dry, full body, intense fruit, herbal, fruity, great structure and balance, long lingering finish.

Grand Cru Vineyards

From Grand Cru Vineyards, Glen Ellen:

Sauvignon Blanc, California, 1982, $9.

Outstanding food wine.
Sight: clear, light straw.
Nose: herbal, fruity, closed.
Taste: dry, clean, fruity, full body, good balance of acid and fruit, long finish.

Grgich Hills

From Grgich Hills Cellar, Rutherford:

Fumé Blanc, Napa Valley, 1982, $9.
Intense Sauvignon Blanc flavor—price has come down from the 1981 wine.
Sight: brilliant, medium straw.
Nose: assertive, grassy, complex.
Taste: dry, full body, fresh, tart, clean, fine structure, well balanced, long acidic finish.

Hidden Cellars

From Hidden Cellars Winery, Talmage:

Sauvignon Blanc, Mendocino County, 1982, $8.
Aggressive fruity style.
Sight: brilliant, light gold.
Nose: clean, herbaceous, floral, grassy.
Taste: dry, medium body, tart, great fruit, good acid, herbaceous character, balanced, lingering finish.

Lakespring

From Lakespring Winery, Napa:
Sauvignon Blanc, California, 1981, $7.50.
Grassy style, with only moderate wood.
Sight: brilliant, light-to-medium gold.
Nose: fresh, clean, fruity, some wood.
Taste: dry, intense fruit, grassy, herbal, medium body, light wood in background, balanced, nice finish.

Monticello Cellars

From Monticello Cellars, Napa:
Sauvignon Blanc, Napa Valley, 1982, $7.50.
Still very young, will improve with another year in the bottle.

Sight: brilliant, pale straw.
Nose: green pepper, celery notes, clean.
Taste: dry, very clean, medium body, intense varietal character, herbal, green pepper flavors, balanced.

Parducci

From Parducci Wine Cellars, Ukiah:

Sauvignon Blanc, North Coast, 1983, $6.25.
Has a touch of spritz and sugar, very clean.
Sight: clear, spritzy, straw.
Nose: clean, grassy, fruity.
Taste: dry, clean, light grass, medium body, good fruit, lingering finish.

Pat Paulsen Vineyards

From Pat Paulsen Vineyards, Cloverdale:

Sauvignon Blanc, Alexander Valley, 1982, $8.50.
Rich and lush style of Sauvignon Blanc.
Sight: clear, light greenish gold.
Nose: clean, melons, herbal, great character.
Taste: dry, clean, full body, good fruit and acid, firm structure, rich flavors on palate, lush, long finish.

Preston

From Preston Vineyards & Winery, Healdsburg:

Cuvée de Fumé, Sonoma County, Dry Creek Valley, 1983, $6.
Lots of character and complexity for age.
Sight: clear, pale straw.
Nose: light, varietal fruit.
Taste: dry, herbaceous, firm tart acidity, crisp on finish.

Simi

From Simi Winery, Healdsburg:
Sauvignon Blanc, Sonoma County, 1982, $9.
Beautiful flavor in a delicate framework.
Sight: pale straw.
Nose: clean, herbal, and fruity.
Taste: dry, medium body, delicate, herbal flavor, great depth and complexity, clean finish.

Recommended

Almadén

From Almadén Vineyards, San Jose:
Sauvignon Blanc, Monterey County, 1982, $5.35.
Intensely herbal style.
Sight: clean, light straw.
Nose: intensely herbal, celery aromas.
Taste: dry, full body, intense fruit and extract, full fruit, herbal and celery, clean finish.

Ballard Canyon

From Ballard Canyon Winery, Solvang:
Fumé Blanc, Santa Barbara County, 1982, $8.50.
Fruity style of Fumé Blanc.
Sight: clear, pale straw.
Nose: clean, perfumy, herbal.
Taste: dry, full body, superfruity, good acid, seems sweet on entry, balanced.

Bandiera

From Bandiera Winery, Cloverdale:
Sauvignon Blanc, Mendocino County, 1982, $5.90.
A bargain in clean, well-balanced Sauvignon Blanc.
Sight: brilliant, light straw.
Nose: varietal, light and grassy.
Taste: dry, medium body, good acid, lots of varietal character, clean fruit, tart, grapefruit flavor, well balanced.

Beringer Vineyards

From Beringer Vineyards, St. Helena:
Fumé Blanc, Napa Valley, NV, $7.50.
Solid food wine.
Sight: brilliant, medium straw.
Nose: herbal, fruit, olives, oaky, complex.
Taste: dry, medium body, good herbal, fruit, chalky, balanced, complex flavors, chalky finish.

Boeger

From Boeger Winery, Placerville:
Sauvignon Blanc, El Dorado County, 1982, $6.
Fruity and clean.
Sight: brilliant, pale gold.
Nose: low intensity, fruity.
Taste: off-dry, good fruit, clean, moderate acidity, well balanced.

Davis Bynum

From Davis Bynum Winery, Healdsburg:
Fumé Blanc, Sonoma County, Rochioli-Harrison Reserve, 1982, $8.
A good wine for seafood—might be too herbal or grassy for some.
Sight: brilliant, pale straw.
Nose: clean, very grassy, herbal.
Taste: dry, very herbal and tart, medium body, medium-to-

high acid which adds structure, some wood, long finish.

Cain Cellars

From Cain Cellars, St. Helena:
Sauvignon Blanc, Napa Valley, 1982, $7.50.
Simple and spicy.
Sight: clear, light gold.
Nose: herbal.
Taste: dry, tart, medium body, fruity, woody, high acid, bitterness on finish.

NAPA VALLEY
SAUVIGNON BLANC

Cakebread Cellars

From Cakebread Cellars, Rutherford:
Sauvignon Blanc, Napa Valley, Decade, 1982, $9.50.
Needs lot of time.
Sight: brilliant, medium gold.
Nose: closed, some sulfur aromas.

Cakebread Cellars

1973 DECADE 1983

Napa Valley
Sauvignon Blanc
1982

PRODUCED & BOTTLED BY CAKEBREAD CELLARS RUTHERFORD
NAPA VALLEY, CALIFORNIA, U.S.A. ALCOHOL 13.1% BY VOLUME

Taste: dry, full bodied, big, intensely varietal, high in acid and alcohol, woody, awkward and unbalanced at this time.

Callaway

From Callaway Vineyard and Winery, Temecula:
Fumé Blanc, Temecula, 1982, $7.25.
Distinctive herbal style.
Sight: clear, light gold.
Nose: clean, fruity, herbal.
Taste: dry, clean, medium body, some fruit, austere flavors, herbal, some wood, balanced.
Sauvignon Blanc—Dry, California, 1982, $7.
Good price, nice food wine.
Sight: brilliant, medium straw-gold.
Nose: fruity, clean.
Taste: dry, medium body, fruity, tart, simple, austere, balanced, not complex.

Cambiaso

From Cambiaso Vineyards, Healdsburg:
Sauvignon Blanc, Sonoma County, Chalk Hill, 1982, $7.22.
Simple but nice one-dimensional wine.
Sight: clear, herbal, floral, fruit.
Nose: clean, light yellow-gold, green tint.
Taste: dry, medium body, good balance, forward herbal Sauvignon Blanc character, focused fruit, one dimensional, lingering finish.

J. Carey

From J. Carey Vineyards, Solvang:
Sauvignon Blanc, Santa Barbara County, 1983, $7.75.
Intense, well-focused Sauvignon Blanc flavors.
Sight: brilliant, pale good.
Nose: celery, clean, herbal.
Taste: dry, tart, very clean, celery & herbal flavors, lingering finish.

Carneros Creek Winery

From Carneros Creek Winery, Napa:
Fumé Blanc, California, 1982, $7.50.
Austere style, drink with food.
Sight: brilliant, medium straw.
Nose: closed, perfumed, fruity.
Taste: dry, closed, full body, good citric fruit underneath, well structured, balanced, short finish.
Sauvignon Blanc, California, 1982, $7.50.
Unusual style; try a bottle first.
Sight: clear, medium straw.
Nose: clean, floral, candied.
Taste: dry, chalky, candied, astringent, balanced, seems woody, a bit short on varietal character.

Caymus Vineyards

From Caymus Vineyards, Rutherford:
Sauvignon Blanc, Napa Valley, 1982, $6.50.
A different style, if you like celery.
Sight: clear, light gold.
Nose: deep celery aromas.
Taste: dry, medium body, strong celery, fruit, black pepper, good acid, lingering finish.

Chalk Hill Winery

From Chalk Hill Winery, Healdsburg:
Sauvignon Blanc, Sonoma County, 1982, $6.
Good price for a lighter style.
Sight: clear light gold.
Nose: clean, herbal, celery.

Taste: dry, medium body, austere, fruity, celery, great balance, good acid, lingering finish.

Chateau Lefranc

From Charles Lefranc Cellars, San Jose:
Sauvignon Blanc, Monterey County, Late Harvest, 1982, $5/350 ml.
Interesting herbal dessert wine.
Sight: brilliant, light gold.
Nose: intense bell-pepper, vegetal, herbal, botrytis underneath.
Taste: sweet, very herbaceous, low in acid, full-bodied, intensely vegetal, some botrytis, long finish.

Chateau M

From Monticello Cellars, Napa:
Sauvignon Blanc, Napa Valley, 1982, $17.50/375 ml.
Complex wine with unusual, spicy, woody flavors. Some will like it, others may not.
Sight: medium gold.
Nose: honeyed, herbal, toasty, woody, edge of nail polish.
Taste: wood flavors predominate, balanced with acid; slightly charred, spicy aftertaste with caramel and honey.

Chateau St. Jean

From Chateau St. Jean, Kenwood:
Fumé Blanc, Alexander Valley, Robert Young Vineyards, 1983, $10.
Forward, assertive Sauvignon Blanc.
Sight: pale straw.
Nose: intense fig, herbal fruit, melons.
Taste: dry, intense, complex fruit flavors, great structure and balance, long clean finish.
Fumé Blanc, Sonoma County, La Petite Etoile, 1982, $10.50.
Superb Fumé Blanc.
Sight: brilliant, light gold-green.
Nose: woody, herbal, citric.
Taste: dry, clean, full body, slightly astringent, tart, great

herbal character, grapefruity, balanced, long finish.

The Christian Brothers

From The Christian Brothers, Napa:
"Napa" Fumé Blanc, Napa Valley, Cuvée 813, NV, $5.
Very young and tart Sauvignon Blanc.
Sight: brilliant, straw.
Nose: clean, green apples and watermelon, lots of fruit.
Taste: dry, full body, tart, citric, lots of grapefruit, balanced, intense citric finish.

Clos du Bois

From Clos Du Bois Winery, Healdsburg:
Sauvignon Blanc, Alexander Valley, 1982, $7.50.
Needs food.
Sight: brilliant, light straw.
Nose: clean, herbal, cheesy, olives.
Taste: dry, medium body, soft simple flavors, tart, good balance, clean finish.

Clos Du Val

From Clos Du Val Wine Co., Napa:
Sauvignon Blanc, Napa Valley, 1983, $7.50.
Lemony flavors, a lot of acid.
Sight: clear, light gold, slight red edge.
Nose: clean, floral, herbal.
Taste: dry, very citric, medium body, lemon-peel flavor, overacidic, otherwise nice flavors.

Concannon

From Concannon Vineyard, Livermore:
Sauvignon Blanc, California, 1983, $7.
Young Sauvignon Blanc with good potential.
Sight: pale straw, a shade brown.
Nose: herbal, varietal fruit.
Taste: dry, full body, lots of clean tart varietal fruit, balanced, clean herbal finish.

R & J Cook

From R & J Cook, Clarksburg:
Fumé Blanc, Clarksburg, 1982, $7.
Costs more than it should—if priced lower would have been more enthusiastically received.
Sight: clear, medium straw.
Nose: clean, herbal, olives, dill.
Taste: dry, medium body, strong olive character, some herbal fruit, slightly flabby, finish falls off.

Cordtz Brothers

From Cordtz Brothers Cellars, Cloverdale:
Sauvignon Blanc, Alexander Valley, 1982, $7.50.
Dry food wine with lots of fruit.
Sight: brilliant, light straw.
Nose: clean, grassy, nice Sauvignon Blanc character.
Taste: dry, full body, ripe fruit flavors, herbal, tart, firm acidity, good structure.

Cosentino Select

From Cosentino Wines, Modesto:
Sauvignon Blanc, Napa Valley, "The Novelist," 1982, $8.
Very grassy style—not overdone though.
Sight: brilliant, medium straw.
Nose: grassy, good varietal aromas.
Taste: dry, medium body, good fruit at first then falls off a bit, crisp acid, very grassy and austere, balanced.

Crystal Valley Cellars

From Crystal Valley Cellars, Modesto:
"Crystal Fumé," California, Limited Reserve, 1982, $7.
Grassy style.
Sight: clear, medium gold.
Nose: low intensity, a bit woody.
Taste: dry, tart, woody, medium body, grassy finish.

Domaine Laurier

From Domaine Laurier, Forestville:
Sauvignon Blanc, Sonoma County, 1982, $9.
Steely, flinty style.
Sight: clear, light gold.
Nose: light, fresh, fruity.
Taste: dry, lively, tart, clean, good flavors, very well balanced, clean finish.

Domaine Laurier
1982
Sauvignon Blanc
Sonoma County

Produced and bottled by
Domaine Laurier, Forestville, Ca. U.S.A.
Alcohol 12.5% by volume 750 ml

J. Patrick Doré Selections

From Coastal Wines Ltd., Sausalito:
Sauvignon Blanc, Santa Maria Valley, 1982, $4.99.
Excellent value.
Sight: brilliant, pale, light gold.
Nose: herbal, bell pepper.
Taste: dry, medium body, very clean, fruity, great acid, bell-pepper character, well balanced, lingering finish.

Dry Creek Vineyard

From Dry Creek Vineyard, Healdsburg:
Fumé Blanc, Sonoma County, 1982, $8.50.
Great food wine.
Sight: clear, pale gold.

Dry Creek
1982
Sonoma County
Fumé Blanc
(Dry Sauvignon Blanc)

PRODUCED AND BOTTLED BY
DRY CREEK VINEYARD, INC., HEALDSBURG, CALIFORNIA, U.S.A.

Vineyard

Nose: herbal, olives, varietal.
Taste: dry, crisp, intense herbal, full body, great balance, long finish.

Fenestra

From Fenestra Winery, Livermore:
Sauvignon Blanc, San Luis Obispo County, 1983, $7.50.
Distinctive; unabashedly Sauvignon Blanc.
Sight: brilliant, medium straw.
Nose: green, grassy, herbal, green peppers, perfumed.
Taste: intense green-pepper flavors are almost overpowering, decent acid and balance, vegetal flavors on finish.

1983
SAN LUIS OBISPO COUNTY
SAUVIGNON BLANC
PRODUCED & BOTTLED BY FENESTRA WINERY
LIVERMORE, CA   ALCOHOL 13.3% BY VOLUME

Fetzer

From Fetzer Vineyards, Redwood Valley:
Fumé Blanc, Lake County (63 percent) & Mendocino County (37 percent), 1983, $7.
Good value in a simply styled Fumé Blanc.
Sight: clear, pale straw-gold.
Nose: grapy, smoky, herbaceous.
Taste: dry, crisp, medium body, has slightly coarse feel, clean finish.

Flora Springs

From Flora Springs, St. Helena:
Sauvignon Blanc, Napa Valley, 1982, $8.
Very clean and crisp style.
Sight: clear, pale straw-gold.
Nose: a bit grassy, a bit appley, some green pepper.

Taste: dry, very tart, medium body, clean, crisp, hints of bitterness.

Louis J. Foppiano

From Louis J. Foppiano Winery, Healdsburg:
Sauvignon Blanc, Sonoma County, 1982, $7.50.
Intense style of Sauvignon Blanc.
Sight: brilliant, light straw.
Nose: intense, herbal, olives, weedy.
Taste: dry, full body, balanced, grapefruit flavors, herbal and grassy, good fruit, long clean finish.

Franciscan Vineyards

From Franciscan Vineyards, Rutherford:
Fumé Blanc, California, 1982, $6.
Bitter and slightly alcoholic; needs time.
Sight: clear, light gold.
Nose: candied, fruity.
Taste: dry, medium body, appley, some heat, bitter on finish.

Girard

From Girard Winery, Oakville:
Sauvignon Blanc, North Coast, 1982, $8.
Pleasant herbal flavor, crisp finish.
Sight: brilliant, medium gold.
Nose: weedy, Sauvignon Blanc, slight sulfur.
Taste: dry, full body, crisp, clean, Sauvignon Blanc, fruit, grassy and herbal, good acid, long finish.

Glen Ellen

From Glen Ellen Winery, Glen Ellen:
Sauvignon Blanc, Sonoma County, 1982, $8.50.
Will take some age.
Sight: brilliant, pale green gold.
Nose: clean, austere, closed.
Taste: dry, full, rich, clean, lots of fruit, good acid, herbal, well balanced, long finish.

1982
SONOMA COUNTY
SAUVIGNON BLANC

ALCOHOL 12.5% BY VOLUME
PRODUCED & BOTTLED BY GLEN ELLEN WINERY
GLEN ELLEN, SONOMA VALLEY, CALIFORNIA B.W. 4911

Groth

From Groth Vineyards & Cellars, Oakville:
Sauvignon Blanc, Napa Valley, 1982, $8.50.
Better on the palate than nose.
Sight: clear, medium gold.
Nose: closed, lemony, smoky.
Taste: dry, fat, fruity, balanced, oily, full bodied, some wood, lacks complexity, medium finish.

Groth

1982
Napa Valley
Sauvignon Blanc

CELLARED AND BOTTLED BY
GROTH VINEYARDS AND CELLARS, OAKVILLE, CALIFORNIA
ALCOHOL 13.1% BY VOLUME

Guenoc

From Guenoc Winery, Middletown:
Sauvignon Blanc, Guenoc Valley, 1982, $6.50.
Nice food wine—tart, austere style.
Sight: brilliant, medium gold, straw hue.

Nose: austere, clean, woody.
Taste: dry, medium body, lots of extract, a bit awkward, good structure, clean, well balanced.

Husch Vineyards

From Husch Vineyards, Philo:
Sauvignon Blanc, Mendocino County, La Ribera Ranch, 1982, $7.50.
Fruity style.
Sight: brilliant, light-to-medium gold.
Nose: lots of fruit and herbal aromas.
Taste: dry, full body, fruity, pineapple, good balance, tart, clean, long finish.

Inglenook Vineyards

From Inglenook Vineyards, Rutherford:
Fumé Blanc, Napa Valley, 1982, $7.
Very tart style. Needs time to settle down.
Sight: brilliant, medium gold.
Nose: clean, floral, Sauvignon Blanc aromas.
Taste: dry, medium body, tart, a bit short on fruit and flavor, lingering tart finish.

Iron Horse Vineyards

From Iron Horse Vineyards, Sebastopol:
Fumé Blanc, Alexander Valley, 1982, $8.75.
Very clean and assertive.
Sight: brilliant, light green-gold.
Nose: floral, herbal, hint of wood.
Taste: dry, herbal, medium body, tart fruit, crisp, wood in background, assertive, well balanced.

Kendall-Jackson

From Kendall-Jackson Vineyards & Winery, Lakeport:
Sauvignon Blanc, Clear Lake, 1982, $7.
Nicely made, fine debut wine.
Sight: brilliant, light gold.
Nose: clean, closed, herbal, some oak.
Taste: dry, herbaceous, grassy, good fruit and acid, medium body, lingering finish.

Lakespring

From Lakespring Winery, Napa:
Sauvignon Blanc, California, 1982, $7.50.
Intense fruit.
Sight: brilliant, pale straw.
Nose: nice fruit, a bit woody.
Taste: dry, intense fruit, clean, assertive, good varietal character, well balanced.

Charles Lefranc

From Charles Lefranc Cellars, San Jose:
Fumé Blanc, Monterey County, 1982, $8.
Assertive fruit and woody style.
Sight: brilliant, pale straw.
Nose: clean, floral, sweet peas.
Taste: dry, full body, good concentrated fruit balanced with wood, some heat, trace of bitterness.

Maddalena Vineyard

From San Antonio Winery, Los Angeles:
Sauvignon Blanc, Santa Barbara County, 1983, $4.95.
Soft, full, vegetal wine, good value if you like the style.
Sight: brilliant, light gold.
Nose: asparagus, green bean, vanilla, flowery.
Taste: off-dry, rich texture, same vegetable flavors as in the nose, soft finish, not likely to age.

Markham

From Markham Vineyards, St. Helena:
Sauvignon Blanc, Napa Valley, 1982, $7.85.
Very herbal and woody.
Sight: clear, light straw-gold.
Nose: herbal, woody, a bit off.
Taste: dry, herbal, somewhat dirty, woody flavor, good acid, lingering finish.

Paul Masson

From Paul Masson, Saratoga:
Fumé Blanc, Monterey, 1982, $7.50.
Simple and pricey.
Sight: light gold.

Nose: figs, olives, lemons.
Taste: dry, simple, herbal, grapefruit flavors, decent balance, short, clean finish.

Matanzas Creek Winery

From Matanzas Creek Winery, Santa Rosa:
Sauvignon Blanc, Sonoma County, 1982, $10.50.
Age may help; an oaky but not heavy wine.
Sight: brilliant, light straw-gold.
Nose: some varietal character, vanilla from wood.
Taste: dry, full body, lots of wood and acid, moderate fruit, understated, smooth on finish.

McDowell Valley Vineyards

From McDowell Valley Vineyards, Hopland:
Fumé Blanc, McDowell Valley, Estate Bottled, 1982, $7.50.
Super wine.
Sight: brilliant, pale straw, light gold.
Nose: a bit herbal, good fruity nose.
Taste: dry, great fruit, excellent acid, a bit of wood in background, restrained, well balanced, long finish.

John B. Merrit

From John B. Merrit Winery, Cloverdale:
Sauvignon Blanc, Mendocino County, Potter Valley, 1982, $7.
Grassy Sauvignon—nose detracts slightly.
Sight: clear, medium straw.
Nose: tanky off-odor, varietal fruit underneath.
Taste: dry, medium body, grassy, herbal flavors, crisp and clean, good acid, balanced, lingering finish.

Mirassou

From Mirassou Vineyards, San Jose:
Fumé Blanc, San Luis Obispo County, 1982, $7.
Light, fruity, and simple.

Sight: clear, light gold.
Nose: fruity, low herbal.
Taste: dry, clean soft fruit, medium body, slightly short finish.
Sauvignon Blanc, Shenandoah Valley, 1982, $7.75.
Interesting style—very crisp and clean.
Sight: brilliant, medium yellow-gold.
Nose: herbal, very clean.
Taste: dry, good fruit, medium body, varietal, nice toasty flavor, crisp acid, well balanced.

Mt. Palomar Winery

From Mt. Palomar Winery, Temecula:
Fumé Blanc, Temecula, 1982, $4.95.
Good everyday wine.
Sight: clear, medium green-gold.
Nose: closed, perfumy, woody.
Taste: dry, medium body, closed, some simple fruit, one-dimensional, balanced, medium finish.

Napa Cellars

From Napa Cellars, Oakville:
Sauvignon Blanc, Napa Valley, 1982, $8.
Varietal, simple, and pricey.
Sight: brilliant, pale straw-gold.
Nose: varietal, some off-odors.
Taste: dry, clean, medium body, tart, intense tangy flavors, simple, a bit short on finish.

Newlan

From Newlan Vineyards & Winery, Napa:
Sauvignon Blanc, Napa Valley, 1982, $8.50.
Assertive, herbal Sauvignon Blanc.
Sight: brilliant, pale straw.
Nose: herbal, very grassy.
Taste: dry, clean, medium body, celery, green-pepper flavors, herbal, good acid, balanced, lingering finish.

Parducci

From Parducci Wine Cellars, Ukiah:
Sauvignon Blanc, Mendocino County, 1982, $6.
Great for cold chicken or fish.
Sight: brilliant, pale straw.
Nose: fresh, fruity, very clean.
Taste: dry, tart, lots of fruit, crisp, good acid, well balanced, nice finish.

Robert Pecota

From Robert Pecota Winery, Calistoga:
Sauvignon Blanc, Napa Valley, 1982, $8.50.
Austere Sauvignon Blanc.
Sight: brilliant, medium straw.
Nose: citric, fruity aromas.
Taste: dry, medium body, great varietal character, herbal, a bit hot, good acid, balanced, long finish.

Robert Pepi

From Robert Pepi Winery, Oakville:
Sauvignon Blanc, Napa Valley, 1982, $8.
Assertive herbal style.
Sight: brilliant, pale straw.
Nose: fresh, fruity, light herbal.
Taste: dry, medium body, intense, tart, clean, vegetal character, herbal, well balanced, lingering finish.

Joseph Phelps Vineyards

From Joseph Phelps Vineyards, St. Helena:
Sauvignon Blanc, Napa Valley, 1982, $9.
Pricey food wine; nicely made.
Sight: clear, light straw.
Nose: herbal, fruity, varietal.
Taste: dry, clean, full body, herbal character, good structure, balanced, long finish.

R. H. Phillips Vineyard

From R. H. Phillips Vineyard, Camino:
Sauvignon Blanc, Yolo County, Dunnigan Hills, 1983, $5.49.
Unique style of Sauvignon Blanc.
Sight: clear, pale straw.

Nose: clean, olives, herbaceous.
Taste: dry, full body, intense herbal olive flavors, balanced, finish falls off a bit.

Preston

From Preston Vineyards & Winery, Healdsburg:
Sauvignon Blanc, Dry Creek Valley, 1982, $8.50.
Lots of herbal flavor.
Sight: brilliant, pale straw.
Nose: celery, vegetal, very clean.
Taste: dry, clean, medium body, lots of good tart fruit, herbal, celery, balanced.

Round Hill

From Round Hill Vineyards, St. Helena:
Fumé Blanc, Napa Valley, 1982, $6.
Intense flavor, good value.
Sight: brilliant, pale straw.
Nose: clean, grassy herbal.
Taste: dry, medium body, clean assertive fruit, grassy, herbal, assertive, balanced, long finish.

Rutherford Ranch

From Rutherford Ranch Vineyards, St. Helena:
Sauvignon Blanc, Napa Valley, 1982, $7.50.
Austere, not fruity style, lean and mean.
Sight: brilliant, deep straw, brassy edge.
Nose: metallic, some slight Sauvignon Blanc fruit, bell pepper.
Taste: metallic, flavor; citric, lean texture, very little fruit, elusive, tart finish, slightly hot.

Sanford

From Sanford Winery, San Luis Obispo:
Sauvignon Blanc, Santa Maria Valley, 1982, $8.50.
Vegetal flavor dominates.
Sight: brilliant, medium green-gold.
Nose: vegetal, earthy, woody.
Taste: dry, medium body, vegetal, fruity, balanced, chalky, somewhat bitter, vegetal finish.

Santa Ynez Valley Winery

From Santa Ynez Valley Winery, Santa Ynez:

Sauvignon Blanc, California, 1982, $7.
Loaded with fruit.
Sight: clear, medium straw.
Nose: clean, green peas, herbaceous.
Taste: dry, tart, herbal with green pea flavor, balanced, medium body, lingering fruity finish.

Sea Ridge

From Sea Ridge Winery, Cazadero:

Sauvignon Blanc, Sonoma County, Scalabrini Vineyards, 1983, $8.
Very unusual style of Sauvignon Blanc.
Sight: clear, light gold.
Nose: spicy, perfumy.
Taste: off-dry, soft fruit, seems to be low in varietal character, perfumy, floral character, soft on palate.

August Sebastiani

From Sebastiani Vineyards, Sonoma:

Country Fumé Blanc, California, 1982, $6.89/magnum.
Clean quaff, good value.
Sight: brilliant, pale gold.
Nose: grassy, low intensity.
Taste: dry, varietal, medium body, some wood and herbal, light style.

Shenandoah Vineyards

From Shenandoah Vineyards, Plymouth:

Sauvignon Blanc, Amador County, 1983, $7.50.
Assertive style: a surprising Sauvignon Blanc from Amador County.
Sight: clear, light gold.
Nose: clean, perfumed, varietal.
Taste: dry, full body, lots of melon fruit, balanced, good varietal character, fruity finish.

Souverain

From Souverain Cellars, Geyserville:

Fumé Blanc, North Coast, 1982, $6.75.
Stylish—has the assertive aroma of Chenin Blanc.
Sight: clear, light green-gold.
Nose: clean, fruity, melons, assertive.
Taste: dry, medium body, clean fruit, crisp acidity, herbal flavors, balanced, a bit short on finish.

Souverain
FUMÉ BLANC
SAUVIGNON BLANC
APPELLATION NORTH COAST
1982

Stag's Leap Wine Cellars

From Stag's Leap Wine Cellars, Napa:

Sauvignon Blanc, Napa Valley, 1981, $9.
Good food wine—needs a bit of time to develop.
Sight: brilliant, light gold.
Nose: woody, very grassy.
Taste: dry, austere, medium-full body, clean, lots of acid, tart, well balanced, lingering finish.

Sterling Vineyards

From Sterling Vineyards, Calistoga:

Sauvignon Blanc, Napa Valley, 1982, $10.
Starting to compete with Chardonnay in price and quality.
Sight: brilliant, light gold.
Nose: austere, clean, low intensity.
Taste: dry, tart, medium body, herbal-grassy flavors, very clean, needs time, well balanced.

Stone Creek

From Stone Creek Cellars, Healdsburg:

Fumé Blanc, Sonoma County, Special Selection, 1982, $5.25.
Well suited for good at the price.
Sight: clear, pale straw.
Nose: clean, slightly grassy.
Taste: dry, medium body, simple flavors, citrus fruit flavors, pleasant style, balanced, lingering finish.

Stonegate

From Stonegate Winery, Calistoga:

Sauvignon Blanc, Napa Valley, 1982, $8.50.
Clean, slightly closed food wine.
Sight: brilliant, pale straw.
Nose: closed, herbal, low intensity.
Taste: dry, very tart, apparent wood, understated, varietal, well balanced, slightly bitter on finish.

Stratford

From Cartlidge, Moser & Forsyth, St. Helena:

Sauvignon Blanc, Napa Valley, 1983, $6.
Fruit just coming through—lots of potential.
Sight: clear, pale straw.
Nose: clean, light herbal.
Taste: dry, full body, nice clean herbal fruit, grassy, fruit expands on palate, tart finish.

MADE & BOTTLED BY CARTLIDGE, MOSER & FORSYTH
ST. HELENA, NAPA VALLEY, CALIFORNIA · ALCOHOL 12.5% BY VOLUME

1983
NAPA VALLEY
SAUVIGNON BLANC

STRATFORD

Sycamore Creek

From Sycamore Creek
Vineyards, Morgan Hill:
**Fumé Blanc, Paso Robles,
1983, $7.50.**
Extremely pungent and off-dry.
Sight: clear, brassy straw.
Nose: grassy, asparagus.
Taste: off-dry, full body, herbal
vegetal character, slightly bitter,
dirty finish.

Tijsseling Family Vineyards

From Tijsseling Vineyards,
Ukiah:
Sauvignon Blanc, Mendocino County, 1982, $7.
Needs time to develop.
Sight: clear, light gold.
Nose: light, herbal, fruity.
Taste: dry, medium body, crisp
fruit flavors, tart, young, long
finish.

MENDOCINO COUNTY
SAUVIGNON BLANC
PRODUCED AND BOTTLED BY TIJSSELING VINEYARDS
UKIAH, CALIFORNIA, USA • ALCOHOL 13.0% BY VOLUME

Vose Vineyards

From Vose Vineyards, Napa:
**Fumé Blanc, Amador
County, 1982, $5.75.**
Assertive Fumé that will mate
well with food.
Sight: brilliant, pale straw.
Nose: nice blend of fruit and
grassy aromas.
Taste: dry, very tart, medium
body, good acid, clean, assertive
fruit, lots of oak, slight bitterness
on finish.

VŌSE Vineyards

FUMÉ BLANC
(100% SAUVIGNON BLANC)
1982 AMADOR COUNTY

PRODUCED AND BOTTLED BY
VOSE VINEYARDS, NAPA, CALIFORNIA
ALCOHOL BY VOLUME 13.5%

Wente Bros.

From Wente Bros., Livermore:
Sauvignon Blanc, Livermore Valley, 1982, $6.15.
A fine woody-styled Sauvignon
Blanc.
Sight: brilliant, medium straw-gold.
Nose: citrusy, fruity.
Taste: dry, medium body, full
woody flavors, clean, fruity, tart,
good acid, balanced.

William Wheeler

From Wheeler Vineyards,
Healdsburg:
**Sauvignon Blanc, Sonoma
County, 1982, $8.**
Grassy style, lots of fruit.
Sight: clear, light gold with a
slight copper tint.
Nose: very grassy and herbal,
perfumy.
Taste: dry, full body, big and
tart, very assertive, clean,
young, lots of extract, grassy flavors, long finish.

Whitehall Lane

From Whitehall Lane Winery,
St. Helena:
**Sauvignon Blanc, 51 percent San Luis Obispo
County, 49 percent Napa
County, 1982, $8.**
Oaky, not complex Sauvignon
Blanc.
Sight: brilliant, medium straw-gold.
Nose: lots of oak, buttery.
Taste: dry, medium body,
clean, lots of woody flavor, not
complex.

Zaca Mesa

From Zaca Mesa Winery, Los
Olivos:
Sauvignon Blanc, California, 1982, $7.50.
Big style without oaky flavors.
Sight: brilliant, light gold.
Nose: bell peppers, asparagus
aromas.
Taste: dry, very tart, medium
body, intense fruit, clean, good
acid, well balanced.

ZINFANDEL

Best Buy

Dehlinger Winery

From Dehlinger Winery,
Sebastopol:
**Zinfandel, Sonoma County,
1981, $4.50.**

A bit alcoholic; fine wine for
the price.
Sight: clear, deep purple-ruby.
Nose: a bit closed, some berry
aroma.

Taste: dry, full body, a bit hot,
good varietal fruit, woody, moderate tannin, long finish.

Highly Recommended

Joseph Phelps Vineyards

From Joseph Phelps Vineyards, St. Helena:

Zinfandel, Alexander Valley, 1980, $6.75.
Great balancing act with tannin and acid.
Sight: medium garnet.
Nose: clean varietal aromas, some oak.
Taste: plenty of nice varietal flavors, good balance of fruit and acid and tannin. Trace of heat on finish.

Zinfandel, Napa Valley, 1982, $5.75.
Beaujolais style—very nice.

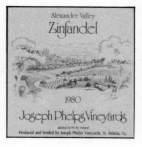

Sight: clear, rich purple.
Nose: lots of Grenache/Zinfandel aromas.
Taste: dry, light, tart, lots of Grenache flavor, easy to drink, good acid.

Ridge

From Ridge Vineyards, Cupertino:

Zinfandel, California, York Creek, 1981, $9.50.
Textbook Zin.
Sight: clear, deep dark ruby.
Nose: attractive, spicy, berries.

RIDGE
CALIFORNIA
ZINFANDEL
YORK CREEK
1981

NAPA COUNTY, 92% ZINFANDEL, 8% PETITE SIRAH
YORK CREEK VINEYARDS   ALCOHOL 13.9% BY VOLUME
PRODUCED AND BOTTLED BY RIDGE VINEYARDS. BW 4488
17100 MONTE BELLO RD., BOX A1, CUPERTINO, CALIFORNIA

Taste: dry, full body, intense, great varietal, big, woody, good acid, long finish

Sycamore Creek

From Sycamore Creek Vineyards, Morgan Hill:

Zinfandel, California, 1982, $9.
Very clean and intense, has concentration of a late-harvest style without the alcohol.
Sight: opaque, dark purple.
Nose: rich, spicy, orange, blackberry, some fermentation bouquet.
Taste: dry, clean, not as alcoholic as expected, very fruity and intense, balanced, lingering finish.

ZD Wines

From ZD Wines, Napa:

Zinfandel, Napa Valley, 1980, $7.50.
Great Zin style for food.
Sight: clear, deep purple.
Nose: clean, ripe, spicy, peppery.
Taste: dry, clean, full body, very spicy, lots of berry fruit, moderate tannin, good acid, very well balanced.

Recommended

Ahern Winery

From Ahern Winery, San Fernando:

Zinfandel, Amador County, 1980, $6.50.
Old style Zinfandel, more winey than fruity.
Sight: deep ruby.
Nose: dank, tanky, not varietal, vinous.
Taste: dry, big and peppery, bitter, bit out of balance, some fruit but too assertive.

Ahlgren Vineyard

From Ahlgren Vineyard, Boulder Creek:

Zinfandel, California, 1980, $7.50.
Huge and tannic; needs a long time.
Sight: clear, deep purple.
Nose: port-like, intense.
Taste: dry, full body, intense, alcoholic, tannic, good fruit, not balanced yet, long finish.

Amador Foothill Winery

From Amador Foothill Winery, Plymouth:

Zinfandel, Amador County, 1980, $6.50.
A good value in varietal Zinfandel.
Sight: clear, medium-deep purple.
Nose: spicy, berries, fresh.
Taste: dry, clean, very nice flavors, full body, varietal berries and spices, balanced, long finish.

Balverne

From Balverne Winery, Windsor:

Zinfandel, Sonoma County, Quartz Hill Vineyard, 1980, $10.

Price is high.

Sight: clear, medium-to-deep garnet.

Nose: light spice, a bit of fruit.

Taste: dry, full body, good varietal character, nice fruit, good wood and balance, restrained character.

Bandiera

From Bandiera Winery, Cloverdale:

Zinfandel, North Coast, 1980, $4.25.

Mature, easy-to-drink Zinfandel.

Sight: clear, medium garnet.

Nose: varietal, some berries and spice.

Taste: dry, light-to-medium body, slight bitterness, good Zinfandel character, balanced, long finish.

Bandiera
Vintage 1980
North Coast
Zinfandel

Produced & Bottled by Bandiera Winery, Cloverdale, CA

Buehler Vineyards

From Buehler Vineyards, St. Helena:

Zinfandel, Napa Valley, 1981, $5.

Light fruity Zinfandel.

Sight: clear, deep ruby.

Nose: pruney, raisiny, woody.

Taste: dry, medium body, clean, good fruit, moderate tannin, balanced, long spicy finish.

Burgess

From Burgess Cellars, St. Helena:

Zinfandel, Napa Valley, 1981, $5.95.

Big Zinfandel.

Sight: clear, deep purple.

Nose: clean, rose petals and peppers.

Taste: dry, full body, little fruit but some Zinfandel fruit comes through heavy tannin, long finish.

Davis Bynum

From Davis Bynum Winery, Healdsburg:

Zinfandel, Sonoma, 1980, $7.50.

Very interesting style of Zinfandel.

Sight: clear, deep ruby.

Nose: spicy, redwood aromas.

Taste: dry, very fruity, medium body, spicy, clean, nice acid, balanced, long finish.

Calera

From Calera Wine Co., Hollister:

Zinfandel, Amador County, 1980, $6.50.

Very stylish Zinfandel.

Sight: clear, deep, black purple.

Nose: berries, jammy, clean.

Taste: dry, full body, tannic, very young, lots of acid, a bit high in alcohol to be balanced, long finish.

Zinfandel, Cienega Valley, 1981, $7.

Pleasant blockbuster Zinfandel.

Sight: brilliant, deep purple.

Nose: raisin, prunes, vanilla.

Taste: off-dry, full body, lots of ripe fruit and tannin, balanced, some heat on finish.

Zinfandel, Cienega Valley, Reserve, 1980, $7.50.

Alcohol is high, but doesn't seem that way.

Sight: clear, deep purple.

Nose: closed, some woody aromas.

Taste: dry, great fruit, full body, berries, varietal, woody, high alcohol, long finish.

Cassayre-Forni Cellars

From Cassayre-Forni Cellars, Rutherford:

Zinfandel, Sonoma County, 1981, $7.50.

Big woody style.

Sight: clear, deep purple-ruby.

Nose: peppery, woody, pruney.

Taste: dry, full body, fruity, lots of wood, slight bitterness in the finish.

Chateau Montelena

From Chateau Montelena Winery, Calistoga:

Zinfandel, Napa Valley, 1981, $8.

Some rough spots but enough fruit to pull through.

Sight: clear, deep purple-ruby.

Nose: Zinfandel berries.

Taste: dry, full body, good lively acid and fruit, balanced, trace of bitterness, tannic finish.

Clos Du Val

From Clos Du Val Wine Co., Napa:

Zinfandel, Napa Valley, 1981, $9.

Big, hard, claret-style Zinfandel, needs to develop further.

Sight: medium ruby.

Nose: Zinfandel, berries, oak.

Taste: dry, very tannic, berryish fruit, closed in, lots of heat on palate, needs developing, a bit woody.

Diablo Vista

From Diablo Vista Winery, Benicia:

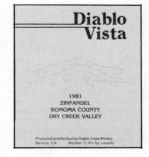

Diablo Vista

1981
ZINFANDEL
SONOMA COUNTY
DRY CREEK VALLEY

Produced and Bottled by Diablo Vista Winery, Benicia, CA   Alcohol 12.4% by volume

Zinfandel, Sonoma County, Dry Creek Valley, 1981, $6.90.
Straightforward, fruity Zinfandel.
Sight: clear, deep wood.
Nose: new wood, berries, balanced.
Taste: dry, medium body, tart, good berry fruit, lots of character without monster tannin, a bit hot on finish.

Dry Creek Vineyard

From Dry Creek Vineyard, Healdsburg:
Zinfandel, Dry Creek Valley, 1980, $7.50.
May be hard to pair with food.
Sight: clear, deep purple.
Nose: rich, currants, berry aromas.
Taste: dry, good fruit, medium body, good acid, somewhat low in tannin, some bitterness in finish.
Zinfandel, Sonoma County, Dry Creek Valley, 1981, $7.50.
Will round out and become more drinkable.
Sight: clear, deep ruby.
Nose: berries, some pepper, low intensity.
Taste: dry, full body, closed fruit, some restraint, good structure, balanced.

Estrella

From Estrella River Winery, Paso Robles:
Zinfandel, San Luis Obispo County, NV, $3.50.
Unbelievable price for a Zinfandel this good.
Sight: clear, medium-to-deep purple.
Nose: fruity, lots of ground pepper.
Taste: dry, clean, full body, lots of fruit and black pepper, tannic, good acid, balanced, long finish.

Fenestra

From Fenestra Winery, Livermore:
Zinfandel, Livermore Valley, 1981, $7.
Good Zinfandel character, lots of peppery berry fruit.

1981 LIVERMORE VALLEY
ZINFANDEL

PRODUCED & BOTTLED BY FENESTRA WINERY
LIVERMORE.CA   ALCOHOL 12.9% BY VOLUME

Sight: medium garnet.
Nose: fresh ground pepper, berries, vanilla, spice.
Taste: Lots of peppery-jammy fruit, balanced with good acid and tannin, long Zinfandel finish.

Fetzer

From Fetzer Vineyards, Redwood Valley:
Zinfandel, Lake County, 1982, $4.50.
Decent wine for the price.
Sight: clear, medium ruby.
Nose: spicy, peppery-smoky.
Taste: dry, full body, a bit too tannic for fruit, peppery fruit, tannic finish.
Zinfandel, Mendocino, 1980, $5.50.
Good value in Zinfandel with some aging potential.

1981
home vineyard
mendocino
zinfandel

GROWN, PRODUCED AND BOTTLED BY FETZER VINEYARDS
REDWOOD VALLEY CALIFORNIA, U.S.A ALCOHOL 13.0% BY VOL.

Sight: clear, medium ruby.
Nose: peppery.
Taste: dry, fruity, black pepper, floral, tannic, balanced, good fruit and acid, clean finish.
Zinfandel, Mendocino County, Home Vineyard, 1981, $8.
Needs time in the cellar.
Sight: clear, light-to-medium ruby.
Nose: clean, light, berryish fruit.
Taste: dry, full body, tannic, good fruit, balanced, tannic finish.
Zinfandel, Mendocino County, Lolonis Vineyards, 1981, $8.
Nicely made.
Sight: clear, medium ruby.
Nose: fresh, pleasant, berryish.
Taste: dry, fresh peppery fruit, grapy, spicy, balanced, tannic, some heat on finish.
Zinfandel, Mendocino County, Ricetti Vineyard, 1981, $9.
A bit woody.
Sight: clear, light ruby.
Nose: a bit closed, some fruit.
Taste: dry, full body, good fruit, tannic, balanced, forward fruit, lingering finish.

Grand Cru Vineyards

From Grand Cru Vineyards, Glen Ellen:
Zinfandel, Sonoma Valley, 1981, $8.50.
Nice with food.
Sight: clear, deep ruby.
Nose: nice, spicy.
Taste: dry, clean, woody, balanced, good fruit flavors, spicy, clean finish.

Green & Red

From Green & Red Vineyard, St. Helena:
Zinfandel, Napa Valley, Chiles Canyon, 1980, $7.
Very classy Zinfandel.
Sight: brilliant, deep purple.
Nose: fruity, ground pepper.
Taste: dry, tart, good fruit, full body, lots of ground pepper, very well balanced, long finish.

Grgich Hills

From Grgich Hills Cellar,
Rutherford:
Zinfandel, Sonoma County, 1981, $10.
Big and lanky, a lot of money for this wine.
Sight: clear, deep purple-ruby.
Nose: cardboard, alcoholic, some fruit under.
Taste: dry, forward, full body, lots of flavor, tannic, a bit alcoholic, long finish.

Guenoc

From Guenoc Winery,
Middletown:
Zinfandel, Lake County, 1981, $5.
Smoky flavor adds to the complexity of this Zinfandel value.
Sight: clear, ruby.
Nose: menthol, ground pepper.
Taste: dry, medium body, tannic, berries, apricots, clean full Zinfandel, soft smoky finish.

Hacienda Wine Cellars

From Hacienda Wine Cellars,
Sonoma:
Zinfandel, California, 1981, $6.50.
Big fruity style.
Sight: clear, medium ruby.
Nose: woody, some fruit.
Taste: dry, big, full body, lots of tannin, woody, good character, long finish.

Haywood Winery

From Haywood Winery,
Sonoma:
Zinfandel, Sonoma Valley, 1981, $6.75.
High alcohol hurts this wine slightly.
Sight: clear, deep purple-ruby.
Nose: a bit jammy.
Taste: dry, full body, clean, ripe, rich, grapy, a bit high in alcohol, long finish.

Hidden Cellars

From Hidden Cellars Winery,
Talmage:
Zinfandel, Mendocino County, 1981, $7.75.

Big-styled Zin.
Sight: clear, medium purple-ruby.
Nose: very spicy, berry aromas.
Taste: dry, medium body, lots of berry flavors, tannic, good acid, alcohol a bit high, thus hot on finish.

Inglenook Vineyards

From Inglenook Vineyards,
Rutherford:
Zinfandel, Napa Valley, 1980, $5.50.
A full rich style of Zinfandel; also a great value.
Sight: clear, medium-to-deep ruby.
Nose: rich berries, nice aroma, slightly piney.
Taste: dry, nice character, medium-to-full body, a bit short, tannic, finish lingers.

Leeward

From Leeward Winery, Oxnard:
Zinfandel, Amador County, 1981, $7.50.
Needs a lot of time.
Sight: clear, medium ruby.
Nose: a bit spicy, some fruit, woody.
Taste: dry, a bit spicy, big, tannic, fruit hidden under tannin, long finish.

Lytton Springs

From Lytton Springs Winery,
Healdsburg:
Zinfandel, Sonoma County, 1981, $7.50.
Needs bottle age.
Sight: clear, medium ruby-purple.
Nose: tar, berries, cooked aromas.
Taste: dry, full body, tannic, wood, some berryish fruit, lingering finish.

Louis M. Martini

From Louis M. Martini, St. Helena:
Zinfandel, North Coast, 1980, $4.45.
Very light style of Zinfandel.
Sight: clear, light ruby.
Nose: low intensity, pruney.
Taste: dry, tart, some fruit,

medium body, soft, round, short, tart finish.
Zinfandel, Sonoma, Special Selection, Monte Rosso Vineyard, 1977, $10.
Ready to drink.
Sight: clear, medium garnet, tawny edge.
Nose: clean, perfumy, varietal.
Taste: dry, medium body, licorice, pepper, wood, balanced, mature and complex.

McDowell Valley Vineyards

From McDowell Valley Vineyards, Hopland:
Zinfandel, McDowell Valley, 1981, $6.25.
Lighter style for current drinking.
Sight: clear, medium, deep ruby.
Nose: light, berries.
Taste: dry, light in body, fruity, a bit thin, tart fruit, berries, good acid, somewhat short finish.

Monteviña

From Monteviña Wines,
Plymouth:
Zinfandel, California, Shenandoah Valley, Winemaker's Choice, Estate Bottled, 1980, $9.
Needs food to stand up to it.
Sight: deep, inky purple.
Nose: intense, jammy, Zinfandel fruit, lots of wood.
Taste: dry, full body, ripe jammy fruit, balanced but lots of wood on finish.
Zinfandel, Montino, Shenandoah Valley, 1981, $5.

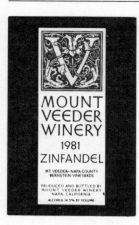

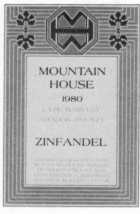

Stylish wine, not a typical Zinfandel.
Sight: clear, deep purple-ruby.
Nose: vinous, woody.
Taste: dry, full body, very woody, low varietal character, fruity on finish, lingering finish.

Parducci

From Parducci Wine Cellars, Ukiah:
Zinfandel, Mendocino County, 1981, $4.50.
Nice, light quaff.
Sight: clear, medium red-ruby.
Nose: light, berries, spice.

Taste: dry, light body, lots of berries and fruit, good acid, balanced, lingering finish.

J. Pedroncelli

From J. Pedroncelli Winery, Geyserville:
Zinfandel, Sonoma County, 1980, $4.50.
Great bargain.
Sight: clear, bright purple.
Nose: earthy aromas, some pepper.
Taste: dry, full body, a bit hot, clean fruit, tannic, some berry and pepper flavors, long finish.

Joseph Phelps Vineyards

From Joseph Phelps Vineyards, St. Helena:
Zinfandel, Napa Valley, 1983, $5.75.
Split personality—can't decide whether it wants to be light, nouveau style or bigger style.
Sight: reddish purple.
Nose: smoky-flowery, you can smell the alcohol.
Taste: dry, light in body, some berry—strawberry fruit, some tannin, especially on finish.

Preston

From Preston Vineyards & Winery, Healdsburg:
Zinfandel, Dry Creek Valley, Estate Bottled, 1981, $6.50.
Good value.
Sight: clear, medium ruby-purple.
Nose: clean, berries, fruity.
Taste: dry, fresh fruit, clean spicy, balanced acid, medium tannin, some heat.

Ravenswood

From Ravenswood, Sonoma:
Zinfandel, Sonoma County, Dry Creek Benchland, 1981, $6.50.
Very high in tannin and alcohol, has character though.
Sight: clear, deep purple.
Nose: nice Zinfandel nose, spicy, berries.
Taste: dry, huge, full body, berry fruit, very tannic, lots of fruit, long finish.

Ridge

From Ridge Vineyards, Cupertino:
Zinfandel, California, Fiddletown, 1978, $15.
Pricey, still needs time.
Sight: clear, medium-to-deep ruby.
Nose: spicy, peppery.
Taste: dry, full body, intense complex fruit, huge, tannic, good acid, puckering finish.
Zinfandel, California, 1981, $6.
Big fruity style.
Sight: clear, deep purple.
Nose: fresh, young, varietal.
Taste: dry, young, full body, lots of berries, clean, spicy, balanced, long finish.
Zinfandel, Fiddletown, 1980, $7.50.
Still needs time.
Sight: clear, medium ruby.
Nose: closed, slight pepper, wood and berries.
Taste: dry, full body, spicy, black pepper, fruity, a bit closed overall on palate, long finish.
Zinfandel, Geyserville, 1981, $9.
Needs time, worth the price.
Sight: clear, deep purple.
Nose: closed, berries, lots of ground pepper.
Taste: dry, full body, excellent varietal character, tannic, well structured, good acid, balanced, long finish.
Zinfandel, Paso Robles, 1981, $8.
Full jammy style.
Sight: clear, deep ruby.
Nose: berries, spicy, clean aromas, jammy.
Taste: dry, jammy fruit, clean, good structure, woody, big, long finish.

Round Hill

From Round Hill Vineyards, St. Helena:
Zinfandel, Napa Valley, 1981, $5.
Good fruit flavors.
Sight: medium ruby-purple.
Nose: pine, mint, Zinfandel fruit.
Taste: dry, full body, good ripe Zinfandel fruit, lots of tannin and wood on palate and finish.

Rutherford Ranch

From Rutherford Ranch Vineyards, St. Helena:
Zinfandel, Napa Valley, 1980, $6.
A bit hot on finish.
Sight: clear, deep ruby-purple.
Nose: perfumy, clean, berries.
Taste: dry, tannic, full body, lots of wood and fruit, spicy, balanced, great varietal character, long finish.

Santino

From Santino Wines, Plymouth:
"Fiddletown" Zinfandel, Special Selection, Amador County, 1980, $7.50.
Good value.
Sight: clear, deep purple.
Nose: fruity, spicy.
Taste: dry, full body, good fruit, tannic, nice berry character, clean, well balanced.

August Sebastiani

From Sebastiani Vineyards, Sonoma:
Country Zinfandel, California, NV $5.59 per magnum.
Moderate varietal character.
Sight: clear, medium garnet.
Nose: spicy, some Cabernet aromas.
Taste: dry, peppery fruit, tannic, full body, balanced, woody finish.

Shown & Sons

From Shown & Sons Vineyards, Rutherford:
Zinfandel, Napa Valley, 1981, $7.50.
Smooth and mellow Zinfandel.
Sight: medium ruby.
Nose: clean, Zinfandel berries, rose petal.
Taste: dry, full body, berry fruit, great structure and balance, smooth and pleasant, clean, lingering finish.

Silver Mountain Vineyards

From Silver Mountain Vineyards, Los Gatos:
Zinfandel, Paso Robles, 1980, $7.

Hard young wine that is short on fruit.
Sight: medium garnet.
Nose: yeast-berry fermentation aromas.
Taste: dry, full body, rough, young, sturdy tannic backbone; varietal fruit is missing.

Smothers

From Smothers–Vine Hill Wines, Santa Cruz:
Zinfandel, Sonoma, 1980, $7.50.
Assertive, varietal Zinfandel.
Sight: brilliant, rich ruby.
Nose: light berries, closed.
Taste: dry, tart, full body, lots of berries, spice, clean finish.

Stony Ridge Winery

From Stony Ridge Winery, Pleasanton:
Zinfandel, Livermore Valley, 1980, $7.
Old-style Italian-Californian red.
Sight: clear, medium garnet.
Nose: pruny, raisiny.
Taste: dry, considerable volatile acidity, short flavors, some fruit.

Storybook Mountain Vineyards

From Storybook Mountain Vineyards, Calistoga:
Zinfandel, Napa Valley, 1981, $7.75.
Alcoholic style—distinctive.

Sight: clear, medium-to-deep purple.
Nose: spicy, earthy, woody.
Taste: dry, full body, tannic, lots of fruit, clean, very woody, acid is strong, long finish.
Zinfandel, Napa Valley, Estate Reserve, 1981, $9.50.
Pricey, racy Zinfandel.
Sight: brilliant, purple.
Nose: clean, raspberry, Zinfandel fruit.
Taste: dry, full body, good ripe fruit, lots of tannin, good structure.
Zinfandel, Sonoma County, 1980, $7.75.
Big-style, complete Zinfandel.
Sight: deep dark purple.
Nose: clean, peppery, berries.
Taste: dry, full berry character, wood flavors, balanced acid and fruit, long finish.

Sutter Home

From Sutter Home Winery, St. Helena:
Zinfandel, Amador County, 1981, $6.25.
A clean and easy-to-drink Zinfandel.
Sight: clear, medium ruby.
Nose: nice berries, fruity, fermentation.
Taste: dry, fruity, light-medium body, soft, mellow flavors, lingering finish.

Zaca Mesa

From Zaca Mesa Winery, Los Olivos:
Zinfandel, California, 1981, $5.50.
Unusual lighter style.
Sight: clear, light ruby.
Nose: low in character, not intense.
Taste: dry, medium body, some character, soft, fruity, berries, balanced, short finish.

SPARKLING WINE

Best Buy

Robin's Glow

From Crystal Valley Cellars, Modesto:

Blanc de Noirs, Brut, California, NV, $5.75.
Good semi-sweet aperitif wine.
Sight: brilliant, medium salmon pink.
Nose: clean, yeasty, floral.
Taste: off-dry, light, clean, good fruit, balanced, light effervescence, short finish.

Recommended

Chateau St. Jean

From Chateau St. Jean, Graton:
Blanc de Blanc, Brut, 1980, $20.
High in acid, well-structured wine.
Sight: brilliant, light gold, steady bead.
Nose: light, yeasty, some fruit.
Taste: dry, tart, very clean, good strong acid, fruity, balanced though sharp.
Brut, 1980, $20.
Pricey, simple, fruity sparkler.
Sight: brilliant, pale gold, steady beading.
Nose: yeasty, light and fruity.
Taste: dry, very tart, clean, good fruit, citrusy, good structure and balance.

Crystal Valley Cellars

From Crystal Valley Cellars, Modesto:
Spumante d'Franchesca, California, NV, $5.75.
Priced right.
Sight: brilliant, medium gold.
Nose: Muscat aromas.
Taste: off-dry, lots of Muscat character, slightly soapy, lacks acid, short finish, pleasant quaff.

Robert Hunter

From Robert Hunter, Graton:
Brut de Noir, Sonoma Valley, 1980, $15.
A bit high-priced for a fairly simple sparkler.
Sight: clear, medium copper, steady beading.
Nose: some yeast and fruit.
Taste: dry, very tart and clean, medium body, good acid, moderate Pinot Noir character, simple flavors, linger finish.

Mirassou

From Mirassou Vineyards, San Jose:
Au Naturel Champagne, Monterey County, 1981, $12.75.
Simple but elegant.
Sight: clear, medium straw, steady beading.
Nose: yeasty, some fruit.
Taste: dry, good acid, medium body, balanced, simple but well made, long finish, lively flavors.
Brut Champagne, Monterey County, 1980, $12.
Well-crafted wine.
Sight: clear, pale straw, light beading.
Nose: clean, yeasty, nutty.
Taste: dry, crisp and clean, medium body, good fruit and balance, long finish.

Other States:
Washington/Oregon/New York

Best Buy

Hinzerling Vineyards
From Hinzerling Vineyards,
Prosser, Wash.:
**Chardonnay, Washington,
Yakima Valley, 1981, $6.99.**
Good complexity for price.
Sight: brilliant, gold.
Nose: apples and butter,
cloves.
Taste: dry, medium body, ripe
apple, lemon fruit, simple but balanced, some wood.

Highly Recommended

Chateau Ste. Michelle
From Chateau Ste. Michelle,
Woodinville, Wash.:
**Fumé Blanc, Washington,
1981, $6.50.**
An excellent value in a fruity
and assertive style.
Sight: clear, medium straw-gold.
Nose: fruity, slightly herbal
and spicy.
Taste: dry, medium body, good
fruit, assertive, tart, some
wood, balanced, long finish.

Recommended

Arbor Crest
From Arbor Crest Cellars,
Spokane, Wash.:
**Johannisberg Riesling,
Washington State, Stewart's**

**Sunnyside Vineyard, Select
Late Harvest, 1982, $7.15.**
A light-style dessert wine.
Sight: clear, medium yellow-gold.
Nose: honey, botrytis.
Taste: lightly sweet, medium
body, tart, clean, orange, honeyed flavors, balanced, lingering
finish.
**Sauvignon Blanc, Washington, Bacchus Vineyard,
Cameo Reserve, 1982,
$7.75.**
Middle-of-the-road style between fruity and woody.
Sight: brilliant, light gold.
Nose: light, some wood.
Taste: seems off-dry, good
fruit, impressive, low wood,
clean finish.
**Chardonnay, Washington,
1982, $10.**
Clean, appley style.
Sight: clear, medium gold.
Nose: clean, ripe apples, figs.
Taste: dry, full body, clean tart
flavors, crisp, balanced, lingering
finish.
White Riesling, Washington, 1983, $6.75.
An interesting, fresh-tasting
Riesling style.
Sight: clear, very pale straw.
Nose: floral, yeasty, fermentation aromas.
Taste: off-dry, yeasty character, good acid, short but complex
flavors.

Champs
From Wahluke Cellars,
Mattawa, Wash.:
White Table Wine, Washington, 1983, $4.99.
Unusually fine structure for a
wine of this price—balanced, not
heavy-handed, very nice fruit.
Sight: medium straw.

Nose: fresh fruit, lots of melon
aromas, flowery.
Taste: melony flavors, long finish, seems slightly sweet but
acidity is sufficient to balance.

Chateau Ste. Michelle
From Chateau Ste. Michelle,
Woodinville, Wash.:
**Cabernet Sauvignon, Benton County, Cold Creek
Vineyards, Chateau Reserve, 1978, $16.**
A bit dumb now—has all the
components.
Sight: clear, medium-to-deep
ruby.
Nose: earthy, herbal, closed.
Taste: dry, full body, fruit underneath tannin now, good acid,
very woody, complex, a bit out of
balance, long finish.
Chenin Blanc, Washington, 1982, $4.50.
Good sipping wine.
Sight: clear, pale straw.
Nose: varietal, melon.
Taste: off-dry, medium body,
good acid, fruity, well balanced.
**Johannisberg Riesling,
Washington, 1982, $4.35.**
More of an apple-styled Riesling.
Sight: clear, pale gold.
Nose: some fruit, low intensity.
Taste: off-dry, cardboardy,
medium body, tart, crisp, good
fruit, short on finish.
Semillon Blanc, Washington, 1982, $5.50.
Fruity dinner wine.
Sight: spritzy, clear, pale
straw.
Nose: floral, fruity.
Taste: dry, medium body, tart,
clean, good fruit, some wood,
balanced.

Gold Seal Vineyards

From Gold Seal Vineyards, Hammondsport, N.Y.:

Chardonnay, New York State, 1981, $10.89.

Another fine effort in New York State vinifera.

Sight: brilliant, medium-deep gold.

Nose: clean, oaky, buttery.

Taste: dry, medium body, tart, fruity, buttery texture, full oak flavors, long finish.

Tualatin Vineyards

From Tualatin Vineyards, Forest Grove, Oreg.:

Pinot Noir, Willamette Valley, 1980, $9.75.

Different Pinot style, needs time.

Sight: clear, medium-to-deep garnet.

Nose: pine aromas, closed, juniper.

Taste: dry, full body, fruity, some wood, closed, varietal, tannic, young, awkward flavors, long finish.

France

BORDEAUX

Best Buy

Prestige

From Yvon Mau, Gironde; imported by Yvon Mau & Fils, New York:
Bordeaux Blanc, Dry, 1983, $3.49.
Fine tart white wine at this price.
Sight: clear, light straw.
Nose: clean, grassy, floral.
Taste: dry, medium body, tart, clean citric fruit, touch of herbaceousness, good acid and balance, tart finish.

Highly Recommended

La Cour Pavillon

From La Cour Pavillon, Gironde; imported by Dreyfus, Ashby & Co., New York:
Bordeaux Blanc, Sec, 1981, $5.50.
A very good wine for seafood or just sipping.
Sight: brilliant, pale straw.
Nose: earthy, herbal, clean.
Taste: dry, light body, tart, crisp, excellent acid and balance, lingering finish.

"R"

From Château Rieussec, Fargues; imported by Lefcourt Cellars Inc., San Francisco:
"R" Bordeaux Blanc, 1981, $6.50.
Good value, great food wine.
Sight: brilliant, pale straw.
Nose: austere, Semillon, a bit of sulfur.

Taste: dry, very tart and restrained, clean, lots of Semillon, nice acid, balanced, medium body, lingering finish.

Recommended

Chevalier de Vedrines

From Chevalier de Vedrines, Bordeaux; imported by Mosswood Wine Co., New York:
Bordeaux Rouge, 1981, $3.50.
Reasonably priced.
Sight: brilliant, medium ruby.
Nose: clean, very herbal.
Taste: dry, medium body, fruit falls off, dry from tannin on finish, short finish.

Château Laurétan

From Château Laurétan; imported by Château & Estate Wines Co., New York:
Bordeaux Superieur, 1981, $3.49.
Good light dinner wine.
Sight: clear, light purple-ruby.
Nose: light, piney, eucalyptus.
Taste: dry, light body, good fruit and acid, clear, woody, short finish.

La Cour Pavillon

From La Cour Pavillon, Gironde; imported by Dreyfus, Ashby & Co., New York:
Bordeaux Rouge, 1979, $5.50.
Nice complex flavors.
Sight: clear, rich ruby red.
Nose: tobacco, herbal, woody.
Taste: dry, clean, good fruit, tannic, nice balance, lingering finish.

Yvon Mau & Fils

From Yvon Mau & Fils, Gironde; imported by Yvon Mau & Fils, New York:
Sauvignon Blanc, Bordeaux, 1982, $3.99.
We suggest drinking this with food.
Sight: clear, pale straw.
Nose: some melons, vinous.
Taste: dry, medium body, tart citric fruit, balanced but some off flavors on finish.

BORDEAUX: GRAVES

Recommended

Château Carbonnieux

From Château Carbonnieux, Léognan; imported by Château & Estate Wines Co., New York:
Graves, Blanc, Grand Cru, 1982, $11.50.
Austere style, seems pricey.
Sight: brilliant, light gold.
Nose: woody, perfumed, some fruit and sulfur.
Taste: dry, full body, good fruit, tart flavor, Semillon, nice structure, lingering finish.

Château la Tour Bicheau

From Château la Tour Bicheau, Portets; imported by Transcontinental Trade Corp., Placentia, Calif.:
Graves, Grand Cru, 1980, $11.25.
Super food wine—a good introduction to Graves.
Sight: clear, medium ruby.

Nose: very spicy, herbal, Cabernet aromas.
Taste: dry, clean, good fruit, full body, simple Cabernet flavors, balanced, long finish.

Château Olivier

From Louis Eschenauer, Léognan; imported by International Vintage Wine Co., Hartford, Conn.:
Graves, Red, 1981, $15.
Needs time, will develop.
Sight: clear, deep ruby.
Nose: spicy, plummy, deep cherry, toasty.
Taste: dry, soft Graves character, woody, stemmy, deep rich fruit, young, chocolaty on finish.
Graves, White, 1982, $15.
Very pungent and not particularly varietal.
Sight: clear, light green straw.
Nose: off odor, lingers.
Taste: dry, tart, fruity, taste of cheese, flavor of the lees, good structure.

Château Piron

From Château Piron, St. Morillon; imported by Woltner & Co., San Francisco:
Graves, 1982, $6.75.
A nice wine on the palate, but the nose puts us off a bit.
Sight: brilliant, medium straw.
Nose: vegetal, burnt matches at first.
Taste: dry, steely, tart, clean, Semillon character, some Sauvignon Blanc, clean finish.

BORDEAUX: MÉDOC/HAUT-MÉDOC

Spectator Selection

Château Margaux

From Château Margaux, Margaux; imported by Kobrand

Corp., New York:
Pavillon Blanc, Bordeaux, 1979, $35.
A superb achievement—will live for many years.
Sight: brilliant, pale straw.
Nose: herbal, grassy, closed, very austere.
Taste: dry, medium body, very assertive Semillon, herbal, very tart and grassy, clean, a bit closed, lots of wood complexity, balanced, long finish.

Recommended

Château la Tour St. Joseph

From Château la Tour St. Joseph, Gironde; imported by Transcontinental Trade Corp., Placentia, Calif.:
Haut-Médoc, 1979, $12.40.
Nicely made; a bit expensive though.
Sight: clear, medium-deep ruby.
Nose: clean, spicy, herbal, anise.
Taste: dry, medium body and fruit, low acid, some herbal character, low tannin.

Château Malescasse

From Château Malescasse; imported by Schieffelin & Co., New York:
Haut-Médoc, Cru Bourgeois, 1979, $8.50.
Needs food.
Sight: clear, medium red-garnet.
Nose: woody, a bit rubbery.
Taste: dry, medium body, vegetal, herbal, a bit thin, fruity, some heat on finish.

Chevalier Lascombes

From Alexis Lichine, Bordeaux; imported by Shaw Ross International, Miami:
Médoc, 1979, $4.99.
Soft and drinkable now.

Sight: clear, medium ruby, purple.
Nose: herbal, rich, barnyard aromas.
Taste: dry, tart, full body, earthy flavors, soft, some tannin, balanced, lingering finish.

André Simon

From André Simon, Lancie, Rhône; imported by Grapevine Consultants, Napa, Calif.:
Château Clos du Gentilhomme, Médoc, 1979, $6.50.
Very simple Médoc, priced well.
Sight: clear, medium ruby.
Nose: slight herbal, minty.
Taste: dry, very tart, medium-to-full body, fruity, simple, a bit woody, balanced, lingering finish.

BORDEAUX: SAINT-EMILION

Recommended

Château Bois-Tiffray

From Château Bois-Tiffray, Lussac; imported by Channel Street Importers, San Francisco:
Lussac-St.-Emilion, 1981, $5.50.
Nice wine for the price, may improve, worth the risk.
Sight: clear, deep garnet.
Nose: spicy, anise, wood.
Taste: dry, moderate tannin, ripe plums, good acid, structured, a bit closed, long finish.

Château de Lussac

From Château de Lussac, Lussac; imported by Woltner & Co., San Francisco:
Lussac-St.-Emilion, 1981, $6.25.
A well-priced table wine.
Sight: clear, medium garnet.
Nose: some perfume, fruit and wood, smoky, toasty.

Taste: dry, medium body, nice fruit, slight oxidation, bit soft, tangy finish.

Château Guibeau

From Château Guibeau, Puisseguin; imported by Channel Street Importers, San Francisco:
Puisseguin-St.-Emilion, 1979, $8.45.
Needs time, seems a bit low on acid.
Sight: clear, medium-to-deep garnet.
Nose: cheesy aroma, some spice, barnyard aromas.
Taste: dry, full body, big, chewy and dense, tannic, woody, short on finish, leathery flavors.

Château Haut-Sarpe

From J. Jonoux, St.-Emilion; imported by Stacole Co., Deerfield Beach, Fla.:
St.-Emilion, 1979, $10.99.
Needs lots of air to open up.
Sight: clear, medium garnet.
Nose: medicinal quality, opens to slight spiciness.
Taste: dry, full body, bitter, medicinal, chalky flavor, after thirty minutes it cleans up and balances out.

BURGUNDY

Best Buy

Domaine de Perignon

From Domaine de Perignon, Nuits-St.-Georges; imported by Park, Benziger & Co., Scarsdale, N.Y.:
Bourgogne Passetout-grains, 1982, $5.
Very assertive and flavorful, a fine value for current drinking.
Sight: clear, deep red-ruby.
Nose: assertive and fruity, ripe, alcoholic.
Taste: dry, full body, lots of character, more Rhône-like than

Burgundian, grapy fruit, lingering finish.

Highly Recommended

Joseph Drouhin

From Joseph Drouhin, Beaune; imported by Dreyfus, Ashby & Co., New York:
Laforet Bourgogne Blanc, 1982, $8.44.
A great white Burgundy for the price—true to form in every way.
Sight: brilliant, pale gold.
Nose: clean, appley, spicy, vanillin.
Taste: dry, full body, full fruit, oily texture, viscous, apples, crisp acidity, balanced oak flavor, very clean overall, lingering finish.

Antonin Rodet

From Antonin Rodet, Mercurey; imported by Channel Street Importers, San Francisco:
Bourgogne Rodet, Pinot Noir, 1978, $6.95.
Great for food; excellent value.
Sight: clear, medium garnet, tawny edge.
Nose: varietal, tea, complex mature aromas.
Taste: dry, tart, clean fruit, medium body, woody, varietal, balanced, lingering finish.

Recommended

Joseph Drouhin

From Joseph Drouhin, Beaune; imported by Dreyfus, Ashby & Co., New York:
Laforet Bourgogne Rouge, 1982, $8.44.
Nice fruit—but wine lacks body and presence.
Sight: clear, light-to-medium garnet.
Nose: rich cherries and spice.
Taste: dry, medium body, good

fruit, a bit thin, pleasant, short on finish.

Louis Jadot

From Louis Jadot, Côte d'Or; imported by Kobrand Corp., New York:
Chardonnay Jadot, Bourgogne Blanc, 1982, $8.50.
Excellent food wine; a good value.
Sight: clear, light straw.
Nose: closed, some fruit, toasty aromas.
Taste: dry, good fruit, full body, appley, good fruit and acid, toasty flavors, long finish.

Antonin Rodet

From Antonin Rodet, Mercurey; imported by Channel Street Importers, San Francisco:
Bourgogne Rodet, Chardonnay, 1981, $6.95.
Good value in French Chardonnay.
Sight: clear, light straw.
Nose: light wood and fruit.
Taste: dry, medium body, tart clean fruit, lots of acid, balanced, moderate varietal character, lingering finish.

BURGUNDY: BEAUJOLAIS

Recommended

Bouchard Père et Fils

From Bouchard Père et Fils, Côte d'Or; imported by International Vintage Co., Hartford, Conn.:
Beaujolais-Villages, 1982, $6.50.
Light, young wine.
Sight: clear, light red-ruby.
Nose: a bit stemmy, good fruit.
Taste: dry, medium body, good tart fruit, clean, light, short finish, nice quality.

Joseph Drouhin

From Joseph Drouhin, Beaune; imported by Dreyfus, Ashby & Co., New York:

Beaujolais-Villages, 1982, $6.49.

Great red wine for light foods.
Sight: clear, medium ruby.
Nose: earthy, stemmy, grapy.
Taste: dry, tart, medium body, clean, good acid, balanced, grapy flavors, lingering finish.

Louis Jadot

From Louis Jadot, Beaune; imported by Kobrand Corp., New York:

Beaujolais-Villages, 1982, $7.

Gamay all the way.
Sight: brilliant, medium ruby.
Nose: rich, grapy, earthy, Gamay.
Taste: dry, good fruit, slight heat, medium body, clean flavors, complex, nicely balanced.

Antonin Rodet

From Antonin Rodet, Mercurey; imported by Channel Street Importers, San Francisco:

Beaujolais-Villages, 1982, $4.95.

Standard quality Beaujolais-Villages with some pleasant attributes.
Sight: medium-light ruby.
Nose: clean, floral, cherry, minty.
Taste: dry, medium body, very ripe fruit, light on palate, a bit tarry, balanced, astringent finish.

André Simon

From André Simon, Lancie, Rhône; imported by Grapevine Consultants, Napa, Calif.:

Beaujolais, 1981, $5.30.

Light quaff; simple, straightforward.
Sight: clear, medium purple.
Nose: intense, grapy.
Taste: dry, light body, grapy flavors, tart acid, balanced, short finish.

BURGUNDY: CÔTE D'OR/CHABLIS

Spectator Selection

Bouchard Père & Fils

From Bouchard Père & Fils, Beaune; imported by International Vintage Wine Co., Hartford, Conn.:

Côte de Beaune–Villages, 1982, $18.40.

Needs time, after about four years will be lovely.
Sight: clear, medium garnet.
Nose: cherry, vanilla spice.
Taste: dry, fruity, clean, cherries, plummy, full body, nice balance, lingering finish.

Highly Recommended

Henri de Villamont

From Henri de Villamont, Savigny-les-Beaune; imported by C. & B. Vintage Cellars, San Francisco:

Corton-Charlemagne, 1981, $23.

Very complex, rich fruit.
Sight: clear, deep yellow-gold.
Nose: complex, pineapple, toasty, rich, figs.
Taste: dry, rich, full body, complex fruit, balanced, buttery, long full finish.

Recommended

Baron Patrick

From Baron Patrick, Chablis; imported by International Vintage Wine Co., Hartford, Conn.:

Chablis Premier Cru, 1979, $12.80.

An earthy, racy Chablis at a good price.
Sight: brilliant, light gold.
Nose: smoky, not much fruit.
Taste: dry, earthy, some fruit, lemony, nice structure, tropical fruit on finish.

F. Beault-Forgeot & Cie

From F. Beault-Forgeot & Cie, Nuits-St.-Georges; imported by French Wine Service, Los Angeles:

Hospices de Beaune, Mazis-Chambertin, Cuvée Madeleine-Collignon, 1980, $56.

Young; made to age, let it lie in your cellar. Yes, the price is correct.
Sight: clear, deep ruby.
Nose: very smoky, violets, lots of depth.
Taste: dry, very intense, lots of character, full body, woody, very full and long on finish.

Nuits-Saint-Georges, Les Plateaux, 1981, $17.

An honest Burgundy, velvety and flavorful.
Sight: clear, good ruby color.
Nose: lots of cherries, spice, rich aromas.
Taste: dry, clean, lots of extract, tart, rich, cherries, moderate wood, long finish, complex.

Bouchard Père & Fils

From Bouchard Père & Fils, Beaune; imported by International Vintage Wine Co., Hartford, Conn.:

Chassagne-Montrachet, 1982, $17.50.

Expensive Burgundy. Not much complexity.
Sight: clear, medium greengold.
Nose: toasty, charred, some fruit.
Taste: dry, full body, lots of acid, not much fruit, chalky, candied finish.

Gevrey-Chambertin, 1982, $18.

A nice red Burgundy; balance is its strong point.
Sight: clear, medium-light garnet.

Nose: vinous, some fruit aromas.
Taste: dry, has some fruit and wood, nice acid balance.
Meursault, 1981, $17.
Hard and tough. Expensive for what you get.
Sight: clear, medium brassy gold.
Nose: charred, toasty, cloves.
Taste: dry, full body, assertive fruit, but a bit harsh, good acid, balanced, lots of toast on finish.
Puligny-Montrachet, 1982, $17.95.
Complex, has rough edges, but will age well.
Sight: brilliant, medium yellow-gold.
Nose: woody, some fruit, resiny.
Taste: dry, tart, has moderate oak flavor, rough, resiny on palate, has complexity.

Henri de Villamont

From Henri de Villamont, Savigny-les-Beaune, France; imported by C. & B. Vintage Cellars, San Francisco:
Chevalier-Montrachet, 1982, $38.
Fabulous depth.
Sight: brilliant, medium-to-deep gold.
Nose: deep fruit, cloves, clean, woody.
Taste: dry, lots of full fruit, full body, clean, lots of toasty wood, full long finish.
Gevrey-Chambertin, 1980, $20.
Slightly pricey.
Sight: clear, deep ruby.
Nose: deep wood and fruit, varietal.
Taste: dry, good fruit, leathery, simple, moderate acid, balanced.

Louis Max

From Louis Max, Nuits-St.-Georges; imported by New World Wines, San Francisco:
Puligny-Montrachet, 1981, $14.
Needs time; priced a bit high.
Sight: clear, light gold.
Nose: closed, oaky, toasty aromas.

Taste: dry, closed, oaky, woody, full body, a bit low in acid, moderate fruit, lingering finish.

Quancard Père et Fils

From Quancard Père et Fils, Beaune; imported by Transcontinental Trade Corp., Placentia, Calif.:
Chablis Premier Cru, "Vaillons," 1980, $13.25.
Will be a long-lived Chablis.
Sight: brilliant, medium gold.
Nose: fruity, lots of wood.
Taste: dry, full body, lots of Chardonnay fruit, complex, crisp acidity, oak in background, well balanced.
Meursault 1980, $15.88.
May simply be young, but lacks complexity.
Sight: brilliant, medium gold.
Nose: oaky, varietal.
Taste: dry, fruity, medium body, full wood flavors, slightly low in acid, balanced, lingering finish.
Puligny-Montrachet 1980, $18.75.
Very woody, but lacks complexity.
Sight: clear, medium-to-deep gold.
Nose: low in fruit, lots of oak.
Taste: dry, a bit chalky, medium body, good acid, falls off in middle, balanced, lots of oak in finish.
Vosne-Romanée, 1977, $27.50.
At its peak for drinking, might be a little high priced.
Sight: clear, medium-to-deep garnet, tawny edge.
Nose: earthy, leathery, very Burgundian, soft and mature.
Taste: dry, full body, soft, mature, good Pinot Noir character, well balanced, lingering finish.

BURGUNDY: MÂCONNAIS

Best Buy

F. Chauvenet

From F. Chauvenet, Nuits-St.-Georges; imported by Park, Benziger & Co., Scarsdale, N.Y.:
Mâcon-Villages Blanc, Les Jumelles, 1982, $6.
A complex and elegant Mâcon, especially for the price.
Sight: clear, medium green-straw.
Nose: floral, perfumed wood aromas.
Taste: dry, tart, grapefruit flavors, full body, good acid, rose petals, well balanced, long full finish.

Recommended

Bouchard Père et Fils

From Bouchard Père et Fils, Côte d'Or; imported by International Vintage Wine Co., Hartford, Conn.:
Mâcon-Villages, 1982, $7.50.
Reasonable price for this Chardonnay.
Sight: clear, light gold.
Nose: closed, woody, some fruit.
Taste: dry, good fruit, medium body, butterscotch, clean, woody, long finish.

F. Chauvenet

From F. Chauvenet, Nuits-St.-Georges; imported by Park, Benziger & Co., New York:
Pouilly-Fuissé, 1982, $8.50.
Average white Burgundy, but not a typical Pouilly-Fuissé; very big and rich.
Sight: clear, medium gold.

Nose: clean, blossoms, floral, fruity.

Taste: dry, full body, balanced, good ripe fruit flavors, but coarse, long full finish.

Louis Jadot

From Louis Jadot, Beaune; imported by Kobrand Corp., New York:

Pouilly-Fuissé, 1982, $13.
Clean Chardonnay flavors.
Sight: clear, light gold.
Nose: citrus, fruity.
Taste: dry, medium body, tart, good fruit and balance, long finish.

Maison Quancard

From Quancard Père et Fils, Beaune; imported by Transcontinental Trade Corp., Placentia, Calif.:

Mâcon-Villages, Réserve, NV, $9.25.
Nice wine; price seems slightly high, though.
Sight: brilliant, medium-to-deep gold.
Nose: light, austere, some perfume.
Taste: dry, good fruit, lots of Chardonnay, crisp acidity, moderate oak, balanced, lingering finish.

Antonin Rodet

From Antonin Rodet, Mercurey; imported by Channel Street Importers, San Francisco:

Mâcon-Villages Blanc, 1982, $5.50.
Nice, stylish Mâcon; a solid value.
Sight: clear, light straw.
Nose: some floral fruit, Chardonnay.
Taste: dry, medium body, good clean fruit at first, good balance, some oxidized flavors, a bit of bitterness on finish.

Pierres Blanches

From Pierres Blanches, Saint-Genoux; imported by Château & Estate Wines Co., New York:

Pinot Chardonnay, Mâcon-Villages, 1981, $4.75.
Good value in imported Chardonnay.

Sight: clear, pale light gold.
Nose: simple fruit, buttery.
Taste: dry, medium body, good fruit, chalky, some bitterness, balanced.

CHAMPAGNE

Spectator Selections

Dom Ruinart

From Dom Ruinart, Reims; imported by Schieffelin & Co., New York:

Brut Rosé, 1975, $34.95.
Worth seeking out.
Sight: clear, medium salmon-orange, steady beading.
Nose: fruity, yeasty, complex.
Taste: dry, great fruit-acid balance, full rich complex flavors, yet delicate, long full finish.

Moët et Chandon

From Moët et Chandon, Epernay; imported by Schieffelin & Co., New York:

Brut Imperial, 1976, $27.95.
With this wine, you get what you pay for.
Sight: brilliant, medium gold, steady beading.
Nose: light, apples, toasty.
Taste: dry, medium body, full flavors, apples, very clean, lightly toasty, balanced, clean finish.

Recommended

Dom Ruinart

From Dom Ruinart, Reims; imported by Schieffelin & Co., New York:

Blanc de Blancs, 1975, $30.
Classy Champagne.

Sight: brilliant, medium-deep gold, very steady beading.
Nose: toasty, complex, clean, woody, yeasty.
Taste: dry, great fruit, good complexity from oak, young, long life ahead,

Moët et Chandon

From Moët et Chandon, Epernay; imported by Schieffelin & Co., New York:

Brut Imperial, 1978, $30.
Distinctive and elegant.
Sight: clear, medium-deep gold.
Nose: yeasty, smoky, toasty.
Taste: dry, medium body, creamy, rich fruit in the mouth, elegant and balanced, distinctive flavors, long finish.
Brut Imperial, NV, $22.75.
Complex, fruity style.
Sight: brilliant, medium gold, steady beading.
Nose: clean, fresh, yeasty.
Taste: dry, very clean, nice fruit, very tart and balanced, long finish.
Brut Imperial Rosé, 1978, $30.
A bit high-priced.
Sight: clear, deep orange-bronze, medium beading.
Nose: yeasty, some fruit, assertive.
Taste: dry, medium body, very assertive, good acid, fruit and balance; a bit cloying and heavy on finish.
White Star, Extra Dry, NV, $18.75.
Great off-dry style.
Sight: brilliant, medium gold, steady beading.
Nose: light aromas, some fruit.
Taste: off-dry, a bit spicy, some oak, very complex and balanced, good spritz.

Perrier-Jouet

From Perrier-Jouet, Epernay; imported by Château and Estate Wines Co., New York:

Fleur de Champagne, 1978, $56.
Defines elegance.
Sight: clear, medium gold, small, steady beading.
Nose: yeasty, complex and toasty, some fruit.

Taste: dry, creamy and syrupy, elegant, subtle, great balance and finesse, good acid and long finish.

Taittinger

From Taittinger, Reims; imported by Kobrand Corp., New York:

Comtes de Champagne, Rosé, 1975, $55.
Many would gladly pay the price for a Champagne like this.
Sight: brilliant, medium salmon, steady beading.
Nose: yeasty, mature, good fruit.
Taste: dry, clean, tart, lots of fruit and yeasty character, nice structure, balanced, long finish.

CÔTES DU RHÔNE

Best Buys

Château d'Aigueville

From Château d'Aigueville, Vachaux; imported by Frank Schoonmaker Selections, New York:

Côtes du Rhône, 1982, $4.75.
Very light, nouveau-style Rhône.
Sight: clear, medium ruby-red.
Nose: light fruit, wood, toasty.
Taste: dry, nice Grenache character, good fruit, clean, very attractive, balanced nouveau style.

Château la Borie

From Château la Borie, Suze-la-Rousse; imported by Park, Benziger & Co., New York:

Côtes du Rhône, 1982, $3.50.
Drink now, good value.
Sight: clear, deep purple.
Nose: fruity, spicy.
Taste: dry, full body, clean,

good fruit, nice acid, balanced, long finish.

Highly Recommended

Domaine de Mont-Rédon

From Domaine de Mont-Rédon, imported by Kobrand Corp., New York:

Châteauneuf-du-Pape, 1979, $12.50.
A wine for the cellar; needs time.
Sight: clear, medium-deep ruby.
Nose: spicy, fresh ground pepper.
Taste: dry, good fruit and tannin, full body, lots of ground pepper, complex, full, wood, big, assertive finish.

Recommended

Bouchard Père & Fils

From Bouchard Père & Fils, Beaune; imported by International Vintage Wine Co., Hartford, Conn.:

Châteauneuf-du-Pape, 1982, $9.
Light simple style.
Sight: clear, light garnet.
Nose: pepper, spice.
Taste: dry, some fruit, not complex, lots of Grenache character, simple.

Château d'Aigueville

From Château d'Aigueville; imported by Château & Estate Wines Co., New York:

Côtes du Rhône, 1981, $3.75.
Good bargain; wait a few years to drink.
Sight: clear, deep purple.
Nose: peppery, a bit of sulfur.
Taste: dry, full body, nice peppery flavors, balanced, needs a bit of time.

Coron Père & Fils

From Coron Père & Fils, Beaune; imported by A. L. Romano Wine Co., San Francisco:

Côtes du Rhône, 1981, $5.35.
Mature, ready to drink. Good simple character.
Sight: clear, medium garnet.
Nose: deep, rich, peppery, spicy fruit, some oxidation.
Taste: dry, very soft and smooth, good acid and fruit, balanced, finish falls off.

Domaine de Vieux Lazaret

From Domaine de Vieux Lazaret, Châteauneuf-du-Pape; imported by Channel Street Importers, San Francisco:

Châteauneuf-du-Pape, 1981, $9.95.
Good value in a big Rhône wine.
Sight: clear, medium red-garnet.
Nose: complex, deep and perfumed.
Taste: dry, full body, closed, intense fruit, complex, well structured, good wood flavor, balanced.

Châteauneuf-du-Pape Blanc, 1982, $9.99.
Distinctive style of wine, needs time to breathe and open up.
Sight: clear, light brassy gold.
Nose: clean, plums, floral.
Taste: dry, medium body, some young coarse fruit flavors, awkward now but very clean.

Guigal

From E. Guigal, Ampuis; imported by Grape Expectations, Emeryville, Calif.:

Côtes du Rhône, 1980, $4.50.
A very smooth and supple wine now—will last and improve.
Sight: clear, deep garnet.
Nose: spicy, peppery, plummy, deep and fragrant.
Taste: dry, ripe fruit, full body, clean flavors, good acid, rich, young, slightly fat, lingering finish.

LOIRE

Best Buy

Barre

From Barre, Gorges; imported by Kobrand Corp., New York:
Muscadet de Sèvre-et-Maine, 1982, $5.50.
Clean, crisp sipping wine.
Sight: brilliant, pale straw.
Nose: fruity, clean floral.
Taste: off-dry, medium body, good acid, steely, crisp, balanced, good fruit, lingering finish.

Highly Recommended

De Ladoucette

From de Ladoucette, Pouilly-sur-Loire; imported by International Vintage Wine Co., Hartford, Conn.:
Pouilly-Fumé, 1982, $15.
Classic Pouilly-Fumé, expensive.
Sight: pale greenish-straw.
Nose: clean, herbal, grassy.
Taste: dry, full body, good ripe, tart Sauvignon Blanc fruit, great balance and structure.

Domaine René Michot et Fils

From Domaine René Michot et Fils, Pouilly-sur-Loire; imported by the Mosswood Wine Co., New York:
Pouilly-Fumé, 1982, $8.50.
Well structured, with aging potential.
Sight: clean, light gold.
Nose: closed, herbal, spicy.
Taste: dry, herbal, balanced acid, tart fruit flavors, long lingering finish, needs time.

Recommended

Baron Briare

From Baron Briare; imported by International Vintage Wine Co., Hartford, Conn.:
"Touraine" Sauvignon, 1979, $6.25.
May have some appeal.
Sight: medium yellow-gold.
Nose: candied, oaky, some fruit, a bit oxidized.
Taste: dry, full body, tart, herbal but simple fruit, tart finish.

Bouvet

From Bouvet-Ladubay, S.A. St.-Hilare–St.-Florent; imported by Kobrand Corp., New York:
Brut, NV, $10.
Good value in a dry sparkler.
Sight: clear, light gold, steady beading.
Nose: appley, yeasty, pleasant aromas.
Taste: dry, medium body, good acid, crisp, tart fruit, balanced, long finish.

Marc Brédif

From Marc Brédif, Rochecorbon; represented by Warren B. Strauss, New York:
Vouvray, 1982, $7.95.
Simple flavors with good structure.
Sight: brilliant, pale straw.
Nose: closed, light fruit, almond.
Taste: dry, medium body, lots of fruity flavors, tart, clean, long finish.

Château Gaudrelle

From J. Monmousseau, Montrichard; imported by C. & B. Vintage Cellars, San Francisco:
Vouvray, 1981, $8.
Worth the price.
Sight: brilliant, pale straw.
Nose: citric, fruity, Chenin.
Taste: off-dry, light, crisp, clean, melony fruit, citric, lots of acid, tart finish.

Clos Le Vigneau

From J.M. Monmousseau, Montrichard; imported by C. & B. Vintage Cellars, San Francisco:
Vouvray, 1982, $7.
Lots of complexity for Chenin Blanc; it will surprise you.
Sight: brilliant, yellow, green-gold.
Nose: juniper, cherries, resin.
Taste: dry, full body, tart, clean fruit, cherries, apples, balanced but rough now, long resinous finish.
Vouvray, 1981, $8.
A Chenin that will age very gracefully.
Sight: brilliant, medium straw-yellow.
Nose: very fruity, lemony, clean.
Taste: dry, tart, medium body, good acid, lots of Chenin Blanc character, strong structure, balanced, long finish.

Comte Lafond

From Comte Lafond, Pouilly-sur-Loire; imported by International Vintage Wine Co., Hartford, Conn.:
Sancerre, 1980, $14.25.
High priced, but lots of character.
Sight: brilliant, medium green-straw.
Nose: green peas, fruit.
Taste: dry, full body, very tart, herbal, clean lingering finish.

Domaine des Chailloux

From Domaine des Chailloux, Nievre; imported by Mosswood Wine Co., New York:
Pouilly-Fumé, 1981, $10.
Assertive Sauvignon Blanc.
Sight: clear, light green-straw.
Nose: intense herbal, grassy, celery.
Taste: dry, medium body, herbal, celery, balanced, intense fruit, lots of Sauvignon Blanc character.

Fournier Père et Fils

From Fournier Père et Fils, Verdigny-en-Sancerre; imported by the Mosswood Wine Co., New York:

Sancerre, Caves des Chauvrieres, 1982, $8.95.
This wine has excellent fruit behind assertive earthy flavors.
Sight: brilliant, light straw, green edge.
Nose: herbal, grassy, fruity.
Taste: dry, firm, full body, steely, earthy, forward fruit, herbal, tart and crisp acidity, very clean finish.

Maison-Blondelet

From Maison-Blondelet, Pouilly-sur-Loire; imported by Cellars International, San Francisco:
Pouilly-Fumé, Les Bascoins, 1981, $8.50.
Very nice, tart food wine.
Sight: clear, medium gold.
Nose: grassy, herbal, lots of wood.
Taste: dry, grassy, tart, medium body, somewhat hard, clean, moderate wood, balanced, nice finish.

Monmousseau

From J.M. Monmousseau, Montrichard; imported by C. & B. Vintage Cellars, San Francisco:
Touraine, Brut, 1981, $9.
Full-bodied sparkling wine that seems expensive.
Sight: brilliant, medium gold, steady beading.
Nose: nutty, yeasty.
Taste: dry, full body, good fruit but some cardboard flavors.
Vouvray, Blanc de Blancs, 1982, $6.
Pleasant Vouvray with lots of spirit.
Sight: brilliant, medium straw.
Nose: lemon, wax, some moldy aromas.
Taste: dry, medium body, lots of assertive lemony fruit, good structure and balance, lemony, waxy finish.

Michel Redde

From Michel Redde, Pouilly-sur-Loire; imported by Kobrand Corp., New York:
Sancerre, Les Tuilieres, 1981, $11.
Beautiful, tart wine.

Sight: brilliant, medium green-straw.
Nose: herbal, grassy, assertive.
Taste: dry, very tart, medium body, citrusy, clean, young and very assertive, moderate wood, balanced.

OTHER APPELLATIONS

Best Buy

Château Villerouge la Cremade

From Château la Cremade, Corbières; imported by Jason Brook Importers, Jericho, N.Y.:
Corbières, 1983, $2.99.
Great value, reminds us of a Rhône wine.
Sight: clear, deep ruby-purple.
Taste: dry, peppery, rich fruit and character.

Recommended

Domaine de Vieux Lazaret

From Domaine de Vieux Lazaret, Châteauneuf-du-Pape; imported by Channel Street Importers, San Francisco:
Côtes de Provence, 1982, $3.99.
Hardy, everyday quaffer; try with some cheese.
Sight: clear, purple.
Nose: lively, full, fruity.
Taste: dry, full body, good ripe fruit, lots of tannin but fairly well balanced, hard on finish.

NON-REGIONAL, NON-VINTAGE BLENDS

Best Buy

Antonin Rodet

From Antonin Rodet, Mercurey; imported by Channel Street Importers, San Francisco:
Maître Rodet, NV, $3.60.
Fantastic value in red table wine.
Sight: clear, medium red-ruby.
Nose: clean Pinot, cherries.
Taste: dry, clean, tart fruit, good acid, soft flavor, balanced, delightful fruity flavors.

Recommended

Jouvet

From T. Jouvet; imported by Stacole Co., Deerfield, Fla.:
Chamboustin Blanc, NV, $1.99.
Excellent buy in everyday wine.
Sight: clear, medium straw.
Nose: clear, floral, fruity, some oxidation.
Taste: dry, medium body, good but simple flavor, balanced, clean and round on palate.

Albert Lucas

From Labouré-Roi; imported by Channel Street Importers, San Francisco:
Red Table Wine, NV, $3.60.
Pleasant table wine.
Sight: clear, deep ruby-purple.
Nose: jammy, stemmy.
Taste: dry, fruity, stemmy, nice flavor, low tannin, balanced, lingering finish.
White Table Wine, NV, $3.60.

Simple sipping wine.
Sight: clear, light gold.
Nose: clean, oaky, some fruit.
Taste: dry, medium body, clean simple fruit, balanced fruit and finish.

Red Cap

From F. Chauvenet; imported by Park, Benziger & Co., Yonkers, N.Y.:
Sparkling Red Wine, NV, $9.
Lots of personality and charm. An interesting and appealing wine. One to look for.
Sight: brilliant, garnet red, fine bead.
Nose: spicy, grapy, cherries, Pinot Noir.
Taste: dry, full body, clean, full, ripe cherries, Pinot Noir fruit, lots of character, some ethyl acetate accentuates fruit rather than detracts.

Antonin Rodet

From Antonin Rodet, Mercurey; imported by Channel Street Importers, San Francisco:
Maître Rodet White, NV, $3.60.
Clean table wine.
Sight: pale, light gold.
Nose: oaky, smoky, some fruit.
Taste: dry, medium body, good clean fruit, balanced, tart, some chalkiness on finish.

Sichel

From Sichel; imported by Schieffelin & Co., New York:
Cuvée Speciale, NV, $3.70.
Standard wine.
Sight: clear, medium garnet.
Nose: vinous, slightly resinous aromas.
Taste: dry, medium body, tart, piney flavor, some bitterness on finish.

Société Woltner

From Société Woltner; imported by Woltner & Co., San Francisco:
"Maitre de Chai," NV, $2.50.
Soft and balanced, this wine is reasonably priced.
Sight: clear, medium-to-deep garnet.
Nose: low intensity, moderate wood.
Taste: dry, fruity, light, short and soft, not much of a finish, balanced flavors.

Wan Fu

From Wan Fu; imported by Shieffelin & Co., New York:
White Table Wine, NV, $4.99.
Decent quaff—for Chinese food.
Sight: clear, light gold.
Nose: oaky, fruity, sweet melon.
Taste: dry, tart, full body, good fruit, a bit out of balance.

Italy

PIEDMONT

Best Buy

Pio Cesare

From Pio Cesare, Alba;
imported by Paterno Imports,
Chicago:
  **Dolcetto d'Alba, 1983,
$7.49.**
  Attractive and pleasant to
drink, with fruit to spare.
  Sight: bright purple.
  Nose: fresh berries.
  Taste: light-to-medium body,
very little tannin, ripe raspberry
fruit, lively and fresh on the palate.

Highly Recommended

Burati

From Burati, Asti; imported by
Monsieur Henri Wines Ltd.,
White Plains, N.Y.:
  Asti Spumante, NV, $6.99.
  A great sparkler for a summer
party.
  Sight: clear, moderate beading, light gold.
  Nose: spicy, clean, nutmeg,
lots of Muscat.
  Taste: sweet, lots of varietal
character (Muscat), clean, medium body, lots of spritz on palate, good acid, lingering finish.

Recommended

Fontanafredda

From Fontanafredda, Alba;
imported by Dreyfus, Ashby &
Co., New York:
  **Asti Spumante, Estate
Bottled, NV, $9.65.**
  Sweet sparkler, a bit high
priced.
  Sight: light gold, steady beading.
  Nose: slightly yeasty, Muscat
aromas.
  Taste: sweet, Muscat spicy flavors, assertive character, balanced, lingering finish.
  Barolo, 1978, $12.75.
  Drinking nicely now—has a lot
of Barolo character.
  Sight: clear, medium garnet.
  Nose: closed, toasty, woody,
mature.
  Taste: dry, olives, herbal, long
finish.

Gavi

From La Battistina, Novi
Ligure; imported by
Mediterranean Importing Co.,
Lake Success, N.Y.:
  Gavi, 1982, $8.
  Serve with food.
  Sight: clear, pale gold.
  Nose: clean, fruit, candied,
woody.
  Taste: dry, medium body, tart,
chalky, some fruit, a bit dirty,
short finish.

Morando

From Morando, Castiglione del
Asti; imported by Mosswood
Wine Co., New York:
  Asti Spumante, NV, $6.99.
  A low price for a good sparkler.
  Sight: brilliant, light gold,
steady beading.
  Nose: orange peel, yeasty,
aromas.
  Taste: off-dry, spicy, fruity,
clean, good balance, acid, clean
finish.

Pio Cesare

From Pio Cesare, Alba;
imported by Paterno Imports,
Chicago:
  **Cortese di Gavi, 1983,
$8.98.**
  Attractive delicate white table
wine.
  Sight: spritzy, light straw.
  Nose: clean, floral, melons.
  Taste: light delicate fruit, floral, nice acid and balance, citric,
grapefruity, tart and clean.
  **Ornato Piemonte, 1982,
$10.95.**
  Rough young wine that needs
time to settle down.
  Sight: medium garnet.
  Nose: leathery, spicy, jammy.
  Taste: dry, intense, concentrated fruit flavors, lots of acid
and tannin, some heat on the
palate, tannic finish.

Renato Ratti

From Renato Ratti, La Morra;
imported by Paterno Imports,
Chicago:
  Barolo, 1979, $18.
  Will reward patient aging.
  Sight: clear, medium garnet.
  Nose: rich, fruity, spicy.
  Taste: dry, big, tannic, good
spicy fruit, well balanced, needs
time.

La Scolca

From La Scolca, Gavi; imported
by Mosswood Wine Co., New
York:
  Gavi dei Gavi, 1981, $17.
  Very earthy and elegant.
  Sight: brilliant, pale straw.
  Nose: clean, floral, earthy aromas.
  Taste: dry, earthy flavors,
crisp, full body, tart, elegant,
firm structure, balanced, long
finish.

TUSCANY

Spectator Selections

Brolio

From Barone Ricasoli, Firenze; imported by Browne Vintners, New York:
Chianti Classico Riserva, 1978, $6.50.
Textbook Chianti; at this price buy a case.
Sight: clear, medium-ruby center, garnet edge.
Nose: clean, tobacco, cherries, complex wood.
Taste: dry, rich, clean fruit, complex, good acid, lots of wood, cedary character, well balanced, long full finish.

Il Poggione

From Il Poggione, S. Angelo in Colle, Montalcino; imported by Paterno Imports, Chicago:
Brunello di Montalcino, Riserva, 1978, $34.95.
Tremendous depth, great elegance; delicious now, but wait.
Sight: clear, deep rich garnet.
Nose: pruney, very complex, woody, perfumed, cassis and spice.
Taste: dry, very deep and intense, full body, very spicy, rich, chocolaty, coffee, expands in mouth, full deep finish.

Best Buy

Il Poggione

From Il Poggione, S. Angelo in Colle, Montalcino; imported by Paterno Imports, Chicago:
Rosso di Montalcino, 1982, $8.49.
A nice Brunello-style wine without the wood.
Sight: clear, deep ruby.
Nose: raisiny, grapy.

Taste: dry, very big and intense, concentrated, grapy flavors, has a lot of fruit on finish without the wood.

Highly Recommended

Nozzole

From Nozzole, Greve; imported by Kobrand Corp., New York:
Bianco Toscano, 1979, $4.99.
Perfect aperitif.
Sight: brilliant, medium straw.
Nose: fragrant, anise, clean.
Taste: off-dry, clean, very tart, medium body, lots of fruit, intense grapy character, good acid, very clean finish.

Ruffino

From Ruffino, Pontassieve; imported by Schieffelin & Co., New York:
Chianti Classico Riserva Ducale, 1979, $8.25.
Needs time—price is hard to beat.
Sight: clear, medium tawny ruby.
Nose: rich, closed, young, full fruit and spice.
Taste: dry, clean, tart, good fruit and acid, full body, still young, developing complexity from wood and bottle age, balanced.

Tenuta Caparzo

From Tenuta Caparzo, Montalcino; imported by Mediterranean Importing Co., Lake Success, N.Y.:
Rosso Toscano di Brunello, 1980, $4.50.
A fresh, fruity low-wood style of Italian wine.
Sight: clear, deep ruby.
Nose: young, closed.
Taste: dry, young and grapy, lots of potential, clean and fresh, crisp acidity, balanced.

Recommended

Abbazia Monte Oliveto

From Abbazia Monte Oliveto, San Gimignano; imported by Francis A. Bonanno, Inc., Miamisburg, Ohio:
Vernaccia di · San Gimignano, 1982, $4.99.
This is a very dry wine. It needs food.
Sight: brilliant, light straw.
Nose: candied, perfumed, ripe fruit.
Taste: dry, medium body, short fruit, slightly better on finish.

Clastidio

From Clastidio-Angelo Ballabio; imported by Eurowines Imports, Vienna, Va.:
Narbusto, 1974, $20.
Very mature, pricey.
Sight: clear, medium tawny red.
Nose: rich, ripe, pruney, complex, peppery.
Taste: dry, mature, full body, deep fruit, peppery, full woody flavor, balanced, long finish.

Mario Innocenti

From Mario Innocenti, Montefollonico; imported by Grape Expectations, Emeryville, Calif.:
Chianti, 1981, $4.75.
Good table wine; not particularly like Chianti, though.
Sight: clear, medium-deep garnet.
Nose: thin, peppery, closed.
Taste: dry, young, tannic, medium-full body, some fruit, lacks complexity, balanced.

Nozzole

From Nozzole, Chianti; imported by Kobrand Corp., New York:
Chianti Classico Riserva, 1978, $7.
A fine pasta wine.
Sight: clear, medium garnet.
Nose: coffee, cedary, complex aromas.

Taste: dry, clean, good acid, rich, medium body, woody, balanced, lots of complexity and maturity.

Ruffino

From Ruffino, Pontassieve; imported by Shieffelin & Co., New York:
Chianti Classico, 1981, $4.90.
Good food wine—not complex in style or price.
Sight: clear, medium red-ruby.
Nose: low intensity, ground pepper.
Taste: dry, medium body, young, simple, nice acid, balanced.
Chianti Classico Riserva Ducale, Gold Label, 1974, $13.75.
Drinking well—a small price to pay for this wine.
Sight: clear, medium tawny red.
Nose: rich, spicy, complex cedar aromas, mature.
Taste: dry, full body, tart, nice fruit, tannic, woody, complex mature flavors, well balanced, long finish.

UMBRIA

Best Buys

Lungarotti

From Lungarotti, Torgiano; imported by Paterno Imports, Chicago:
Chardonnay, Umbria, 1982, $9.
Outstanding value in Chardonnay.
Sight: brilliant, light straw.
Nose: clean, apples, light oak.
Taste: dry, intense apple flavor, crisp, medium body, very well balanced, crisp long finish.
Rubesco Riserva, 1975, $16.
Just beginning to show its colors.

Sight: brilliant, medium red-garnet.
Nose: rich, complex, spicy, pepper.
Taste: dry, closed, tannic, good fruit and acid, still-young flavors, lots of spicy cedary flavors, woody finish.

Ruffino

From Ruffino, Pontassieve; imported by Schieffelin & Co., New York:
Orvieto Classico, 1982, $4.50.
Excellent value in a wine for both sipping and food.
Sight: brilliant, pale gold.
Nose: slightly sweet aromas, fruity.
Taste: dry, tart, light body, crisp, clean, slight spritz, tart flavors, well balanced, lingering finish.

Recommended

Ruffino

From Ruffino, Pontassieve; imported by Schieffelin & Co., New York:
Orvieto Classico, 1983, $3.99.
A standard Orvieto—basic dry Italian wine.
Sight: clear, dullish light gold.
Nose: oxidized, apples, nutty.
Taste: dry, some nice fruit, light chalky almond flavor.

VENETO

Best Buys

Santa Sofia

From Santa Sofia; imported by Kobrand Corp., New York:
Soave Classico Superiore, 1980, $4.50.

Great value for sipping, but also has structure for food.
Sight: clear, medium straw-gold.
Nose: light, fruity, very clean and perfumy.
Taste: dry, light body, very tart, great character, clean, lots of fruit and acid, balanced, lingering finish.

Torresella

From Cantine Torresella, Fossalta di Portogruaro; imported by International Vintage Wine Co., Hartford, Conn.:
Merlot di Pramaggiore, 1982, $5.25.
Drink now, very pleasant, textbook Merlot.
Sight: clear, medium-deep ruby.
Nose: cherry, rich fruit, young, slight mint.
Taste: dry, clean, soft fruit, good character, not complex but very interesting.

Recommended

Pomposa

From Cantine Scalambra, Codigoro; imported by Wines of the World, New York:
Chardonnay del Veneto, 1983, $2.99.
Decent drink for the price.
Sight: light gold.
Nose: spicy, fruity.
Taste: dry, tart, clean Chardonnay fruit, good acid and balance, simple fruit, short chalky finish.

Torresella

From Cantine Torresella, Fossalta di Portogruaro; imported by International Vintage Wine Co., Hartford, Conn.:
Cabernet di Pramaggiore, 1981, $4.99.
Good value.
Sight: clear, medium ruby, light in color.
Nose: herbal, wood, cherries.

Taste: dry, simple, light-medium body, clean and soft, nicely fruity, lingers.

Chardonnay delle Venezie, 1982, $5.75.
Lean-style Chardonnay; crisp, with a fruity-almond character.
Sight: brilliant, pale straw.
Nose: fruit and almonds, some oxidation.
Taste: dry, full body, crisp, clean, lean Chardonnay fruit, some bitterness on finish.

Pinot, 1982, $4.99.
Typical Italian white wine, a blend of Pinot Grigio and Pinot Bianco grapes; serve with food.
Sight: clear, medium straw.
Nose: typical aroma, lightly oxidized.
Taste: dry, nice fruit, tart, some oxidized flavors, citric.

Pinot Grigio del Veneto, 1982, $4.99.
Good value in a Pinot Grigio.
Sight: brilliant, pale straw.
Nose: fresh, varietal aroma.
Taste: dry, clean fruit, fine flavors, crisp, clean finish.

OTHER WINE REGIONS/NON-REGIONAL BLENDS

Spectator Selection

Mastroberardino
From Mastroberardino, Atripalda; imported by Mediterranean Importing Co., Lake Success, N.Y.:
Lacryma Christi del Vesuvio, 1979, $6.25.
Very distinctive and stylish wine.
Sight: clear, deep ruby.
Nose: ground pepper.
Taste: dry, very distinctive flavor, clean, peppery, lots of character, long finish.

Best Buy

Bollini
From Bollini, Mezzocorona; imported by Premium Wine Merchants, Greenwich, Conn.:
Pinot Grigio, Valdadige, 1981, $5.50.
Very stylish light food wine.
Sight: brilliant, medium gold.
Nose: butterscotch, watermelon aromas, clean.
Taste: dry, clean, light-to-medium body, good acid, lots of fruit, pleasant flavors, very well balanced.

Recommended

Bollini
From Bollini, Spilimbergo; imported by Premium Wine Imports, Greenwich, Conn.:
Cabernet Sauvignon, Grave del Friuli, 1980, $4.25.
Nice, impressive Cabernet Sauvignon, lots of green pepper character.
Sight: clear, medium-deep garnet.
Nose: green pepper, vegetal aromas.
Taste: dry, medium body, clean fruit, green pepper, light tannin, balanced, slightly sour on finish.

Casal Thaulero
From Casal Thaulero, Roseto Degli Abruzzi; imported by Mediterranean Importing Co., Lake Success, N.Y.:
Montepulciano d'Abruzzo, 1980, $2.
A good value; serve with food.
Sight: clear, deep inky purple.
Nose: pruney, stemmy, coffee, tobacco.
Taste: dry, pruney and stemmy, clean, good acid, balanced, lingering finish.

Castello di Gabbiano
From Castello di Gabbiano, Monferrato; imported by Wine

Imports Ltd., San Francisco:
Vino da Tavola, 1974, $8.25.
A bit expensive for an Italian table wine.
Sight: clear, medium-deep garnet.
Nose: perfumy, lots of wood.
Taste: dry, plummy, clean, woody, medium body, tart, slight volatile acidity, balanced.

Corvo
From Corvo Duca di Salaparuta; imported by Paterno Imports, Chicago:
Colomba Platino, 1983, $7.50.
Clean, crisp wine with good structure.
Sight: brilliant, pale straw.
Nose: bananas, almonds.
Taste: dry, tart, some clean fruit, almond, nutty character.

Colomba Platino, 1982, $7.
Old-style Italian white wine.
Sight: clear, pale gold.
Nose: sweaty, sweet-peas aroma.
Taste: dry, medium body, good fruit, low in acid, a bit chalky, lingering finish.

Gancia
From F. Gancia & Co., Canelli; imported by Paterno Imports, Chicago:
Spumante, Extra Brut, NV, $5.
Good value in Italian sparkling wine.
Sight: clear, very pale straw, medium beads.
Nose: clean and fruity, spicy.
Taste: dry, medium body, clean and simple, good fruit, some bitterness, short finish.

Herrnhofer
From Herrnhofer, Atesino; imported by Terra Trading Co., Santa Monica, Calif.:
Chardonnay, Atesino, 1981, $7.
Full, varietal, definitely *Italian* Chardonnay.
Sight: clear, light green-gold.
Nose: perfumed, appley, fruity, almond flavors.
Taste: dry, medium body, soft,

ripe fruit, well structured, appley flavors, some bitterness on finish.

Mastroberardino

From Mastroberardino, Atripalda; imported by Mediterranean Importing Co., New Hyde Park, N.Y.:

Greco di Tufo, 1982, $7.50.

Old-style Italian wine with good structure. Best enjoyed with food.

Sight: yellow-gold.

Nose: clean, perfumed, almonds.

Taste: dry, nice acid and structure, light and delicate flavors, finish fades.

Principe Pallavicini

From Principe Pallavicini; imported by Kobrand Corp., New York:

Frascati Superiore, 1980, $4.50.

Nice wine for sipping.

Sight: clear, medium gold.

Nose: sweet, nutty aroma.

Taste: dry, nutty character, light body, clean, a bit fat, balanced.

Rosso Col d'Orcia

From Rosso Col d'Orcia, Montalcino; imported by Mosswood Wine Co., New York:

Vino da Tavola, 1979, $4.99.

Well made, mature table wine.

Sight: clear, medium garnet.

Nose: rich, fruity.

Taste: dry, tart, medium body, clean, well balanced, good acid, lingering finish.

Spain

PENEDÉS

Best Buy

Paul Cheneau

From Paul Cheneau, San Sadurní de Noya; imported by Mosswood Wine Co., New York:
Blanc de Blancs, NV, $4.99.
A great value in sparkling wine for any occasion.
Sight: clear, medium yellow-gold, large bubbles.
Nose: yeasty, some fruit.
Taste: dry, medium body, tart, good fruit, simple clean flavors, balanced, lingering finish.

Recommended

Castellblanch

From Castellblanch, San Sadurní de Noya; imported by Shaw Ross Importers, Miami:
Cristal, 1978, $5.99.
An easy-to-drink sparkling wine.
Sight: brilliant, yellow-green tint, good beading.
Nose: soapy, floral.
Taste: off-dry, medium body, balanced, Muscat, good acid.

Dom Yago

From Santyago Vinicola, Alto Ebro; imported by Monsieur Henri Wines Ltd., White Plains, N.Y.:
Brut, NV, $4.99.
Bargain in quality sparkling wine.
Sight: brilliant, light, large bubbles, pale straw.
Nose: light fruit, vinous.
Taste: off-dry, fruity, creamy, tart, medium body, lingering finish.

Freixenet

From Freixenet, San Sadurní de Noya; imported by Slocum & Sons, West Haven, Conn.:
Brut Barroco, $10.
Just a bit expensive.
Sight: brilliant, medium gold, moderate beading.
Nose: very light, fruity, some wood.
Taste: dry, clean, medium body, lots of spritz, good acid, slightly bitter on finish.

Jean Leon

From Jean Leon, Pla del Penedés; imported by Classic Wines Ltd., Culver City, Calif.:
Cabernet Sauvignon, Penedés, 1978, $6.49.
Tannic and bitter style is not for everyone.
Sight: clear, deep purple.
Nose: ripe berries, pepper, jammy, woody.
Taste: dry, full body, sour, some volatile acidity, tannic and harsh, lots of wood, same on finish.

RIOJA

Best Buy

Bodegas Ellauri

From Bodegas Ellauri; imported by Jason Brooke Imports, Jericho, N.Y.:
Rioja, Viña Zabal, 1975, $3.25.
Great buy for the price.
Sight: clear, medium garnet, amber edge.
Nose: spicy, woody, leathery.
Taste: dry, tart, clean fruit, medium body, leathery and woody, good balance, lingering finish.

Recommended

Bodegas Velasquez

From Bodegas Velasquez, Cenicero; imported by Mosswood Wine Co., New York:
Rioja, 1978, $4.29.
Drink now—a round soft red wine.
Sight: clear, medium-to-deep garnet.
Nose: spicy, nice bottle bouquet.
Taste: dry, soft fruit, mature, full body, spicy, slight oxidation and volatile acidity, pleasant flavors.

Privilegio del Rey Sancho

From Bodegas Domecq, Alava; imported by Domecq Importers, Larchmont, N.Y.:
Rioja, 1978, $2.99.
Mature, woody, what you would expect in a Rioja.
Sight: clear, browning, some garnet.
Nose: some fruit, but mostly wood aroma.
Taste: dry, grapy, fruity, moderate acid, woody, long woody finish.
Rioja, Reserva, 1978, $5.
Pleasant, woody and mature Rioja.
Sight: clear, deep mahogany, some garnet.
Nose: very woody, charred, smoky.
Taste: dry, silky feel, a bit low on fruit, high on wood, mature, lingering finish.

Rioja Ellauri

From Bodegas Ellauri; imported by Jason Brooke Imports, Jericho, N.Y.:
Carabel Rioja, NV, $1.99.
Lots of wood and character for such a low price.
Sight: brilliant, red garnet.
Nose: cherries and wood.
Taste: dry, light body, good ripe clean fruit, lots of wood, clean finish.

Other Countries

AUSTRALIA

Recommended

Mark Swann

From Mark Swann, Australia; imported by The Wine Express, Pleasanton, Calif.:

Cabernet Sauvignon, Conawarra Valley, 1982, $7.50.
Nice Cabernet flavors, too much wood almost hurts this wine.
Sight: clear, deep purple-ruby.
Nose: rose petals, fruity aromas.
Taste: dry, medium body, nice fruit, black cherry flavors, lots of wood on finish.

Shiraz, Eden Valley, 1980, $6.50.
A different style of wine with lots of character.
Sight: clear, medium ruby.
Nose: clean, earthy, piney, leathery.
Taste: dry, clean, peppery, medium body, earthy fruit flavors, good structure, spicy, tannic, long finish.

Vintage Port, Australia, 1980, $10.
Good buy in port; young, needs time.
Sight: deep purple-ruby.
Nose: alcohol, tropical fruit.
Taste: off-dry, good tropical fruit flavors, balanced, alcoholic but good backbone, nutty finish.

Taltarni

From Taltarni Vineyards, Moonambel, Australia; imported by Areti Wine Imports, Napa, Calif.:

Cabernet Sauvignon, 1980, $6.75.
Good value, great varietal character, especially on the nose.
Sight: clear, medium-deep red-ruby.
Nose: nice eucalyptus, perfumy, herbaceous.

Taste: dry, full body, balanced, nice fruit, good acid and structure, short on finish, pleasant.

Shiraz, Victoria, 1980, $6.75.
Tremendous complexity on nose but rough on palate.
Sight: clear, medium-to-deep purple.
Nose: clean, complex, spicy, cedar aromas.
Taste: dry, full body, spicy, rough and tannic, good balance, fine structure, lingering finish.

AUSTRIA

Best Buy

Burgenländischer Winzerverband

From Burgenländischer Winzerverband, Rust, Austria; imported by Preiss International, Los Angeles:

White Stork, Ruster Riesling, 1982, $3.25.
Good, clean grapefruit flavor.
Sight: light gold.
Nose: pleasant, floral, grapefruit aroma.
Taste: off-dry, full-bodied, good balance, racy, light grapefruit character, clean finish.

Highly Recommended

Burgenländischer Winzerverband

From Burgenländischer Winzerverband, Rust, Austria; imported by Preiss International, Los Angeles:

Ruster Trockenbeerenauslese, 1981, $19.50.
Great complexity and finesse for the price.

Sight: brilliant, deep gold, greenish edge.
Nose: honeyed, apricot-or-ange, slightly floral, very complex.
Taste: very rich and sweet, complex honey-orange flavors, oily but not heavy, texture is elegantly balanced, finishes clean despite sweetness.

Recommended

Burgenländischer Winzerverband

From Burgenländischer Winzerverband, Rust, Austria; imported by Preiss International, Los Angeles:

Red Stork, Ruster Blaufränkisch, 1982, $3.25.
OK, if you can get past the nose.
Sight: black-cherry red.
Nose: slightly moldy.
Taste: off-dry, medium body, some fruit, good acid, simple and short finish.

Gumpolskirchen Winzergenossenschaft

From Gumpolskirchen Winzergenossenschaft, Austria; imported by Preiss International, Los Angeles:

Neuberger, 1982, $3.99.
Coarse, soft flavors and not much fruit; a simple sipper.
Sight: light gold.
Nose: wet cardboard, melons.
Taste: off-dry, full body, some fruit, a bit fat, some dirty flavors on finish.

Schlumberger

From Sektkellerei Schlumberger, Vienna, Austria; imported by Preiss International, Santa Fe Springs, Calif.:

Sekt, Blanc de Blancs, Brut, NV, $15.69.
Austere style of sparkling wine. Some may find it too bitter; others pleasingly complex.

Sight: light yellow, light bead.
Nose: yeasty, slightly floral, cardboard edge.
Taste: dry, floral-peachy edge to yeasty flavors, finishes slightly soapy and bitter.

GERMANY

Best Buy

Baum
From Philipp und Heinrich Baum Weinkellerei, Bad Kreuznach, Germany; imported by Baum Wine Imports, Franklin Park, Ill.:
Moselblümchen, Mosel-Saar-Ruwer, 1983, $3.25.
A lot of fruit and delicacy for your money.
Sight: very pale straw.
Nose: nice floral, fruity.
Taste: dry, medium body, good, clean, delicate peach and pineapple flavors, crisp and clean, good acid, long finish.

Highly Recommended

Fürst von Metternich
From Fürst von Metternich Sektkeller, Johannisberg, Germany; imported by Elliot Fine & Co., San Francisco:
Riesling, Sekt, Extra Trocken, 1981, $13.
Elegant sparkling wine with lots of style.
Sight: brilliant, medium gold, good beading.
Nose: clean, yeasty, elegant.
Taste: dry, crisp, tart, clean fruit, elegant and mouth-filling, nice style, mile-long finish.

Recommended

Baum
From Philipp und Heinrich Baum Weinkellerei, Bad Kreuznach, Germany; imported by Baum Wine Imports, Franklin Park, Ill.:
Piesporter Michelsberg, Mosel-Saar-Ruwer, 1983, $3.79.
Simple, perfumy style.
Sight: very pale straw.
Nose: clean, piney, floral fruit.
Taste: dry, medium body, good balance, good clean floral fruit, perfumy, medium finish.

Goldener Oktober
From Goldener Oktober, Bingen, Germany; imported by C. & B. Vintage Cellars, San Francisco:
Rheinhessen, 1982, $5.
Good Riesling character.
Sight: clear, pale straw.
Nose: clean floral, complex pine aromas.
Taste: off-dry, light body, good fruit flavors, balanced, lingering finish.

Weingut Toni Jost
From Weingut Toni Jost, Germany; imported by Baum Wine Imports, Franklin Park, Ill.:
Bacharacher Hahn, Mittelrhein, Riesling, Kabinett, 1982, $6.99.
A fleshy Riesling.
Sight: brilliant, medium gold.
Nose: floral, fruity, Riesling.
Taste: off-dry, medium body, good fruit and lively acid but short on the middle, cardboard finish.
Bacharacher Schloss Stahleck, Mittelrhein, Riesling, Auslese, 1976, $15.99.
Not one of the better Ausleses from 1976, pricey.
Sight: brilliant, deep, bright gold.
Nose: botrytis, concentrated aromas, sugary.
Taste: off-dry, sugary, simple, lacks complexity, a bit viscous, lemon candy.

SOUTH AFRICA

Recommended

Nederburg
From Nederburg Wines, Paarl, South Africa; imported by Centurion Wines & Spirits Ltd., Cleveland, Ohio:
Baronne Superior, Coastal Region, 1978, $5.50.
Sight: clear, medium-garnet.
Nose: pleasant, woody, some Cabernet?
Taste: dry, medium body, very fruity, clean, pleasant, nice acid, woody, soft flavors.
Edelkeur Superior, 1979, $26.50/350 ml.
Very expensive for a delicious wine.
Sight: clear, medium amber.
Nose: intense honey, caramel, gardenia.
Taste: sweet, honey, lots of caramel, one-dimensional, good structure, lingering finish.
Fonternel, Semi-Sweet, 1981, $5.50.
Acceptable slightly sweet table wine.
Sight: clear, pale straw.
Nose: vinous.
Taste: off-dry, fruity, light body, good acid, bitter on the middle, short on finish.
Paarl Riesling, Dry, 1981, $5.49.
Understated wine for food.
Sight: clear, medium gold.
Nose: vinous, fruity.
Taste: dry, light body, a bit flat on palate, fruity, balanced, lacks lively and fresh flavor.
Premier Grand Cru, Extra Dry, NV, $5.99.
Good price for an all-purpose wine.
Sight: clear, medium gold.
Nose: vinous, a bit spicy.
Taste: dry, some appley flavors, medium body, some chalkiness on middle and finish, tart lingering finish.
Rosé-Sec, Coastal Region, 1981, $5.49.
Dry style of rosé which would go well with food.

Sight: clear, medium orange.
Nose: restrained, low intensity, fruit.
Taste: dry, fruity, light body, moderate acidity, balanced, clean flavors.

Zonnebloem

From Zonnebloem, Oude Libertas, South Africa; imported by Centurion Wine and Spirits Ltd., Cleveland, Ohio:
Grand Mousseaux, Vin Doux, NV, $7.79.
Very clean and attractive sparkler.
Sight: brilliant, pale straw, steady beading.
Nose: fruity, very fresh, lively.
Taste: sweet, very fruity, creamy, clean, light body, good acid, very well balanced.
Premier Grand Cru, Extra Dry, NV, $5.64.
Very woody and stylish wine.
Sight: clear, medium gold.
Nose: woody, spicy.
Taste: dry, tart, soft and woody, some fruit, good acid, short finish.

OTHERS: BULGARIA/ HUNGARY/ PORTUGAL

Best Buy

Sandeman

From Sandeman, Oporto, Portugal; imported by Château & Estate Wines Co., New York:
Founder's Reserve Port, NV, $12.50.
Good alternative to higher-tannin, higher-alcohol California ports.
Sight: clear, medium-to-dark garnet.
Nose: raisiny, pruney aromas.
Taste: sweet, full body, very smooth and mature, lots of wood, clean, well made, well balanced.

Recommended

Egri Bikavér

From Monimpex, Budafok, Hungary; imported by International Vintage Wine Co., Hartford, Conn.:
Red Table Wine, 1980, $6.
Clean and simple table wine.
Sight: clear, deep garnet.
Nose: cooked, slightly salty aroma.
Taste: dry, soft fruit, short and simple, nice spicy flavor, clean on finish.

Trakia

From Vinimpex, Sofia, Bulgaria; imported by Monsieur Henri Wines Ltd., New York:
Cabernet Sauvignon, Suhindol Region, 1978, $2.99.
Good value; drink now.
Sight: clear, medium garnet.
Nose: woody, vinous, some Cabernet character.
Taste: dry, medium body, very soft, fruity, mature, woody, balanced.

Cellar Selections

CALIFORNIA

Acacia

From Acacia Winery, Napa, Calif.:

Pinot Noir, Napa Valley—Carneros, Iund Vineyard, 1982

Release date: Aug. 1984
Availability: national
Current price (bottle retail): $15
Current price (case retail): $180
Total production: 650 cases

Some of the finest Pinot Noirs in California have been produced by this Carneros-area winery. This wine, from the Iund Vineyard, has a distinctive black-pepper character and complexity which sets it above the other four Pinots Acacia produces. It is definitely a wine to be patient with, since it may take several years for the depth in the nose and palate to open up and become accessible to the consumer.

Date Recommended: July 16, 1984

Caymus Vineyards

From Caymus Vineyards, Rutherford, Calif.:

Cabernet Sauvignon, Napa Valley, Special Selection, 1978

Release date: spring 1984
Availability: national, but in very selected outlets and in small quantities

Current price (bottle retail): $30
Current price (case retail): $360
Total production: 600 cases

This wine is hard to find, but if you are a California Cabernet lover, it is worth the effort. It is big, tannic, and oaky, yet demonstrates great complexity and depth as well. A bit hard to drink now, it will age gracefully for many years to come.

Date Recommended: June 16, 1984

Clos Du Val

From Clos Du Val Wine Co., Napa, Calif.:

Cabernet Sauvignon, Napa Valley, 1980

Release date: Jan. 1, 1983
Availability: national
Release price (bottle retail): $12.50
Current price (bottle retail): $14
Current price (case retail): $168
Total production: 15,000 cases

Winemaker Bernard Portet traditionally blends with about 12 percent Merlot. This wine is fruity and charming now, with good complexity and elegance. According to Portet, the wine has great aging potential.

Date Recommended: Feb. 1, 1984

Zinfandel, Napa Valley, 1981

Release date: spring 1984
Availability: national
Current price (bottle retail): $9
Current price (case retail): $108
Total production: not available

Bernard Portet, winemaker at Clos du Val, has built a reputation or Zinfandels that have elegance and finesse in their youth and yet have the structure and backbone to age gracefully. This reputation was reinforced by the showing of his 1973 Zinfandel at the recent California Barrel Tasting in New York.

Date Recommended: May 16, 1984

Jekel Vineyard

From Jekel Vineyard, Greenfield, Calif.:

Johannisberg Riesling, Monterey County, Late Harvest, 1981
Release date: summer 1983
Availability: national at release
Current price (bottle retail): $10/375 ml.
Current price (case retail): $240
Total production: limited quantities

This is a light-styled sweet wine that is suitable anytime a sweet yet crisp white wine is called for. This wine has plenty of life ahead, and will no doubt become more complex in the next few years. At $10 per half-bottle it is also one of the more affordable premium dessert wines on the market.

Date Recommended: June 1, 1984

Jordan

From Jordan Vineyard & Winery, Healdsburg, Calif.:

Cabernet Sauvignon, Alexander Valley, 1978
Release date: April 1982
Availability: national
Release price (bottle retail): $14
Current price (bottle retail): $17.50
Current price (case retail): $210
Total production: 45,000 cases

This is the third commercial vintage for the Jordan winery and their first estate-bottled Cabernet Sauvignon.

The wine is made of a blend consisting of 93 percent Cabernet Sauvignon and 7 percent Merlot. It has 12.8 percent alco-

hol. It spent twenty-two months in oak before bottling.

This Cabernet has excellent structure and will age well. Although it is drinkable now, it will begin to show its potential after an additional five or more years in the bottle.

Date Recommended: July 1, 1983

Robert Mondavi Winery

From Robert Mondavi Winery, Oakville, Calif.:

Cabernet Sauvignon, Napa Valley, Reserve, 1978
Release date: Oct. 1982
Availability: national
Release price (bottle retail): $40
Current price (bottle retail): $50
Current price (case retail): $360
Total production: 11,000 cases (estimate)

The Cabernet Sauvignon Reserve is Robert Mondavi's premium wine release.

The wine is a blend of 92 percent Cabernet Sauvignon, 5 percent Cabernet Franc, and 3 percent Merlot. The grapes for the wine were harvested at 23.3 degrees Brix. It was finished with 13 percent alcohol. It spent twenty-five months in French oak before bottling.

This is a wine that, although forward now, has good acidity and tannin to ensure a long cellar life.

Date Recommended: Aug. 1, 1983

Opus One

From Robert Mondavi—Baron Philippe de Rothschild, Oakville, Calif.:

Napa Valley, 1980
Release date: April 1984
Availability: limited availability
Release price (bottle retail): $50
Current price (bottle retail): $50
Current price (case retail): n/a
Total production: 2,000 cases

Because of the tremendous pre-release demand, a very limited supply, and the one-of-a-kind nature of this wine, it is bound to be a collector's item.

The 1980 Opus One is made entirely of Napa Valley grapes. The majority of the blend is Cabernet Sauvignon (96.1 percent) with the balance in Cabernet Franc.

Date Recommended: April 1, 1984

Joseph Phelps Vineyards

From Joseph Phelps Vineyards, St. Helena, Calif.:

Insignia, Napa Valley, 1980
Release date: June 1984
Availability: national
Current price (bottle retail): $25
Current price (case retail): $300
Total production: 1,900 cases

This is a Cabernet Sauvignon

of classic proportions. Blended with 15 percent Merlot, this wine exhibits tremendous depth and complexity. There is no doubt in our minds that it will develop even more of the complexity it already has with additional bottle age. Well worth the price.

Date Recommended: July 1, 1984

Scheurebe, Napa Valley, Late Harvest, 1982
Release date: March 1, 1984
Availability: selected markets
Current price (bottle retail): $15
Current price (case retail): $180
Total production: 443 cases

This wine has a rare quality not often found in California dessert wines—a light, feathery feel on the palate with great intensity of flavor. This is not a heavy, syrupy wine. (Scheurebe is a German grape which makes wine very similar to Riesling.)

Date Recommended: April 16, 1984

Ridge

From Ridge Vineyards, Cupertino, Calif.:
Cabernet Sauvignon, Santa Cruz Mtns., Monte Bello, 1978
Release date: June 1983
Availability: national (at release)
Current price (bottle retail): $30
Current price (case retail): $360
Total production: 1,800 cases

This is clearly the flagship of the Ridge line of fine wines. A

big, aggressive Cabernet with full fruit and hard tannins, it is destined for a long life. The warm fall of the 1978 vintage, according to the winery, did not affect the ripening of the grapes for this wine—breezes cooled the top of the hill where the vineyard is located.

The wine spent twenty months in small oak cooperage and was lightly fined with egg whites late in its second year.

Because of high demand and low availability, it is likely that this wine will become very hard to find on retail shelves. As is customary with Ridge Cabernets, its price will grow substantially in the coming months and years. The time to purchase is now.

Date Recommended: Oct. 16, 1983

Stag's Leap Wine Cellars

From Stag's Leap Wine Cellars, Napa, Calif.:
Cabernet Sauvignon, Napa Valley, Stag's Leap Vineyards, Cask 23, 1977
Release date: Sept. 1, 1983
Availability: national
Current price (bottle retail): $30
Current price (case retail): $360
Total production: 800 cases

This reserve wine has been a major success at Stag's Leap since the winery's inception. It is made almost entirely from Cabernet Sauvignon with, as winemaker Warren Winiarski says, "a small percent of Merlot for 'grace.' "

The wine received approximately sixteen months of barrel age and additional bottle age at the winery before release. The 1977 vintage was a drought year, but the vines compensated for the dryness. The wine is concentrated, with an almost cedary quality, robust and complex. It is not as briary as the 1976 bottling or as fleshy as the 1978 (not yet released).

The 1977 Cask 23 is drinking well now for those who like a robust fruity wine. For those who prefer a more attenuated, austere flavor, it would be best to wait another five-or-so years.

Date Recommended: Dec. 1, 1983

FRANCE

Château Ducru-Beaucaillou

From Château Ducru-Beaucaillou, Saint-Julien-Beychevelle, Gironde, France:
Saint-Julien, 1980
Release date: May 1983
Availability: national
Current price (bottle retail): $13.50
Current price (case retail): $162
Total production: 8,000 cases
Here is a wine for the first-time Bordeaux drinker. The 1980 vintage has produced wines which are balanced and accessible while young and reasonably priced. While this wine will not enjoy the longevity of more classic years, it will still improve in the bottle for several years. It is a beautiful lesson in the Bordeaux style of winemaking.
Date Recommended: March 1, 1984

Château d'Yquem

From Château d'Yquem, Sauternes, France:
Sauternes, Premier Grand Cru, 1975
Release date: fall 1979
Availability: national
Release price (bottle retail): $55
Current price (bottle retail): $85
Current price (case retail): $960
Total production: 8,833 cases
Harvest dates for this wine were between Sept. 29 and Nov. 17, 1975.

This wine is a blend of 80 percent Semillon and 20 percent Sauvignon Blanc.
Of all the Sauternes, Château d'Yquem has unquestionably demonstrated the greatest potential for longevity and appreciation.
Count Alexandre de Lur-Saluces, the proprietor of Yquem, believes the 1975 is the most likely candidate in recent vintages to last one hundred years.
Date Recommended: July 16, 1983

Château Lafite-Rothschild

From Château Lafite-Rothschild, Pauillac, Gironde, France:
Pauillac, 1978
Release date: spring 1981
Availability: national
Current price (bottle retail): $95
Current price (case retail): $1,125
Release price (case retail): $375
Total production: 16,500 cases
High demand for this classic claret from the first-growth Lafite, combined with unusually small supply (Lafite's average production is 20,000 to 30,000 cases), has sent prices for the popular 1978 soaring.
The 1978 Lafite is composed of 71 percent Cabernet Sauvignon, 20 percent Merlot, and 9 percent Cabernet Franc.

Grapes for the wine were harvested between Oct. 5 and 24.
It is a complex, beautifully structured wine that will last well into the next century, but will become drinkable by the end of this decade.
Date Recommended: Sept. 1, 1983

Château la Mission Haut Brion

From S.C. des Domaines Woltner, propr. à Talence, Gironde, France:
Graves, Cru Classé, 1979
Release date: fall 1981
Availability: national
Current price (bottle retail): $48
Current price (case retail): $570
Release price (case retail): $312
Total production: 7,000 cases

This wine is a blend of 65 percent Cabernet Sauvignon, 30 percent Merlot, and 5 percent Cabernet Franc. The harvest began on Oct. 5 and ended on Oct. 25, 1979.
La Mission is a wine that has become increasingly in demand over the past decade. It is renowned for its harmony, and comparisons between it and Château Haut-Brion (La Mission's new owner) are inevitable.

Moreover, the 1979 vintage remains a good value because of the decline in the value of the French franc. Prices have begun to climb as the wine has become less available.

Date Recommended: Sept. 16, 1983

Château Margaux

From Château Margaux, Margaux, France:
Margaux, Premier Grand Cru Classé, 1980
Release date: May 1983
Availability: national
Current price (bottle retail): $30
Current price (case retail): $360
Total production: 20,000 cases

For anyone who has always wanted to try a Château Margaux, but could never part with the $50 to $60 a bottle it usually costs, the 1980 is the perfect way to experience the Margaux style with a bit less tannin and for a lot less money. But don't let the (relatively) low price fool you; this wine still has a long life ahead of it.

Date Recommended: May 1, 1984

Château Palmer

From Château Palmer, Margaux, France:
Margaux, 1978
Release date: spring 1981
Availability: major markets
Current price (bottle retail): $35
Current price (case retail): $325
Release price (case retail): $215
Total production: 7,000 cases

For several years, Château Palmer has been priced well in excess of its third-growth status, due to strong demand. Carefully controlled vinification and rigorous vat selection have resulted in a highly sought-after wine.

It has good color, a fruity nose, full, round fruit, and is balanced with typical finesse. Palmer is made from 45 percent Cabernet Sauvignon, 40 percent Merlot, 10 percent Petite Verdot, and 5 percent Cabernet Franc. The 1978 should first become drinkable by 1988.

Date Recommended: Nov. 1, 1983

Château Pichon-Lalande

From Château Pichon-Lalande Comtesse de Lalande, Pauillac, Gironde, France:
Pauillac, Grand Cru Classé, 1980
Release date: winter 1983
Availability: national
Release price (bottle retail): $9.50
Current price (bottle retail): $14
Current price (case retail): $112
Total production: 17,500 cases

The second-growth Pichon Lalande produced one of the best examples of the '80 vintage. It is a blend of rigorously selected Cabernet Sauvignon (45 percent), Merlot (35 percent), Cabernet Franc (12 percent), and Petite Verdot (8 percent). The vat selection accounts for the wine's success in an otherwise maligned vintage. It is fruity, elegant, and complex. The wine is not one of great depth, but it should develop for another few years.

Date Recommended: March 1, 1984

Château Suduiraut

From Château Suduiraut, Preignac, Gironde, France:
Sauternes, Premier Cru, 1979
Release date: April 1982
Availability: major markets
Release price (bottle retail): $12
Current price (bottle retail): $19
Current price (case retail): $228
Total production: 8,500 cases

A blend of 80 percent Semillon and 20 percent Sauvignon Blanc, the 1979 Château Suduiraut is a classic, rich Sauternes. Considered better than the 1978 in quality, the 1979 vintage rivals the 1975.

Deep gold in color with a powerful bouquet, the wine displays lovely complexity and great finesse. It is a wine that can be enjoyed now, but will surely benefit from extended aging. This Suduiraut will most likely reach its optimum drinkability by the end of this decade.

Date Recommended: Feb. 16, 1984

Joseph Drouhin

From Joseph Drouhin, Beaune, France:
Beaune, Clos des Mouches, 1978
Release date: 1981
Availability: major markets
Current price (bottle retail): $36
Current price (case retail): $432
Total production: 2,500 cases

Clos des Mouches is one of the most famous first-growth vineyards of Beaune in Burgundy. It is considered a "signature wine" of the Joseph Drouhin establishment. Drouhin, a well-respected Burgundy shipper, owns, vinifies, and bottles the wine produced from his thirty-acre parcel of the Clos des Mouches vineyard.

The wine is made of 100 percent Pinot Noir, has a pronounced spicy bouquet, good balance, and great finesse. While it is drinkable now, it should improve over the next ten-to-fifteen years. (Drouhin also makes a white wine from the Clos des Mouches from 100 percent Chardonnay.)

Date Recommended: Jan. 1, 1984

OTHER COUNTRIES: ITALY/PORTUGAL

Fattoria dei Barbi

From Fattoria dei Barbi,
Montalcino, Italy:
**Brunello di Montalcino,
1978**
Release date: Oct. 1982
Availability: major markets
Current price (bottle retail):
$10.60
Current price (case retail):
$127.20
Total production: 9,167 cases
(estimated)

Already comparisons are being
made between the 1978 dei Barbi
and earlier classics such as the
1964, '70, and '75. The youngest
available dei Barbi Brunello on
the market, the '78 is perfect for
laying down now and sampling in
a decade.

The dei Barbi is expected to
live up to its reputation as a powerful, rich, austere, and long-lived wine. It is made of 100
percent Sangiovese Grosso
grapes. It has 13.2 percent alcohol. Judging from preceding price
spirals, the 1978 dei Barbi could
very likely command $600-to-
$700 a case by 1986.

Date Recommended: Oct. 1,
1983

Graham

From Graham, Oporto,
Portugal:
Vintage Port, 1977
Release date: fall 1982
Availability: national
Release price (bottle retail):
$17
Current price (bottle retail):
$27.50
Current price (case retail):
$330
Total production: not available

Now thought to eclipse the
classic 1963, this wine has great
color, an intense bouquet, and is
very full bodied. It is expected to
mellow as it matures, but will not
be ready to drink for at least
another decade. However, as
prices have climbed substantially
since its release, we recommend
that you purchase this port now.

Date Recommended: March
16, 1984

Taylor Fladgate

From Taylor, Fladgate &
Yeatman, Oporto, Portugal:
Vintage Port, 1977
Release date: early 1981
Availability: major markets
Release price (bottle retail):
$17.50
Current price (bottle retail):
$22.50
Current price (case retail):
$225
Total production: not available

According to the tradition of
the port trade, the precise production of a shipper's declared
vintage is a closely guarded secret. Vintage Port production,
however, represents a minute
fraction of total port production—between 2 percent and 5
percent.

There is no question that demand for the 1977 vintage, which
is already being favorably compared with the classic 1963, is
very strong. Taylor, for a long
time, has commanded a marked
edge over its competition. Rich
and concentrated, it has outstanding depth of flavor and elegance.

Even though the Taylor will
not be drinkable for another decade, nor reach its peak of drinkability for an additional twelve
years or so, it has already begun
to move up in price.

Now is the time to lay away
some if you want to ensure a
future supply at an accessible
price.

Date Recommended: Dec. 16,
1983

About
The Wine Spectator

The Wine Spectator is a twice-monthly consumer newspaper on wine. It is read regularly by more than 100,000 consumers as well as by members of the wine trade—vintners, distributors, importers, retailers, and restaurateurs.

Each year *The Wine Spectator* selects and honors those restaurants that have the finest wine lists in the United States, with its "Grand Award" and certificate programs. And every October *The Wine Spectator* California Scholarship Foundation sponsors a "wine weekend" of seminars and tastings in San Francisco—the California Wine Experience. Registrants, both consumer and trade, attend from all over the world.

Serious collectors and fun-loving amateurs alike follow its regular coverage of the wine scene in California and Europe, in which it not only reviews wines and vintages but presents special profiles of the people behind the news.

Subscribe to *The Wine Spectator* today. Send $15 for a six-month trial subscription ($30 annual subscription) to: *The Wine Spectator*, 400 East 51st Street, New York, NY 10022.